1,000 HOUR WAR : COMMUNICATION
DS79.739 .A14 1994

MY 6 '2

DEMCO 38-296

The
1,000
Hour War

Recent Titles in
Contributions in Military Studies

THE
1,000
HOUR WAR

Communication in the Gulf

Edited by
Thomas A. McCain
and
Leonard Shyles

Contributions in Military Studies, Number 148

GREENWOOD PRESS
Westport, Connecticut • London

Library of Congress Cataloging-in-Publication Data

The 1,000 hour war : communication in the Gulf / edited by Thomas A.
McCain and Leonard Shyles.
    p. cm.—(Contributions in military studies, ISSN 0883–6884 ;
no. 148)
    Includes bibliographical references and index.
    ISBN 0–313–28747–3 (alk. paper)
    1. Persian Gulf War, 1991—Press coverage. I. McCain, Thomas A.
II. Shyles, Leonard. III. Title: Thousand hour war.
IV. Series.
DS79.739.A14   1994
956.7044′3—dc20   93–12979

British Library Cataloguing in Publication Data is available.

Library of Congress Catalog Card Number: 93–12979
ISBN: 0–313–28747–3
ISSN: 0883–6884

First published in 1994

Greenwood Press, 88 Post Road West, Westport, CT 06881
An imprint of Greenwood Publishing Group, Inc.

Printed in the United States of America

The paper used in this book complies with the
Permanent Paper Standard issued by the National
Information Standards Organization (Z39.48–1984).

10 9 8 7 6 5 4 3 2 1

Contents

Illustrations

FIGURES

TABLES

Introduction

Thomas A. McCain

This is a book about communication practices during 1,000 unique hours in time—January 17 to February 27, 1991. There is no pretense about inclusivity; lots of communication occurred during the Gulf War that is not covered in these pages. But this collection of chapters does describe and analyze several aspects of communication and technology vital to the prosecution and news coverage of the conflict; hence, they are vital to our understanding of the important role of communication in the events known as the Persian Gulf War, and they warrant our attention.

In general, the authors assume that understanding communication principles and practices is required for understanding the complex nature of modern warfare. The role of communication is particularly germane to understanding the 42 days that are the subject of this book. Communication practices influenced the prosecution of the war in manifold ways; the unprecedented air and ground attacks on Iraq and Kuwait by allied forces under U.S. command were orchestrated through a dazzling array of integrated communication technologies. That these technologies were tested for the first time under fire in the deserts of Saudi Arabia and Kuwait, home of some of the richest oil fields in the world, is also important. That the war was prosecuted through the cooperation of people allied for the first time against an Arab neighbor is also of key importance. For the allies to succeed, the communication surrounding the events and circumstances in the Gulf required that many bridges would be built; there were many new assumptions to negotiate in a short amount of time; successful communication had to overcome countless opportunities for error and misunderstanding. There were gulfs of uncertainty among the participants; moreover, classic adversarial conditions challenged the press and the military as they attempted, frequently at cross purposes, to execute their missions. Viewers around the world had much to make sense of and little time in which to do it.

The chapters assembled in these pages are collected to help the reader understand the communication challenges constituting these special circumstances and also the role of communication technologies and practices that shaped the events known as the Gulf War. The communication principles and models offered are meant to illuminate some of the salient issues, practices, and images that made a difference in these unique 1,000 hours. Some of the writers handle their subject from a macroscopic view and some, microscopically. Some deal with relationships between communication systems and society; others describe important aspects of individuals' communicative behavior. The key communicative aspects of the Gulf War treated here perforce deal with a plethora of complex issues, including the encoding and decoding of messages, their distribution systems, their symbolic meanings, and the human values and expectations that motivated and shaped participants' perceptions and subsequent behavior during the conflict. Questions about the structures that determined the nature of information transfer and the values exchanged during the crisis are articulated and explored.

COMMUNICATION SYSTEMS' ALTERATION OF SOCIAL CONCEPTS OF TIME AND SPACE

The lineage of communication systems goes back thousands of years, beginning with toolmaking and primitive art. With the development of papyrus and cuneiform, the oral traditions of humankind were supplemented by writing in the ancient cultures of China, Phoenicia, Babylon, and Egypt. Centuries later, Chinese moveable type was introduced, then Guttenberg's printing press. Electricity brought the telephone and telegraph; then wireless telegraphy joined these earlier nineteenth-century technologies. Modulation of the ether soon found its voice on radio. Television followed relatively quickly. In the 1990s conventional broadcasting has been augmented, and in some cases replaced, by satellite and cable video. These late innovations have recently been conjoined with computers, Fax machines, integrated circuits, and modems. In the twenty-first century, fiber-optic technology and digital electronics promise a new generation of dazzling gizmos to press human societies toward a virtually instantaneous worldwide communication capability.

What all of these communication technologies have in common is that they emerged during times when societies altered the ways in which time and space were constructed and construed. The potential speed and distribution of information in the 1990s has become so fast compared to those of only a decade ago that most users of these new technologies are no longer as concerned with how to get information to an audience or another person as they are with how people will handle the bombardment of information they are physically able to receive. In the 1990s a one-page message can be sent 10 million times faster than the Spanish Armada could have delivered it, even on a windy day. New digitized information allows the light-based technologies of glass and satellites to send the equivalent of the entire *Encyclopaedia Britannica*, including all the color graphics, a total of six times in one minute. This rapid distribution of information was witnessed in the homes of the world, "live and in color," during the Gulf conflict.

In this instance, the concepts of distance and time were altered by the ability of new communication systems to distribute the same messages instantly to global publics. Of course, the rate at which people can read and comprehend stories and information hasn't changed much at all since Guttenberg's time. So while events unfolding in the Gulf were distributed globally in startlingly rapid fashion, and were carried in expanded formats as the lead story on nearly every television system in the world, as David L. Swanson and Rebecca A. Carrier report in this volume, the Persian Gulf War will take far longer to understand than it took to report.

The shrinking of distance and time by communication technologies redefined the war for various media audiences from communication, political, and military perspectives. For example, Chava E. Tidhar and Dafna Lemish describe Israel's expert tracking systems, which the allies used to monitor Iraqi SCUD missile attacks and which allowed Israeli civil defense systems to activate warnings within seconds of enemy launches. Israeli citizens routinely benefited from televised warnings to take cover in sealed rooms, allowing them to find safe quarters while SCUD missiles were still airborne. This is one example of how mass-mediated information transformed events in the Gulf as they happened. In this way, media systems contributed significantly to outcomes rather than merely reporting them.

By contrast, Jay M. Parker and Jerold L. Hale describe the leaflet dropping on Iraqi soldiers on the front lines as relatively low tech. Parker noted in remarks to the Speech Communication Association meeting, that these thousands upon thousands of paper leaflets "could just as easily have been dropped from a piper Cub" (Chicago, Illinois, November 1992). Hence, analysis of the various communication systems operating in the Gulf and their feedback features (or lack thereof) offers the opportunity to explore the extent to which unique communication processes themselves dramatically altered events as they happened. The role played by Cable News Network (CNN) is a mainstream example of how communication changed events simply by reporting them. A full appreciation of the role of communication in understanding the Gulf War recognizes the inherently blurred distinction (and the futility of distinguishing) between reporting news and making news. From both journalistic and military perspectives, Gulf War communication analysis should begin with the fundamental premise that nothing communicated was left in pristine condition. An important feature of the communication systems that operated during these 1,000 hours is that they profoundly altered time and space relationships for a war, its conduct, and coverage.

COMMUNICATION SYSTEMS AS PART OF THE SOCIETAL INFRASTRUCTURE

Societies create communication systems consonant with and reflective of their dominant values and power structures. Telecommunications and mass media industries, and even normative conversational behavior, constitute systems that a society must create in order to function. As with other infrastructures (e.g., public utilities, transportation, monetary systems), the functioning of a communication system is maximized when awareness of the mechanisms used to create it are transparent to persons' experiences while they are using it (Horwitz, 1989). Infrastructures are so labeled because much of their successful functioning happens below the surface of immediate experience. Simply put, people take for granted that money will buy things they want; roads will take them where they want to go; water comes out of the tap when the spigot is turned. So it is with communication systems and technology. People take it for granted that communication systems will perform the functions of distributing, storing, and transforming information and messages. So, when a person picks up the phone to call someone, the particulars and complexities of the specific electronic interconnection are not contemplated or viewed as problematic. One dials, another answers, and the object of the call is a conversation. Likewise, people don't need to know how a toaster works, the history of electrical appliances, the advantages and disadvantages of two- and four-slice models. Mostly, people just want toast. Similarly, when people watch television or listen to the radio or read the morning newspaper, the processes of gathering and distributing news and information are to the user essentially irrelevant. What people come to expect from their communication systems is a transparent set of interconnections and regulative norms that allow them to take the gory details for granted. To remain transparent, the systems and norms of communication are generally in keeping with the social values and expectations of the society or culture in which they operate. But when crises strike, then systems once transparent themselves become a focal point. During times of stress, the values and norms that collectively shape policy and structure for communication systems become salient, even problematic. Their viability is again subject to critical evaluation. So it is in the Persian Gulf War. Seminal values of free press, as well as issues of censorship, access, ownership, government control, and the like, are heightened. It is critical that the communication structures created to uphold social values of a democracy be carefully scrutinized and evaluated. These are the issues that William J. Small explores from the background of a television news executive and professor of journalism. Small's perspective is contrasted by that of M. David Arant and

Michael L. Warden, who provide a view that includes the thinking of the military establishment.

As an infrastructure, the communication systems used in both covering and prosecuting the Gulf War challenged many of the taken-for-granted aspects of communication and media as viewed from the perspective of societies' numerous norms and values.

TECHNOLOGY, MARKETS, AND POLICY AS INTERDEPENDENT COMMUNICATION SYSTEMS' COMPONENTS

The important components of any infrastructure, including communication systems, include its technological, political, and economic aspects. To understand a communication system, therefore, is to understand the interdependence of these three components: technology, markets, and policy (McCain, 1992). The nature and character of communication systems are defined by the interaction of these components. Communication markets are largely determined by a host of entrepreneurial efforts, marketing, and technological innovations, as well as by government regulation and policy. It is critical that the concept of a communication system, like those operating during the Gulf War, be understood in terms of these three interlocking parts. To change existing configurations with new technologies, be they fiber-optic cables rolled out along the desert or portable up-links with live video from Kuwait, is to change not only technology but policy and the nature of the economic marketplace. Similarly, to advocate a change in policy for new technologies is to privilege one market or market component over others. The technology of television is essentially the same everywhere in the world, but such issues of media control and ownership as how they are financed and regulated and what their function is vary significantly from country to country. So, for example, the use of satellite technology by CNN has changed the nature of the market for news worldwide. The same technology has been available to many for some time. Yet, the technology did not act alone, nor was it necessarily the prime factor related to CNN's coverage. Because communication technologies are fundamentally conditioned by political and economic forces, they should be understood in the matrix of regulation and public policy.

That technology, markets, and policy are necessarily interdependent is shown in this volume in a number of ways. For example, the nature and mission of mass media institutions in Arab countries are substantively different from those of the media institutions in the United States and Europe regarding ownership, access, content, economics, and purview. These differences placed tremendous pressure on the Western press and on its communications systems to conform to a very different set of norms of the host states. Since the Gulf War was fought on Arab soil and troops were stationed in friendly Saudi territory, the practices of the Saudi Arabian mass communication infrastructures (frequently at cross purposes with Western press ideology) had to be acknowledged and respected.

Douglas A. Boyd details the impact of the communication norms of the Arab states and provides insight about what these differences meant to the communication systems that "belonged" to Western countries but which were allied with important Arab countries with divergent communication values. As Boyd reports, the juxtaposition of Western press organizations on Arab soil led to quite a bit of grumbling by U.S. journalists; both Small and Arant and Warden note this in their pieces about military-press relations.

Communication infrastructure differences are also illustrated in Parker and Hale's analysis of the leafleting of Iraqi troops by the Psychological Operations Forces (PSYOP) of the allies. What eventually became one of the most effective leaflets in promoting surrenders among young Iraqi soldiers was a message that had originally been rejected by the U.S. chain of command as "inappropriate." This leaflet showed two young Arab men, one in traditional clothing, the other in uniform, walking hand in hand into the sunset together. Holding hands is a rather common practice for Arab men, but it was viewed as "unmanly" by the U.S. command. Eventually PSYOP specialists convinced their superiors that this was a cultural practice of long standing in the Gulf region.

Linda Jo Calloway's detailing of the scarcity of portable up-link units further emphasizes the obvious—you have to have a market demand for a technology before it can be produced and distributed. Since there had been only limited demand for this technology prior to the war, most news organizations did not have it. CNN's coverage, which catapulted the network into a position of news leader, was not successful because of superior technology, but rather, as Calloway shows, because CNN capitalized on the political realities of the region, a choice that provided it with the insight to install an outgoing telephone line from Baghdad to Jordan rather than to Saudi Arabia or some other Western ally that was instantly cut off when the bombing started. Hence, as these articles show, the importance of past and current government policies and the nature of existing markets and uses for communication technology were as important as technical expertise and capability in shaping content and coverage.

INTERACTIVE CONTEXT AND CIRCUMSTANCES AND PARAMETERS FOR COMMUNICATION NORMS

In his 1940s study of communication effects, Bernard Berelson said that the "context and circumstances of any communicative interaction set unique parameters for appropriate norms of communication." This quotation is often used with exasperation to demonstrate how little we know about the process of mediated communication. He concluded from his analysis that "some kinds of communication, on some kinds of issues, brought to the attention of some kinds of people under some kinds of conditions, have some kinds of effects" (Berelson, 1948). What communication researchers have done since the time of Berelson's pronouncement is to specify the contexts and circumstances that contribute to direct and indirect effects of media on individuals and society. Denis McQuail

(1990), for example, summarized and categorized numerous studies documenting some of the influences and relationships the media have with individuals and society. It is a commonplace that the exigencies of context, including relevant situational conditions and historical and material factors, that are in place when information is exchanged are among the most important considerations in understanding communication effects. Communication during war is therefore different in substantive ways from communication in peaceful circumstances. Clearly, the salience of information is increased. When information becomes critical to the preservation of life, different information-processing procedures come to the fore. Highly involving or highly salient issues invoke different approaches than do issues that are ephemeral or of low importance (Ray et al., 1973). People communicate differently about the weather when they need to know it for strategic military purposes than when they are making small talk with neighbors. The behavior of the communication media and of military leaders in a war context, featuring particular participants, in a particular place, at a particular time needs to be understood in its unique context. The 1,000 hour war in the Persian Gulf was different from the Six-Day War or the Vietnam War or the 1983 U.S. invasion of Grenada in very important ways. As several authors point out, this was a "war by appointment." Everyone knew that the United States had publicly set January 17 as the day it would take action. Further, it was a war in the sand, not in the jungle. The implications of this were that highly efficient communication systems could quickly be put in place across the desert, allowing for rapid and immediate distribution of information, as Calloway details. The specific context of the war in the Gulf, with Israel nearby and in range of enemy missile attack, allowed for the development of the first radio station without programming, as evidenced by the account of Tidhar and Lemish. Leonard Shyles and Robert M. Fischbach document the bipartisan war debate in the deliberations of the U.S. Congress carried live on C-SPAN. This special political communication context is essential for understanding the issues most salient for the American people, who wanted desperately to ensure that they would "commit the nation before they commit the troops" and, by so doing, avoid another Vietnam. It was a war in which the flow of information between family members and soldiers in the field was faster than that which reached the chain of command of the military. The circumstance of having the Joint Chiefs of Staff watch the same television coverage as did transnational publics was a new context in and of itself. This war melded context and circumstance as never before and allowed artists and printers to produce psychological appeals targeted toward the enemy, based on daily exchanges in intelligence about Saddam Hussein's forces and what might motivate them to surrender.

As a principle of communication, the context and exigency of sending and receiving messages has consistently been found to be an important explainer of communication effectiveness. The authors who write in this volume provide extensive examples that this was indeed the case.

SOURCE CREDIBILITY AS A DETERMINANT OF COMMUNICATION EFFECTIVENESS

The credibility of the sources of information for the public and the press was of great importance in the 1,000 hour war. The quality and character of information sources are vitally important factors for determining the veracity of information and ultimately of public opinion. The key spokespersons who emerged to report the progress of the war included President George Bush; Chairman of the Joint Chiefs of Staff Colin Powell; Pentagon spokesperson, Assistant Secretary of State Pete Williams; and Commander of Allied Forces in the Gulf, General H. Norman Schwarzkopf. These men, as Marion K. Pinsdorf reports, were profoundly different in their communication styles, but all were accorded enormous respect and high credibility by those who watched them on television. They came across as believable and expert; their levels of dynamism were varied but complementary. And the images of these sources of information went directly to television sets in the homes of people around the world, often unedited and unchallenged by the press.

Television audiences are different from readers of newspapers. "Serious war reporters" in the World War II tradition of Ernie Pyle were by and large absent from the Gulf War. The changing relationship of time and space made reflection and interpretation nearly superfluous to the immediate live images of the generals. For the daily press briefings, military sources were the "Norm." However, the spokespersons were seen as honest, thoughtful, and knowledgeable. Audiences identified with them. Overall, the credibility of the military spokespersons was high.

COMMUNICATION MESSAGES AS COMPREHENSIBLE TOPICS AND NARRATIVES

People use information to tell and understand the stories of their lives. The news media's coverage of the 1,000 hour war was told in stories with dramatic elements and recurring themes. The debates in the U.S. Congress were likewise both topics and stories. The war will be remembered by military and civilian viewers alike in terms of lessons learned and dramatic events and stories told. The CNN stories detailed in this volume by Lynda Lee Kaid, Roger Myrick, Mike Chanslor, Cynthia Roper, Mark Hovind, and Nikos Trivoulidis speak to three underlying stories—the Americanization of the war, the role of participation of the media in the war, and the "gee whiz" use of military and telecommunications technology as a determining factor. But this should not be interpreted to mean that everyone got the same story, for as Swanson and Carrier report, the national news networks of 20 different countries in the world produced essentially 20 different spins on the event. These different narratives reflected different national sentiments toward the Gulf War and its participants as well as the strength of each country's involvement in or distance from it.

Several communication themes or narratives seem to be persistent in human history, regardless of its war context. They occurred during the 1,000 hour war as well.

Kill the Messenger Responses

The bashing of the press by the military and the public has been a persistent theme in military-press relationships. The most notable example from history is that of the marathon runner—ancient Greece's equivalent of fiber optics—who was killed after a heroic run because he brought bad news. This predilection to finger pointing at the carrier of information for the content of the message, especially when the news is bad, is a matter of record in nearly every war. It also functions in families, in companies, and in political circles. There is an irrational need to find blame for bad news or for uncertainty. More often than not, the media and the people who carry such information and news of others are subjected to angry attack. Blaming the carrier of bad or disturbing news was evident in the conduct of the Gulf War. The criticism of the press in general, and of Peter Arnett of CNN in particular, for distributing and carrying information and opinion that seemed unsupportive of the allied forces is the most obvious case.

Technology as Salvation Myth

The belief that science and technology are on the side of good and winning has been a persistent theme in American life, and elsewhere in the world as well. During the 1,000 hours of Gulf War conflict, much attention was placed on the superiority of American technology. Kaid et al. note that this was a consistent theme in the CNN coverage. Much of the postwar evaluation focuses more on the technology than on the issues of economics and policies.

These findings reinforce the notion that communication infrastructures reflect the values of a country that is embodied in that country's technology, markets, and policies.

FINAL THOUGHTS

An examination of communication during the Gulf War allows for reflection upon the ways in which communicative institutions and processes function. Communication infrastructures, which are under a profound transformation at present in all parts of the world, can benefit from reflection upon the events of these 1,000 hours. There is a need to resist accepting the easy answer that technological superiority is the most important lesson learned. Communication technology must have a market and a means of support, and it has always been the subject of public policy. These principles have been clearly illustrated by the Gulf War episode. There is not a technological fix for things, only a human and social transformation in the way communication technology is used. The speed and distance insensitivity of new communication technologies require serious study. The institutions that use these technologies will evaluate their applications and consequences best when they come to be viewed as a complex interdependent mix of policy, technology, and economics. For example, the watchdog function of the press needs to be enhanced and rejuvenated. The press in future conflicts should be prepared to be a sorting, cataloging, and interpreting press, more than an information-distributing press. Government should continue to find direct links to the public with information and opinion. The press must be diligent in order to preserve its credibility—its level of expertise on complex topics and its ethics will determine how the public will perceive its product. The press needs to understand that government and the military have the same tools for reaching the public as they do. Hence, the conduct of future wars will have new tools for persuasion as well as coercion. The military's use of sophisticated telecommunications technology will be sharper than ever in reaching audiences with information and disinformation. The military and government will need to be held to tougher standards of ethics and accountability in their uses of these new communication systems. The press will need to be prepared to explain and reflect on events as they occur and help lead the audience to reflect on these events after they have transpired. Reflecting on professional journalists' narratives during and following times of crises can allow for the public to understand the important stories of our time.

Part I

Communication Issues in Press-Military Relationships

1

The Gulf War: Mass Media Coverage and Restraints

William J. Small

On August 2, 1991, President Saddam Hussein of Iraq sent his troops into Kuwait and within a week, U.S. President George Bush was sending American troops to Saudi Arabia to prevent an Iraqi invasion there and to prepare for a military confrontation with Saddam. What followed was a rarity, a war by appointment, one carried out on the precise date set by Bush: January 16, 1991.

An air war began on the date set just at prime time for television in the Eastern Time Zone (it was early morning, January 17, in Iraq) and, on February 23, a ground war that lasted less than five days, called the "100-Hour War" by some. With a speed that eclipsed even that of Israel's 1967 Six-Day War, the coalition forged by the American president and headed by his massive military power swept over Saddam's overestimated but quickly overcome forces, and a surrender was issued from Baghdad.

The big loser was Saddam Hussein. The other loser was traditional American journalism, which also found itself outmatched by the Bush forces and while not surrendering its First Amendment function, independent reporting, found that function seriously compromised. As for the global press, it was even more seriously handicapped. Too much of the domestic American and the world press relied too much on the output of cable's 24-hour news service, the Cable News Network (CNN), and far too often on a carefully orchestrated news management by military and White House sources.

It was not journalism's finest hour. Worse yet, in the United States, at least, the public didn't seem to care.

A Princeton Survey Research Associates poll for the Times-Mirror Company showed that over three-fourths (76%) of Americans knew that Gulf news was being censored by the American military and a larger number (79%) thought that was a good idea. As for broadcasts from the Iraqi side, more people (45%) disapproved of American outlets carrying censored news from Baghdad than the number (43%) who wanted to see or hear those reports (*Quill*, March 1991).

The public seemed perfectly happy with the news it got, even if it felt that the media was being spoonfed by the military. An NBC–*Wall Street Journal* poll said three out of four Americans thought that the military gave the public sufficient information (Stone, 1991).

Many in journalism, from the start, felt that the output of the media was too jingoistic and not critical enough. The *Wall Street Journal* ran a story titled "TV Faulted as U.S. Cheerleader in Gulf." Sam Donaldson of ABC News said, "I'm worried the networks are whooping up war fever. I was surprised and dismayed by the jingoistic tone of some of my colleagues. The public didn't object." In contrast, when Dan Rather and Ted Koppel reported from Baghdad in the prewar period, *Newsweek* reported that the president was angry at "Iraqi cheerleading by television newspeople" (Small, 1990).

The "appointment" to start the war was unusual in that President Bush had given Iraq 45 days to get out of Kuwait. The networks played it up constantly as the deadline approached. CBS News called it "Countdown to Confrontation." The clock starting ticking on November 30, when Bush proposed U.S.–Iraqi talks. On January 16, the air war finally started—on time as Bush proposed. He went on television two hours later and talked to the largest audience in television history (*Tyndall Report*, 1991). This was followed by the carefully orchestrated pattern of briefings in Riyadh and Washington, virtually the only sources outside Baghdad where CNN and its prime reporter, Peter Arnett, became the only American presence to report. The Pentagon imposed pools on reporters, laid down ground rules, ignored journalistic protests, and found its reward was news as the administration would have it and popular reception by readers and broadcast audiences.

A German newspaper, *Die Zeit* of Hamburg, in an article "Reporters in the Gulf Rally 'Round the Flag," wrote of the U.S. Defense Department success "in launching a surprise attack on the public" and complained that German newscasters had fallen "under the spell of Cable News Network (CNN) and video clips from the Pentagon" (Reporters in the Gulf, 1991).

The Pentagon ground rules called for small pools of reporters, escorted by the military, and followed by a security review by the military. The original rules prohibited impromptu interviews and the photographing of severely wounded or dead soldiers. These requirements were dropped after news organizations complained, but the pools and reviews remained.

Throughout the air war phase in January and most of February, media complaints were airily dismissed. The chief Pentagon spokesman, Assistant Secretary of State for Public Affairs Pete Williams, told Congress on February 20 that pools were needed because "over 1,400 reporters, editors, producers, photographers and technicians" were registered with Joint Information Bureaus (JIBs) in Dhahran and Riyadh; in contrast, during World War II only 461 reporters signed up to cover D-day, and only 27 went ashore with the first wave of forces. In procedure unlike that during the 1983 U.S. invasion of Grenada (which even Williams called "a journalistic disaster"), journalists weren't being kept away until the fighting was over (Williams, 1992).

Of course, unlike those on the Normandy shore D-day, no journalists went on air flights during the pre-land phase of the Gulf War. They waited for planes to return and then got carefully monitored interviews. They used still photos and videotape handed to them by the Pentagon.

Williams also testified that no World War II–type of censorship was being imposed. Instead, there was a procedure that "allows us to appeal to news organizations—before the harm is done—when we think material in their stories would violate the ground rules. And the final decisions belong to journalists" (Williams, 1991a).

As we later learned, the so-called noncensorship involved military eyes, often several layers of them, clearing copy. It meant hours and often days of delay. Sometimes, the copy had to be changed in ways unrelated to the ground rules, out of concern with image. Some material never emerged from the desert sands of the Gulf War. The noncensorship controlled where reporters could go and whom they could see and which military "minder" would be present.

Even before the air war ended, the *New York Times* would report on angry protests by reporters on the scene who were held for up to eight hours for trying to cover the war on their own without military escorts. Chris Hedges of the *New York Times* was detained for five hours and when he picked up his credentials, Army Major William Fellows told him, "You have an attitude problem" (Correspondents Protest Pool System, 1991). Reporters heard a senior Air Force officer bluntly assert, as he began a press briefing, "Let me say up front that I don't like the press. Your presence here can't possibly do me any good, and it can hurt me and my people. That's just so you'll know where we stand with each other." The longtime military spokesman in Vietnam, Major General Winant Sidle, said, "The guys who are generals today were majors and colonels in Vietnam and they were the ones who hated the press the most" (Notes and Comment, 1991).

It was Sidle who headed a panel to discuss coverage of military actions after the blocking of press coverage during Granada until after the fighting. A member of that group, Scott Cutlip, pointed out that pools were never meant to exist after the first 72 hours. Cutlip, dean emeritus of journalism at the University of Georgia, wrote that it was "never intended (that) the pool system be used in the high-handed way that Bush, [Secretary of Defense Dick] Cheney, and [General Norman] Schwarzkopf used it" (*Washington Journalism Review*, April 1991).

Examples abound of abuses of the system imposed by the Pentagon. Fred Bruni of the *Detroit Free Press* described buoyant bomber pilots returning, as "giddy" with the success of their mission. The military changed "giddy" to "proud" and after Bruni protested, allowed "pumped up." They also held the story for two days before releasing it (Military Obstacles Detailed, 1991). Military security certainly was not at issue here, image was.

Said Bruni, "The instructions from the top were to watch us carefully, not help us" (*Editor and Publisher*, 1991).

In July, an Ad Hoc Media Group on problems of news coverage in the Persian Gulf War wrote Secretary of Defense Cheney about many of the shortcomings of the system. For example, anything resembling a religious observance by Americans was usually vetoed for news coverage because of Saudi religious sensitivities.

Stephanie Glass of the *San Antonio Light* told of public affairs officers (PAOs) who frequently finished sentences for those being interviewed or answered for them entirely (Military Obstacles Detailed, 1991). When she asked that the airmen be allowed to finish their own sentences, she was told not to be a "smart ass" or she would be put back on the bus.

Albert Hunt of the *Wall Street Journal* wrote about public affairs officers who stepped into the middle of interviews and stared down military people saying things the PAOs didn't like. Edie Lederer of the Associated Press similarly told of a PAO who sat "facing the person being interviewed and shaking his head yes or no as to whether a question should be answered" (Military Obstacles Detailed, 1991).

A retired army colonel David Hackworth, writing for *Newsweek*, said that when his photographer tried to take a picture through a car window, "U.S. soldiers fixed bayonets and charged us. I had more guns pointed at me by Americans or Saudis who were into controlling the press than in all my years of actual combat" (Military Obstacles Detailed, 1991).

On February 25, when a SCUD missile killed 28 U.S. soldiers bivouacked in Dhahran, a "quick reaction pool" of reporters was headquartered only a few miles away but was never deployed. Official information came—later—from Riyadh, 150 miles away (Military Obstacles Detailed, 1991).

When pool reporters prevented from witnessing the fighting at Khafji were briefed, they were told of the strong presence of Saudi and Qatari troops in recapturing the city from the Iraqis. Clearly it was the American forces who did most of the fighting, but for political or diplomatic reasons, the military passed out most of the praise to the others. They also understated the fierceness of Iraqi resistance. The best accounts of Khafji came from journalists who got there on their own, in violation of Pentagon ground rules (Apple, 1991).

Even the Pentagon spokesman, Pete Williams, confessed that there were problems. "We know of cases where stories were approved in the field only to be delayed for over a day on their trip back to the press center in Dhahran. The first stories written about the stealth fighters were, for some reason, sent all the way back to the F-117's home base in Nevada to be cleared" (Military Obstacles Detailed, 1991).

On January 21 Bob Simon, the highly respected CBS News correspondent, and his crew also tried to avoid the military "minders" and get to the border.

They were picked up by the Iraqis and kept in prison until the war ended. They survived 40 days of ordeal that might have been avoided had restrictions not been so tight.

Pools, the Pentagon said, were needed because of the large number of correspondents, but Barry Zorthian, the U.S. Mission spokesman in Vietnam for four years, has said that roughly 2,000 reporters were accredited in Vietnam during his time there. Uncensored, hundreds of thousands of stories were filed. Only five or six security violations occurred, most of them accidental or based on a misunderstanding. He said none actually endangered life or jeopardized military operations (Schanberg, 1991a).

After the Gulf War ended, Pentagon officials would keep insisting that the system worked well. Pete Williams, the chief spokesman, said "the press gave the American people the best war coverage they ever had." A senior military official dismissed any media gripes as "sour grapes" (*Washington Post*, 1991).

From the earliest days, prominent journalists expressed concerns. David Gergen, editor-at-large of *U.S. News & World Report*, told a Columbia University audience in late January that the common images Americans had about what happened in the war were no longer being provided by the networks or the anchormen or by the correspondents, they were increasingly the releases of the government (Gould, 1991).

In contrast, Mortimer Zuckerman, owner of the same magazine, was among the few in journalism who was not critical of the military's performance vis-à-vis the press. He told the media department of Ogilvy & Mather on March 8 that "I am astonished by the availability and the access that we have had both to the Pentagon and to the information we feel we needed to cover and report the war. The press, in my judgment, seems petulant, self-concerned, self-centered and really downright silly, particularly when you compare the rather mature intelligence of some of the military briefers compared to the stupidity of some of the questioners." He said, "We're not just journalists; we're also Americans." After repeating that he was "absolutely thrilled" with the access "to what was really happening in the war," he said "I think it showed up in the coverage." In *Newsday*, a sardonic Sydney Schanberg added two words: "It did" (Schanberg, 1991b).

The coverage that got the most attention, certainly in the period prior to the start of the brief land land war, was that of the Cable News Network. In its wildest dreams, the leadership of CNN could never have imagined the lavish praise and, in time, heavy criticism that would come its way.

This war at this time was tailor-made for this 24-hour news service. CNN could bring blanket coverage, including live coverage of briefings in the Pentagon and by military officers, both U.S. and British, in the Gulf. The volume was immense. It also was exclusive in Baghdad for many, many weeks. It was the only one capable of broadcasting from the scene on January 16 when the first air raids began over Iraq and, though audio only, it was a stunning scoop. The measure of CNN's elevation to top rank television came when Tom Brokaw on

NBC ("swallowing hard," said *New York* magazine) interviewed CNN's Bernard Shaw, who was in Baghdad at the time.

Salutes like "CNN'S Triumph" (Diamond, 1991a) were not uncommon. Media critic Edwin Diamond said the CNN team had what every other news organization wishes it had: "implicit recognition on the part of Iraqi authorities that it is the preeminent news-gathering force in the world" (Diamond, 1991b). In the opening hours of the war, CNN's usually modest audience swelled tenfold to nearly 11 million viewers. With exposure to just over 60 percent of television homes, on January 16, CNN was getting audiences in prime time as large as the three networks with their 98 percent coverage (War Boosts CNN, 1991).

The turn to CNN coverage seemed to be worldwide. In Cairo, Kuwaitis were making a run on shops to buy new color sets to watch CNN and the newspaper that said, "The whole world is watching CNN" (*Al-Hayat*, 1991).

A regional paper in Germany said, "CNN is on the ball whilst German broadcasters were in deep slumber" (*Abend zeitung*, 1991). An Arab newspaper looked halfway around the world to note that "in spots that barely make it onto maps, people are hearing about the Gulf and watching CNN. . . . In the Solomon Islands a local telephone company, that managed to tap into Cable News Network satellite broadcasts, was mobbed by locals" (*al-Anwar*, 1991).

In Liege, a national Belgian daily headlined "Nous Voulons CNN"—We Want CNN (*Libre, Belgium*, 1991) and in Oslo, a Norwegian national paper said NRK was not enough—"License Payers Are Rushing to Get CNN," that the local cable company was out of stock with decoders, unable to meet the demand (*Morgenbladet*, 1991). In Egypt, Minister of Information Sawat El-Sherif ordered Egyptian television to start carrying CNN (*Akher Saa*, 1991). In Japan, CNN was so popular that people started carrying CNN tote bags and wearing CNN T-shirts (*Quill*, March 1991).

Clearly, the claims of CNN's chairman and founder, Ted Turner, that his network was the world's most important was getting a degree of support that even he might not have envisioned. A Cairo paper said, "Ted Turner has become the most famous media person in this decade . . . thanks to CNN" (*al-Mussawar*, 1991); and a Spanish paper's headline said, "CNN, A Great TV Empire, Born Out of the Hand of Ted Turner" (*Heraldo De Aragón*, 1991).

In Norway, the headline was "Alle vil ha CNN"—Everyone Wants CNN (*Rana Blad*, 1991). In Venice, the local paper wrote of competition between CNN and the Italian networks and concluded "without any doubt, the American CNN dominates" (*Messagero Veneto*, 1991). A French national daily said, "As the sole reporter left in Iraq, Peter Arnett's reports remained a window to the world" in an article headlined "L'irresistible succes de CNN"—The Irresistible Success of CNN (*La Croix*, 1991). In Spain, one headline read "Bendita CNN"—God Bless CNN (*La Crónica de León*, 1991).

What a glorious time for CNN. However, before long, criticism also came flooding in—especially for CNN's reporter Peter Arnett, the only television correspondent reporting from Baghdad.

CNN's President, Tom Johnson, said, "CNN has been ground zero for critics, for colleagues, for viewers, for families, for the military, for the newsmakers and the news haters. . . . The people here have made news policies and decisions that have never been faced by journalists prior to this time. For so much of this there were no guidebooks, there were few rules and there were a lot of professional land mines" (War Takes Its Toll, 1991). The "land mines" ranged from a live and unedited Arnett interview with Saddam to the audience reaction to press behavior at briefings, something that was largely new to American viewers, who have usually seen only more sedate presidential news conferences.

There was a modest flap when Bernard Shaw came out of Baghdad and refused the military's request for a debriefing. Shaw said he was a journalist and felt he had to remain "neutral." Most journalists would agree, but Hollywood actor Charlton Heston, on a morning television show, said, "Who does he think he is—Switzerland?" (Rabinowitz, 1991). It might be argued that at that time, in that set of world conditions, Bernard Shaw was far more important than Switzerland. In fact, one European newspaper in a moment of editorial excess had contended that Shaw "today is better known in the whole world than (President) Bush himself" (*La Crónica de León*, 1991).

The heaviest attacks on CNN came from Wyoming's Senator Alan K. Simpson, the Republican whip in the Senate. Simpson, writing in *USA Today*, called it "ridiculous that millions of dollars were spent to bomb and sever Saddam's communication link to the outside world only to have CNN restore it" (Simpson, 1991).

Simpson directed his harshest criticism at CNN's man in Baghdad, Peter Arnett, whom he called "a sympathizer." Later, in a letter to the *New York Times* in March, he amended that, since he had no proof, and simply described Arnett as a "dupe" or "tool" of the Iraqis. *Newsweek* called it "a half-baked apology" (Calling a Truce, 1991).

The Republican National Committee, in an orchestrated campaign, sent out 500,000 appeals asking recipients to sign letters complaining about media coverage in the Persian Gulf. The appeals were signed by Senator Simpson (Press-bashing Hero, 1991). Simpson, who said Americans "are appalled to see that kind of coverage coming out of an enemy country," had himself visited Saddam the previous April and had told the Iraqi leader that "I believe your problems lie with the Western media, and not with the U.S. Government." He cited a *Newsweek* cover headline, "Butcher of Baghdad," as one example of negative reporting (Smear from the Whip, 1991). He told Hussein that America has "a haughty and pampered press. They all consider themselves to be political geniuses. . . . They are very cynical" (Greenberger, 1991).

The number one target was Arnett. *Time* called him "the lightning rod for most of these complaints" (Zoglin, 1991a). It noted that CNN had gotten over 55,000 letters, phone calls, and faxes in the early weeks of the war, about 60 percent of them negative. In late February, the Time/CNN poll showed that 88 percent of America supported the censorship in the Gulf, that 79 percent said they were getting enough information about the war (Zoglin, 1991b).

CNN's reputation was enhanced on live television when both Defense Secretary Richard Cheney and Joint Chiefs Chairman Colin Powell said they watched CNN and felt its coverage was the best. General Powell referred to Bernard Shaw familiarly as "Bernie" (Zoglin, 1991b). But by the end of March, the dominant military figure in the Gulf War, General H. Norman Schwarzkopf, would be on television saying, "I did resent CNN aiding and abetting an enemy who was violating the Geneva Convention." The four-star general, head of the forces in the Gulf, said he understood there was a First Amendment and a "public's right to know," but with considerable agitation he went on, "I just think that in the future when people choose to justify their actions based upon the American public's right to know, they'd better check with the American public first because the American public has made it very clear to me, in all the literally hundreds of thousands of letters I have gotten, how they felt about the term 'the American people's right to know' as it was being used by the people who were doing that sort of thing" (Tyler, 1991).

What had CNN done that caused such a strong response from General Schwarz-kopf? It had shown American prisoners paraded before television cameras by Iraqi captors. The Iraqis may have violated the Geneva Convention, but an act of self-censorship by CNN or the commercial networks (which also carried the footage) might, in the long run, have caused greater concern among thoughtful Americans than viewing the CNN presentation.

As for Arnett, among the particulars that angered the military and the White House was his report on the bombing of a baby-formula factory. White House Press Secretary Marlin Fitzwater sharply rebuked Arnett and stated flatly, "Disinformation. That factory is, in fact, a production facility for biological weapons."

Arnett the next day said, "I learned in Vietnam to believe only what my eyes have seen as [opposed to] anything I hear from any official of any government or from any person. I have an inborn skepticism because I am a journalist . . . I can only confirm what my eyes see." Arnett also reported that two things seemed untouched by the bombing—a newly painted sign, both in English and Arabic, that said "Baby Milk Plant" and a large painting of Saddam comforting a distressed child. This curious survival of these two items amidst the "twisted and blackened" remains of the plant was a clear message to all viewers that the Iraqis were engaging in heavy-handed propaganda (*Washington Journalism Review*, 1991).

Arnett later was to say, "I think it was a mistaken bombing. . . . It seems to me that it was an unlikely place for a chemical plant. It was beside a main highway with no security fences around it. . . . I see a lot of other installations around here that are probably less important than a facility of that nature, and the security is incredible. I just cannot conceive (of their having) the limited kind of security that they had if it was such a secret installation. I mean, it's Iraq, why pretend: they can build it underground, they can put it anywhere" (Does Bloody Footage, 1991).

Another report that infuriated the military was Arnett's report on the bombing of a bunker that the Pentagon said was an underground military command center. Arnett said he saw no evidence that it was anything other than a civilian bomb shelter (*Newsweek*, 1991b, p. 20).

The perennial nag of America's press, Reed Irvine, chairman of Accuracy In Media, said, "In war time, the rules change. The press can not stay neutral." He noted that after World War II, William Joyce, Lord Haw, and Iva Toguri, who had broadcast as Tokyo Rose, were arrested and tried. The British hanged Joyce as a traitor. Later, asked if Arnett should get similar treatment, Irvine said, "I'm not saying that should happen to Arnett" (Group Launches Campaign, 1991).

There were those who worried not about the press abandoning its role as an observer, a neutral observer, but rather that the new technologies and the availability of live coverage were a problem. Was television giving its audiences too much too fast? A German publication observed that

the impatient television gobbles up all time for consideration, all time for checking and weighing information—time that democracy urgently requires. Thus the triumph of the news could spell the demise of democracy, which would be replaced by the rule of speed. The highest-speed journalism avails itself of military methods, draws near the military, and thus risks losing its independence and credibility. Democracy can protect itself only by rediscovering slowness. (Reporters in the Gulf, 1991)

Those Americans who flocked to watch television and listen to radio throughout the Gulf crisis would disagree. Their appetite for as much as they could learn and as quickly as it could be learned was obvious. Further, inaccuracy in fact or due to nuance could be corrected later by experienced broadcast editors.

One surprise result of live coverage was that it lifted the veil of mystery off the press briefing. Reporters know the helter-skelter nature of press questioning, but to a nonjournalist the reporters can seem rude and at times ignorant. Reporters may believe there are no improper questions, only improper answers; but watching an unedited news conference that in other times would not be seen by the average American, that average American is sometimes, or at least possibly, surprised if not shocked by the manners of the press.

A former vice-president of CBS, Oscar Katz, in a letter to this author, observed that

The problem is that broadcast briefings permit the public to "eavesdrop" on a meeting originally set up as part of the *newsgathering* process. Before the public was able to attend, the only important component at a briefing was the information provided by, or elicited from, the briefer. But, I suspect that the viewer at home reacts not only to the information developed, but even more to the behavior of the participants; and the reporters involved emerge as the heavies to most of the audience.[1]

The perceptive Katz feels that reporters emerge this way "because many of their questions fall into one of the following categeries: just plain dumb; repetitious; sometimes arrogant; a get-the-story-at-any-cost attitude even though human life may be at stake; showing bias or pre-judgment; obscure'' (personal communication, February 27, 1991).

Never before had the media faced the dilemma of the impact of a genuine ''live on television'' war or the admission of the public into the briefing room. The future of television news is not in locking that public out nor in blocking live coverage where technical and other circumstances permit. The future lies in deciding how to deal with these problems.

Meanwhile for the commercial networks, the future also raises serious questions as to the costs of this kind of coverage. In the past, during the four days of the coverage of the assassination and burial of President John F. Kennedy or the times in 1981 when Ronald Reagan and Pope John Paul II were shot, network news stayed on for hours, and all commercials were dropped. That was ''then,'' when the traditional three networks were highly profitable and had different ownership. The new owners of the traditional networks are all bottom-line oriented, and the new economic picture at the networks is one of a badly eroded audience (at times, half the prime-time audience that the three networks had 10 or 15 years ago) and, in 1991, severely depressed advertising sales.

The networks did preempt many hours for Gulf War specials and expanded their nightly newscasts. On 32 weekdays during the war, NBC expanded to a full hour, CBS on 22 of those weekdays, and ABC on 13, but many affiliates carried only the normal half-hour they usually allow for evening network news. Worse still, in the early weeks, a number of affiliates, including some major ones, dropped their network and carried CNN (*Tyndall Report*, 1991).

The CNN scoops and victories of the early going faded once the ground war began on February 23, and the three traditional networks regained their footing. Also, the ground war moved so quickly that the pool rules were ignored. In the sweep to recapture Kuwait City, Bob McKeown of CBS News got there and was on the air before American troops arrived. He and others had discovered that following Saudi and Egyptian forces into Kuwait was a way to escape the heavy handed Pentagon rules. With portable uplinks, network reports poured out. Richard Threlkeld of CBS News, at a position west of the city, found Iraqi troops willing to surrender to him and his crew. Others had similar experiences. ABC's Forrest Sawyer, NBC's Bruce Willis and CNN's Charles Jaco and Brian Jenkins came to Kuwait City within hours of McKeown (*Tyndall Report*, 1991).

The over-the-air network news organizations, like the allied forces, made a very strong finish, but the cable news people had scored early and often. They would read media critics saying things like ''CNN has become the preeminent world-news service'' and even speculating that after CNN brought the briefings into the homes live, the *New York Times'* role as repository of ''the record'' was being supplanted (Who Won the Media War?, 1991).

CNN had long claimed, and world leaders have confirmed, that it is watched in all major world capitals. Reports held that Saddam watched it throughout the war. It certainly was monitored by Iraqi leadership if not by Saddam himself.

In the United States questions for the press generally and television in particular remained, questions about the impact of a government's success in getting the kind of press coverage it so much wanted during the Gulf War. Polls showed that President Bush's popularity was at a point higher than that of any other president since the late 1940s and some polls even showed that at the war's end, the president may have had the highest public approval of *all* time (at least since polling started). The polls showed that the American military was right up there among the most admired of American institutions.

What administration could resist concluding that the taming of the press in the Gulf had paid off? The assertion by military officers was that if you could handle the press properly and keep them out of your way, you could really do your job right.

There was also in the military an increased sophistication since Vietnam in "managing" the news. One senior military officer put it this way (to the *Wall Street Journal* in an article entitled "U.S. Used Press as Weapon"): "Some people say the media is the enemy but in fact the media is really a battlefield and you have to win on it." The article went on to give examples of how the press was "used" in military briefings that served up contradictory or confusing figures about battle damage, about Iraqi ships declared out of action and later reemerging as targets, and—most of all—about leaving the impression that a Marine landing was planned when in fact it was a means to convince Iraq that it had to deploy troops to block an invasion from the sea. As Pentagon press officer Pete Williams put it, "We were not trying to deceive the press. We were trying to fool Saddam Hussein." He said a Marine trial exercise was scheduled and the television reporters clamored to cover it (Mossberg, 1991).

Hodding Carter, a former State Department spokesman, has noted, "Our government is in the business of propaganda, which is not the same thing as lying, but definitely not the same thing as truth" (Gould, 1991). The Pentagon-released pictures of precision-guided "smart" bombs going down chimneys of Iraqi targets left an impression that we rarely missed, but these were a small part of the total bomb load dropped in 43 days of aerial attacks. Some 82,000 tons of unguided bombs were dropped, and their accuracy rating was 25 percent, not the 90 percent of the smart bombs. Of 88,500 tons of bombs dropped, 70 percent missed their targets (Wicker, 1991). That was not the impression left by the hand-out videotapes.

The president of the Associated Press, Louis Boccardi, said, "Lots of stories went into the headquarters review process and died. Reporters are now emerging from the pools and finding that these stories that they thought were back home in print never went anywhere. And that's an intolerable condition" (Media in the 21st Century, 1991).

Pentagon officials keep insisting that there really was no censorship, and they drew no distinction between censorship per se and limiting access to key areas. For example, they barred access to Dover Air Force Base, traditional location for returning bodies to this country from conflicts overseas. Pete Williams, speaking before the National Press Club, stated that there was nothing special about Dover: "There really wasn't anything happening at Dover other than the caskets being unloaded and shipped on" (1991a). Of course, that was precisely why the press wanted the access it had had in the past, to see if a large number of casualties were coming out of the Gulf. From the military's point of view, the image of caskets was one it wanted to avoid. And it succeeded in doing just that.

The Pentagon people said that pools in the Gulf were needed because there were just too many reporters, editors, producers, photographers, and so on over there (Correspondents Protest Pool Systems, 1991). Less than one in three reporters ever got into a pool. Almost all of these represented American news organizations. The non-American press complained bitterly and even threatened in mid-February to drive en masse to the Kuwait front (Ibid.).

In an attempt to break the restrictive nature of the pools, three lawsuits were filed. On January 10, on behalf of 13 journalists and news organizations that were locked out of pools, a suit was launched on the grounds that the press restrictions constituted prior restraint and interfered in the ability to gather news. A second lawsuit, one month later, by Agence France-Presse (AFP) complained that the U.S. military had banned it, but not the Associated Press (AP) and Reuters. A third suit was filed by the American Civil Liberties Union over the issue of banning the public and the press from Dover Air Force Base. None of the suits succeeded (personal communication, Gannett Foundation, June 1991).

Stanley Cloud, *Time*'s Washington Bureau chief, said, "Throughout the long evolution of the Department of Defense pool, the press willingly, passively, and stupidly went along with it. That is the original sin which got us where we are and I don't blame anybody as much as I blame us" (personal communication, Gannett Foundation, June, 1991).

In a letter to the *New York Times*, the executive director of the Fund for Free Expression, Gara LaMarche, noted that

The U.S. had plenty of company in the censorship business. Turkish state television barred scenes of anything hinting at U.S. bombing raids originating in that country. Saudi Arabia censored all foreign publications, banning those with articles dealing with the Palestine Liberation Organization or civilian bombing casualties. The newest U.S. ally, Syria, detained 80 writers and intellectuals for expressing support for Iraq. No surprise, Syrian repression, but France banned any pro-Iraqi publications and the BBC dropped a report on the export to Iraq of British-built superguns on the grounds that the tone is wrong. (In Bad Company, 1991)

THE AFTERMATH

Did other countries notice how well censorship worked? When, after the Gulf War, El Salvador detained foreign journalists, it rationalized the practice by citing U.S. press policies in the Gulf (Back Up the Bombing Boasts, 1991).

It was long after the war ended that Americans learned about some of the things that had gone unreported. In September, Patrick Sloyan, writing for *Newsday*, reported on "a grisly innovation" used by three brigades of the First Mechanized Infantry Division once the ground war began. With combat earth-movers, they had bulldozed 70 miles of trenches and buried thousands of Iraqi soldiers alive (*Newsday*, 1991a).

Those tactics may have been the kind of thing that happens in war, but clearly the Pentagon had no desire to make it known at the time or after. Shortly before the "buried-alive" story surfaced, Secretary of Defense Richard Cheney, in an interim report to the Congress, made no mention of it. Apparently it didn't fit in the armed forces' picture of a quick and sanitary victory.

Cheney did tell Congress that part of the success in the land war was due to dropping clusters of bomblets, millions of them, on Iraqi troops. These mini-bombs, ranging in size from a golf ball to a softball, could create serious casualties and do great damage to morale. What Cheney did not report—but Sloyan did in September—was that thousands of these bomblets were duds that littered the battlefields and proved to be a serious problem for the incoming American troops. Sloyan reported that there may have been more American casualties than Iraqi wounded and dead from these minibombs. Fourteen American deaths and over 100 wounded were the result of American soldiers' stumbling on or playing with the bomblet duds (*Newsday*, 1991a).

On April 2, at Fordham University, a panel discussion of the Gulf War concluded that—in the words of CNN's Bernard Shaw—"The American people, readers, viewers, and listeners were short-changed." CBS correspondent Richard Threlkeld said, "The history of this war is probably going to be lost"; and Shaw added, "You never did get a complete picture at any point in time and it was intentional."

One of Shaw's bosses at CNN, Executive Vice President Ed Turner, in an October Johns Hopkins "Conference on Television and the Gulf War: The Impact on Strategy and Decision Making" said

The fact of the matter is that you have not seen the ground war yet. You have not seen the videotape and you have not seen the still pictures. That footage exists, thousand and thousands of feet of it, on tape and film and still pictures in the Washington area and may be released by 1994. There is no doubt that for some, the display of this videotape could undermine the will to pursue this kind of foreign policy. However, the war is the public's business. The viewers are grown-ups. They really can take bad news. (*Broadcasting*, October 7, 1991)

At that meeting, Richard N. Hass, a special assistant to the president and senior director for Near East and South Asian affairs on the National Security Council, said, "television was the chief tool for selling our policy."

Governments, that of the United States included, try to put the best face on their actions, try to hide embarrassing matters, mislead reporters if it serves their goals. In a free society, the press in its traditional role as witness and watchdog should ferret out as much fact as it can. In the euphoria that followed the Gulf War and with the tremendous public acclaim for the president and the military, these were not issues that the journalist could press, at least with any expectation of public support.

Experienced journalists say they are not in a popularity contest, but many recognize how difficult it is to deal with the arrogance of public figures with immense public approval. They also realize that many government officials freely use the American press as a scapegoat when talking to heads of state and other foreigners who might be displeased with actions of the United States. This happened in the case of Iraq and Saddam Hussein.

In April 1990, U.S. Ambassador to Iraq, April Glaspie, felt compelled to tell Hussein that "if the President had control of the media, his job would be much easier." She said this in the course of an exchange with the Iraqi dictator who had, just one month earlier, hanged Farzad Bazoft after an Iranian British journalist was arrested near an Iraqi military facility.

The Glaspie-Saddam exchange was taped and released by the Iraqis later that summer. It was a year later before the U.S. government, in Ambassador Glaspie's testimony before Congress, claimed that parts of it had been edited by Iraq.

Glaspie cited an interview that ABC's Diane Sawyer had done with Saddam. Said Glaspie to him, "I saw the Diane Sawyer program on ABC. And what happened in that program was cheap and unjust. And this is a real picture of what happens in the American media—even to American politicians themselves. These are the methods that the Western media employs. I am pleased that you add your voice to the diplomats who stand up to the media" (Collins, 1990).

What had Sawyer done to Saddam that Glaspie found so cheap and unjust? Sawyer had asked him about reports of his using chemical weapons, even against his own people. She had asked him whether reports were true that he personally had killed a member of his own cabinet. She had pointed out that he had been called "the most dangerous man in the world" and "the butcher of Baghdad." Of course, Saddam denied all allegations.

When Senators Alan Simpson and Robert Dole were in Baghdad at about the same time, Simpson sympathized with Saddam over the arrogance of the American press, and Dole apologized for a Voice of America commentary criticizing Iraq's human rights record (Gigot, 1990).

The commentary in question, "No More Secret Police," simply said, "The secret police are still widely present in countries like China, North Korea, Iran, Iraq, Syria, Libya, Cuba and Albania." Ambassador Glaspie cabled Washington that Iraq protested this "flagrant interference in the internal affairs of Iraq," and the State Department then asked that all VOA editorials on Iraq go to State for clearance before they aired. One that the State Department killed was especially prophetic—it said that the United States was committed to supporting its friends in the Persian Gulf and would take very seriously any threat that put this country at risk (Correspondents Protest Pool System, 1991).

All of this is disturbing to friends of free speech. But governments do this kind of thing, always have, and always will. What was new in the Gulf War was the extent to which the military successfully spoonfed the press until conditions permitted journalists to break away from those restrictions, and also the extent to which the new technologies spawned by satellite communications permitted the public to be a witness to the raw material of press coverage.

As stated earlier, there are those in journalism who are very much concerned about instant news. Surely many a meeting of newspeople will discuss the impact of this kind of television in the future. But, in the words of Ed Turner of CNN, "The technology we have today can't be disinvented" (Diamond, 1991b). What needs to be discussed is: how it is to be used; how live coverage is to be identified; how the public is to be educated as to its nature. To try to stop it or slow the transmission is futile.

These are the items for the press's agenda as it discusses the future: what to do about the new technology with us now and that still to come. And, perhaps more important, what to do about government moves to manage the news.

Jack Nelson, the *Los Angeles Times* Washington bureau chief said, "If you look at it from the outset, I think, the press was reflecting the views of the government and it never really changed. Bush and the people around him did a masterful job controlling exactly what the American people were seeing" (personal communication, Gannett Foundation, June, 1991).

Newsweek's Jonathon Alter adds, "The sad truth is that we 'covered' the war but we didn't report the war" (personal communication, Gannett Foundation, June, 1991). An angry Sydney Schanberg wrote

The Pentagon generals kept telling us they were savvy about the war—sure, they said, we know war is foul and brutish, never neat or pretty. And then they turned around and, with straight faces, proceeded to prettify it for us—with hand-picked footage that showed precision air strikes on Iraqi buildings, enemy rockets being burst in midair by Patriot missiles, etc., etc. . . . and never a picture of an American boy wounded in the sand. . . . A thousand reporters went to the gulf to cover the war and were treated as POWs. Why aren't they reclaiming their birthright now? (*Newsday*, 1991b)

News executives and reporters are petitioning the Pentagon to see that it doesn't happen again. But the success of the Pentagon, and the fact that the public at large has lost interest, mitigate against any change in policy. Indeed, an administration, having learned how it could contain the press, is not likely to overlook that lesson either in future international conflicts or domestic political ones.

The battle for a free press never ends. The battleground, thanks to the events of early 1991, make it more difficult than ever for the press to prevail.

NOTE

1. Cited in William J. Small, "A Report—The Gulf War and Television News: Past, Future, and Present," *Mass Communications Review*, *19*(1-2) (1992), pp. 3-13.

2

The Military and the Media: A Clash of Views on the Role of the Press in Time of War

M. David Arant and Michael L. Warden

With regard to publicity, the first essential in military operations is that no information of value shall be given to the enemy. The first essential in newspaper work and broadcasting is wide-open publicity. It is your job and mine to try to reconcile these sometimes diverse considerations.

—General Dwight D. Eisenhower
(From regulations for war correspondents accompanying Allied Expeditionary Forces in World War II, 1945)

When in August 1990 the United States deployed troops to challenge the Iraqi invasion of Kuwait and in January 1991 went to war against Iraq, the Bush administration and the military implemented restrictions on the press in reporting from the war zone. The restrictions ignited an acrid debate over the need for controls. Journalists charged that the government was trying to muzzle the press and control the reporting from the war zone in order to shape American public opinion about the war. Tight restrictions on access and implementation of security review of all copy from reporter pools created new tensions in the military-media relationship that had soured in the aftermath of Vietnam. Most journalists vociferously objected to the implementation of press pools and security review in the coverage of the military in the Persian Gulf (Henry, 1991; Nessen, 1991; Sloyan, 1991). A few media organizations and journalists initiated lawsuits against the U.S. Department of Defense in an effort to challenge the constitutionality of war zone restrictions and the limitations on access to Dover Air Force Base. Neither produced any definitive resolution of the issues.

This chapter analyzes the debate between the media and the military over restrictions on press coverage of the Persian Gulf War for the explicit and implicit assumptions about the role of the press in society, and especially for assumptions about its role in society in time of war. First, the ways in which the media view their role in covering government—and in particular how they see their role in reporting U.S. military operations in wartime—are considered. Then, how the military views the media's role in covering the military is explored. Sources for these views of the role of the press are the commentary and debate by the military and media on the press' role in the Persian Gulf War. Also, the ways that changes in media and military technologies exacerbated the tensions in the media-military relationship in the Persian Gulf War are considered.

The conflict about the amount of access that should be granted the press in covering the operations of the U.S. military seems to boil down to different conceptualizations of the role of the press in society, and especially different expectations for the press in time of war. At its essence, the access issue is first a question of what function the press should have in relationship to government in a democratic society and, second, a question of whether that function changes in times of war or other societal stress.

MEDIA'S RELATIONSHIP TO THE GOVERNMENT

This section discusses how American journalists have conceived the role of the press in a democratic society and whether journalists believe that role changes in time of war. Journalists seem to be articulating concepts of the press that echo the libertarian and social responsibility models outlined by Fred S. Siebert, Theodore Peterson, and Wilbur Schramm (1956). On the one hand, some media commentators contend that the press's role is to remain aloof of the government and serve as a watchdog of the government and the military, a classic libertarian or fourth-estate model of the press. Others suggest that the press, particularly during time of war, has a responsibility to line up behind the government and the military to support the war effort. After considering some models of the media's relationship to government we shall discuss some journalists' perspectives on the role of the press in covering the U.S. military in the Persian Gulf War.

John C. Merrill and Jack Odell (1983) said that a nation's journalism must reflect the political philosophy of the government, or else it becomes dysfunctional. In turn, journalism's relation to government determines its basic function or purpose in a society. Americans historically have valued open and free political debate and have given special protection to speech and press in the courts in order to promote the self-governing function. From the nation's inception in the eighteenth century, the U.S. media functioned under a libertarian press model. Under this model, the media served to inform and entertain the people, but more important functions were to help discover truth and to check government abuses. A model of the press similar to the libertarian is that of the press as the fourth estate, an unofficial branch of government. The autonomous press functions as a watchdog on the government, publicizing abuses and arousing citizen interest. In his discussion of the First Amendment's press clause, David A. Anderson (1983) suggested that the framers of the amendment understood the unique role of the press as a check on government and wrote in protection of the press to guard against government control of the press. In his discussion of the meaning of the First Amendment, Vincent Blasi (1977) argued that though the press had several roles in American society, the central one is its checking function on government action.

In the middle of this century, debate on the U.S. media's role in society led to the articulation of the social responsibility model. Proponents of this model argued that because the press had been given special freedom in American society, the press had an obligation to carry out certain essential functions for society. Among press responsibilities under this model are servicing the political system by providing debate on public affairs, enlightening the public so that it can govern itself and serving as a watchdog against government abuses (Siebert, Peterson, and Schramm, 1956). The Commission on Freedom of the Press (1947), chaired by Robert M. Hutchins, found that press performance fell short of its responsibilities to society. The commission recommended that some independent or governmental agency was needed to monitor the press for accountability to its responsibility. The social responsibility model was already the model for U.S. broadcasters, who were encouraged by federal regulations to serve the public interest. Under the social responsibility model of U.S. media, the freedom of the press is restricted by having to answer to some agency that determines the press' responsibility to society. In broadcasting, the Federal Communication Commission defined what that responsibility was.

A third model of press performance, authoritarianism, is at the other end of the freedom-control continuum from the libertarian model. Under the libertarian model, the press enjoys the greatest freedom from government control, while under the authoritarian model, the government imposes the greatest restrictions on the media. Social responsibility falls somewhere in the middle, in the direction of press freedom. In an authoritarian system, the press exists to serve the state or ruler. Diversity of views is not tolerated. The state controls what is published through licensing, censorship or postpublication punishment.

MEDIA'S RELATIONSHIP TO THE MILITARY AND GOVERNMENT IN WARTIME

Though one ideal of press function may characterize a society's press in peacetime, a nation's media model is not static. The tendency to impose limitations on free press is magnified when the government faces a crisis, such as war. For example, a government and its people that normally support extensive freedom for the press may redefine press responsibilities in time of war and try to restrict the media to a role supportive of government. In his study of English press freedom, Fred S. Siebert (1952) found that the area of freedom of press contracts and the enforcement of restraints on the press increases as stresses on the stability of government and of the structure of society increase. In time of national crisis, such as an impending war, the limits on press freedom increase when compared to those in peacetime.

When the United States has faced a crisis, the people and the government have expected the media to serve as an additional means to mobilize support for the national effort. Public support for a freewheeling press in American society does not carry over into times of crisis, such as the onset of war. In almost every instance when America has gone to war, the media became allies with the government in the war effort. In wars before Vietnam, the American media for the most part served the government's goals and objectives in their reporting of the war. News stories of battle confirmed the government and military point of view. In World War I and World War II, the media were factored into the execution of the war, and after the United States entered these conflicts, the mainstream media cooperated in the war effort. During World War II, the U.S. director of censorship, Byron Price (1942), praised the media for demonstrating great patriotism in voluntarily submitting to restrictions on what they published. Except for reporting during the early stages of the Korean conflict, the press voluntarily cooperated with the U.S. government and the military in reporting the war (Knightley, 1975).

The alliance of government and media in time of war seemed to break down in Vietnam, America's most recent lengthy military engagement. In Vietnam the press refused to "join the team," as urged by the Kennedy and Johnson administrations (Knightley, 1975). Although the American media fell into line for nearly a decade of the U.S. military's adviser relationship with South Vietnam (1954–64), the relationship changed as the United States escalated its role in conflict in the 1960s. As Vietnam became a large-scale U.S. operation, an increasing number of U.S. correspondents were sent to Vietnam and reported news from the front that conflicted with the assessments and public pronouncements of the administration and the Pentagon. In response to the media skepticism, the Pentagon and the administration launched a public relations campaign to sell their version of the war to the American press and the American people (Hammond, 1988). Short tours were offered to reporters from middle America in hopes of getting more favorable press coverage (Knightley, 1975). However, by making every facet of the war unusually accessible to any correspondent who turned up in Saigon, the military lost control of the flow of information. During the late stages of American involvement in Vietnam, Vice-president Spiro Agnew attacked the media for failing to support the military effort in Vietnam. He suggested that the media had a responsibility to mobilize public support for the war. The *New York Times'* and the *Washington Post*'s publication of the Pentagon Papers, in defiance of the Nixon administration, raised further question about the press's willingness voluntarily to withhold information that the government contended harmed the war effort.

Since Vietnam, many in the military have come to regard the media as adversaries (Braestrup, 1991; Matthews, 1991). Some blamed the U.S. press for losing the war in Vietnam. Many low-ranking officers who served in Southeast Asia believed the news media were at least partly responsible for the U.S. military's failure in Vietnam (Kaiser, 1983). Later, when some of these officers went on to become senior military leaders in the 1980s, they were determined to keep the media from undermining their efforts in combat. When forced to deal with the press in the Persian Gulf, many of these officers sought to impede the press instead of cooperating.

Additionally, the structure of the military itself creates tension with a free-wheeling press in wartime (Dugan, 1991). The U.S. military is an authoritarian structure authorized by the democratic government and ultimately under civilian leadership. The military itself, however, is an organization of command and control, with the command leaping from the highest-ranking military officers to the democratically elected president, commander in chief of the armed forces. The incongruity of the model of U.S. media structure and function and the model of the U.S. military structure and function creates a conflict when the two cultures try to operate in the same arena in time of war. In the Persian Gulf, the military tried to incorporate the media into its authoritarian structure by establishing formal lines of control, such as the pool system. Because the U.S. model of journalism's relationship to the government is, for the most part, a model of pluralism and adversarialism to the government, its attempt to function in the authoritarian structure of the military generated conflict.

On the other side, the press, especially since Vietnam, has viewed its role, not as a team player with the military for the greater cause of victory, but as a check on government: to evaluate the effectiveness of U.S. military execution of policy. During wartime, when historically the government and the military had looked for support from the national media, journalists still clung to traditional Western libertarian ideals in reporting the war. The result of these conflicting visions of the press was two systems in conflict.

The failure of the American military effort in Vietnam, coupled with the failure of its policy toward the press, made inevitable a change in the U.S. military-media relationship. Because in Vietnam the press proved that it would not adapt its model to the government's and military's need to mobilize and maintain public support, the administration and the Pentagon reevaluated their relationship to the press. The government's and military's new attitudes toward the press were seen in 1983 in Grenada. The Reagan administration excluded the press from the war zone in its invasion of Grenada and controlled the early pictures and information of the battle. In Panama in 1989 pools were set up to ensure that the media had access to a breaking war. However, the pools were kept at bay until much of the action was over.

When U.S. troops initially were deployed to the Persian Gulf in response to Iraq's August 2, 1990, invasion of Kuwait, the Defense Department did not initially activate the standing reporter pool that the U.S. media had expected to accompany any breaking military operation. After the media criticized the exclusion of the press from the deployment, the U.S. government pressured the Saudi government to grant visas to American news organizations, and the Saudis agreed to accept a strictly controlled pool of Western reporters. As part of preparations for conflict with Iraq, a Pentagon public affairs team went to Saudi Arabia to assess how the media should cover the increasingly likely hostilities. The team concluded that open coverage of ground combat operations was impractical because of the distances involved in Saudi Arabia, the probable speed of the advance of U.S. forces, the possible use of chemical weapons, and the violence of a large-scale armor battle (Department of Defense, 1991). On December 14, 1990, Pete Williams sent a memo to the Washington bureau chiefs, in which he outlined a plan for media coverage of hostilities. The plan called for the organization of press pools. When hostilities were imminent, the pools would be assigned to combat units. Reporters had to remain with military escorts at all times. All interviews would be on the record, and all media products would be subject to security review by the public affairs escort at the location where the information was gathered. The ground rules accompanying Williams's memo included the categories of information that journalists could and could not release. These rules generally protected broad categories of information to maintain tactical security during and after the buildup of U.S. and coalition forces. In January the military told arriving journalists that they could function only in pools and could not freely travel to the front and to U.S. military units on their own.

MEDIA REACTION TO PERSIAN GULF WAR
RESTRICTIONS ON THE PRESS

Media reaction to the proposed rules was intense. In the press debate over the restrictions on coverage of the Persian Gulf War, opinions on how much access should be granted the press and how much control should be asserted by the military turned on which model of the press one held. Media response to the formulation and implementation of press pools and security review in coverage of the Persian Gulf War conveyed strong libertarian sentiment. When the Pentagon released the ground rules for coverage of the war, Ron Nessen (1991), vice-president for news of NBC Radio/Mutual Broadcasting, said that the U.S. military had won the last battle of the Vietnam War in the sands of Saudi Arabia: the defeat of the free, critical reporting that the military believed undermined the Vietnam war effort. Nessen said that the requirements that news copy and pictures undergo security review and news personnel be accompanied by public affairs officers amounted to censorship of the media. "In Saudi Arabia, Pentagon officials have the press right where they want us: under their control," Nessen said (p. A21). *Newsday*'s Patrick Sloyan (1991) believed that because of the pool restrictions, the public would get a government-controlled version of hostilities. "Under the guise of ground rules for reporters covering Operation Desert

Shield, the administration is attempting to censor written and filmed accounts of any desert conflict while limiting media reports to government-controlled pool coverage," he said (p. C2). NBC News senior commentator John Chancellor (1991) criticized the government's attempts to control images of killing and death in the war. "The control of the images of war by the authorities, this sanitation of the horrors of war, takes away something important from those of us at home," he said (p. 17).

Many media critics claimed that the military pool and review systems were imposed for political, not military, security purposes. Sydney Schanberg (1991a) said that the security issue was a red herring because except for rare exceptions the U.S. press honored security rules in past wars. The media watch group Fairness and Accuracy in Reporting charged that the restrictions were not to protect lives but aimed "at protecting the Bush administration's popularity by keeping unpalatable images away from the U.S. public" (Spin Control Through Censorship, 1991, p. 14).

Many journalists who opposed the wartime restrictions on the press were unwilling to believe the government's version of the war. After the initial weeks of the air war against Iraq, a *New York Times* editorial questioned the integrity of the government version of the air war (Back up the Bombing Boasts, 1991). In the *Washington Times*, columnist Fred Reed (1991) said he wanted to know what thousands of sorties of bombers had accomplished. He argued that the military gave the major media, which have the political clout to be dangerous, just enough access to the troops to keep them quiet. But the access they got to soldiers was to find out how they feel. "This isn't coverage," he said. "It's pablum. Whether the war is really going well, we don't know" (p. G3).

Many journalists criticized those who covered the war because the press had failed to perform its historical role of watchdog over government action and abuse. They accused the U.S. media of becoming boosters of the war effort. ABC's Sam Donaldson criticized his peers for what he called their war psychosis in letting all pretense of objectivity vanish with the start of the air campaign (Hertsgaard, 1991). On the op-ed page of the *New York Times*, Anthony Lewis (1991) complained that the American press failed to be a detached or critical observer but instead became "a claque applauding the American generals and politicians in charge" (p. A15). He singled out television as the "most egregious official lap dog during the war" because the networks simply transmitted official images of a neat, painless war. An editorialist in *The Nation* (No News: Bad News, 1991) said he could not believe that the Pentagon was worried that an unrestrained press might sabotage the war effort because, as it turned out, the press was practically leading the charge to war.

The critics who sided with the media complaints about access and who complained about the failure of the media to scrutinize the government's rush to war articulated classic libertarian expectations for the press in a democracy. Joan Lowy (1991), who covered the Persian Gulf War for the *Rocky Mountain News*, feared that the tight controls on press coverage of war reduced the press to the function of a propaganda tool for the Pentagon. Other critics complained that because the press was so patriotic and compliant and served as mere scribes for the military in time of war, it failed to provide the information the public needed to evaluate the policies and actions of its government and military leaders. This libertarian view of press function had its most explicit expression in *Nation* v. *The Department of Defense* (1991), the lawsuit a few journalists and media organizations filed in response to the Pentagon's restrictions on the press in the Gulf. Lawyers for the journalists argued that the military should not be allowed to impose any form of pool restrictions on the press, even in time of war. Especially during a war, independent press coverage was critical to checking government action. To keep an eye on government in its important war-making function, the press needed freedom from tight restrictions on reporting.

Not all journalists assumed a libertarian posture in the debate over the restrictions imposed in the Persian Gulf War. Countering the libertarian-minded critics of war coverage were journalists whose views of the media's role in time of war emphasized the press' responsibility to support the war effort. Though these journalists might be open to greater press freedom during time of peace, they saw a need for constriction of open debate in time of societal crisis, such as war. *U.S. News & World Report* editor David Gergen (1991) said journalists covering the war had an antiwar attitude. He said because the draft ended in 1973, most journalists had never worn a uniform and "would rather write than fight" (p. 57). In reporting the war, the American press revealed its antiwar perspective. He suggested that the whining reporters badgering the military briefers and the negative and nit-picking press reports that followed showed the American public just how antiwar the press was. As a result, the public's distaste for the press increased.

This perspective was echoed by Dorothy Rabinowitz (1991) in a column in the *Wall Street Journal*. She said American journalists such as Edward R. Murrow had not pretended to be impartial when the United States went to war and that journalists' extreme adversarial relationship with government born of Watergate did not play well with the American people when the nation was at war. In the *Washington Times*, columnist Thomas Sowell wrote that tight control over the press was needed in the Gulf because the press had changed since the press went to war with the troops in World War II. During the earlier war, the press understood that "it was a part of American society and conducted itself with a sense of responsibility toward that society" (Sowell, 1991, p. G3). Sowell said the modern day press' adversarial stance toward government makes the press "a loose cannon, firing away without any regard to who gets hurt" (p. G3). Former war correspondent Joachim Maitre (1991) said that the American people favor restrictions on press freedom when the nation is at war. What those journalists clamoring for greater access forgot, but what the American public recognized, argued Maitre, is that "the paramount objective of war is victory" (p. 11). Maitre said that everyone, including the press, understood this, although journalists objected on principle to press restrictions.

American journalists who attempted to present balanced reporting of the war met hostility from the public and the government. When media outlets aired alternative interpretations of the U.S. war with Iraq, some condemned the media for giving comfort and aid to the enemy. Senator Alan Simpson accused Cable News Network's Peter Arnett of complicity with Iraq for his reporting the Baghdad government's side of the war. At CNN's Atlanta headquarters, pickets protested the network's coverage of the enemy's perspective. Other U.S. media entities that tried to present Baghdad's side of the crisis were criticized for giving a perspective other than that of the United States. Readers of the *Philadelphia Inquirer* objected to a headline about the bombing of the civilian bunker in Baghdad because it gave too much credence to the Iraqi government's contention that the building was a civilian bomb shelter and not a military command and control center, as asserted by the U.S. military (Jones, 1991).

Though there was no unanimity in their attitudes toward press restrictions in the Gulf War, most journalists continued to cling to the traditional Western libertarian values of media performance, even in reporting the Gulf War. Though some found the restrictions on coverage reasonable, most said the restrictions were too severe and complained that the controls there made it difficult for the press to fulfill its responsibility of providing an independent source of the progress of the war as a check on the military. The military, on the other hand, had a very different view of the role of the press in society and, in particular, its function in covering the military in time of war.

MILITARY VIEW OF THE MEDIA-MILITARY RELATIONSHIP

The difficulties experienced between the military and news media representatives seeking to cover the Persian Gulf War are nothing new. Viewed in the historical context of war reporting, the cries of protest from editors in the rear over restrictions imposed on correspondents at the Gulf War front bear a haunting resemblance to denouncements of past wartime encounters between soldiers and scribblers. Striking the proper balance between the people's "right to know" and the military's "need for secrecy" has always been a contentious rhetorical battleground. But, as Supreme Court Justice Oliver Wendell Holmes wrote in his decision affirming the conviction of an antiwar pamphleteer during World War I: "When a nation is at war, many things that might be said in time of peace are such a hindrance to its effort that their utterance will not be endured as long as men fight" (*Schenck* v. *United States*, p. 51). The Persian Gulf has not made the battleground any less contentious.

Much has been made, and continues to be made, of the media's viewpoint in the relationship. Little has been written of the military's perspective except in military professional journals (Baker, 1991; Matthews, 1991; Metcalf, 1991; Williams, 1991b) and uncirculated service war college studies (Venanzi, 1982; Humphries, 1983; Rogers, Erickson and Watson, 1983; Lunt, 1984; Martin,

1987; Sergeant, 1988; Coleman, 1989; Diehl, 1989; Watson, 1989; O'Brien, 1991). And much of what has been popularly written and widely circulated unfairly characterizes the military's attitudes toward the press in a democracy and offers the Persian Gulf War experience as a caricature of the military-media relationship today.

First, it is important to stipulate "for the record" that the military does accept and readily acknowledge the important role that the press plays in a democratic society. The important role the press plays in defense is institutionalized in the very building that symbolizes the armed forces in Washington, D.C.—the Pentagon. Every day reporters for most of the major news dailies, wire services, news magazines, and broadcast radio and TV networks come to work at the Pentagon to cover the national security "beat." Not just during the war, every day. And of course, Wolf Blitzer, CNN's internationally known military correspondent—the broadcast reporter who clocked more air time on TV sets during the Persian Gulf War than even Vanna White—also works out of the Pentagon. He, and dozens of correspondents like him, regularly covers news on the defense beat from the Pentagon, part of the "golden triangle" of reporting in Washington, D.C. (Hess, 1984).

Visitors to the Pentagon, especially foreigners, are often surprised to learn that reporters are permitted to roam the hallways freely amidst thousands of soldiers and sailors, admirals, and generals. But in a free and democratic society, even the military must be open to scrutiny. The press knows that. The military knows it as well. The symbol of that openness, the institutionalization of the military-media relationship in peace and in war, is the press room maintained in the Pentagon, populated from time to time by the more than 200 journalists accredited to cover the Department of Defense. In peacetime only about two dozen "regulars," correspondents like Wolf Blitzer, cover national defense daily from inside the Pentagon. During this period others came infrequently to attend the twice-weekly press briefings conducted by then Secretary of Defense spokesman, Pete Williams, or to cover routine news events and announcements, or to check on the latest military developments during crises, or to cover wars. During the Persian Gulf War, over 300 additional reporters were accredited to cover the Pentagon—scene of one of the two daily briefings that took place during Operation Desert Storm, one from Riyadh and the other from a dingy television studio across the corridor from Williams's office.

The TV studio Williams and his predecessors briefed the press corps from is located in a "corridor" in the Pentagon that is dedicated to these reporters. Correspondents Corridor, as it is named, is like the several commemorative corridors dedicated throughout the Pentagon—corridors dedicated to Medal of Honor winners, to women in the armed forces, to Generals Hap Arnold, Douglas MacArthur, and Omar Bradley. And at the end of Correspondents Corridor stands a small "shrine" in tribute to the greatest war reporter of modern times—at least from the American military's point of view—Ernie Pyle, and 60 others who, like him, lost their lives covering American military operations. The shrine stands in lasting tribute not only to a great war reporter, but for a time when the military's relationship with the news media was a subject for collegial autobiographies, not the topic of heated debate and scholarly textbooks.

But there is a debate about the military-media relationship, and it has become a very public debate over the most recent public manifestation of that relationship in the microcosm of the Persian Gulf War. One of the first salvos fired in the debate came shortly after the war concluded, when the executive news editors of 15 of the country's major national news organizations sent a letter to Secretary of Defense Dick Cheney complaining about the press policies of the Pentagon during Desert Storm (Editors, 1991). In that letter, the editors stated that

The Defense Department seems to think . . . that the press gave the American people the best war coverage they ever had. We strongly disagree. . . . We are deeply concerned about the abridgement of our right and role to produce timely, independent reporting of Americans at war. . . . We are intent upon not experiencing again the Desert Storm kind of pool system. . . . We cannot accept the limitations on access or the use of monitors to chill reporting. Nor do we want a repeat of the disaster that resulted from unacceptable delays in the transmission of our stories and pictures because of security review requirements.

That letter, and the many news stories that accompanied its release, illustrate what the military consider to be the three myths concerning media coverage of Desert Shield and Desert Storm. Those myths are:

1. The myth that the press did not do a good job covering Desert Storm;
2. The myth that reporters could not do their jobs because of the system of press controls established by the military for coverage of combat, and finally;
3. The myth that the military censored news coming from the Gulf.

MYTH THAT THE PRESS DID NOT DO A GOOD JOB

How do you define what constitutes a good job of reporting a war? It depends on whom you ask.

To Walter Cronkite, a veteran correspondent of World War II, coverage of Desert Storm was lacking. "With an arrogance foreign to the democratic system, the U.S. military in Saudi Arabia is trampling on the American people's right to know," he wrote. "An American citizen is entitled to ask: 'What are they trying to hide?' " (Smith, 1992, p. 47).

The government, in contrast, was understandably pleased with the news coverage in the Gulf. "What public in what other conflict can possibly have been given as much information as the American people in this war?" Pete Williams remarked in an appearance before the National Press Club after the war. "Thanks to reporters the American people could see what our troops, our commanders and our weapons were doing. . . . [T]hose reporters who long for the good old days of Vietnam should visit the archives. . . . [T]hey would find no historical precedent for the expensive and detailed Desert Storm coverage,'' Williams (1991b) claimed.

It is obvious that the Pentagon and the press evaluate the news media's performance in the Gulf War differently. Which view is correct? Perhaps neither protagonist is objective enough to judge the reporting. Another measure of the press's performance is what the public thought of the news coverage. If the press, as it claims, represents the ''people's right to know'' and serves only as their surrogate in covering the American military, then how do the people feel their surrogates did? According to a Times Mirror survey (1991), eight out of every ten Americans thought that the press told about as much as it should have during the war. For them, apparently, the amount of information and coverage provided by the press was just about right. And the public was satisfied with the press as well. A *Newsweek* magazine poll showed that almost six in ten Americans thought better of the news media than they did before the war (Williams, 1991a).

Who could argue with the dramatic coverage beamed almost instantaneously into homes and command centers around the world? If there was a riveting moment in the conflict, it was the sights, sounds and shudders captured by CNN's broadcast team caught in the Al Rashid hotel as F-117 stealth fighters and cruise missiles began their systematic attacks on downtown Baghdad. When the first bombs dropped on Baghdad, we all saw and heard some of the most extraordinary war coverage, live, in journalistic history. All that was lacking was a ghostly reappearance by Edward R. Murrow telling the world, ''This is Baghdad.''

If Vietnam was the first ''television war,'' then the Persian Gulf was truly the first ''live'' television war (Hiebert, 1992). And what the public saw, largely through the unfiltered eye of live television, was their military—their sons and daughters—at war. The public soon discovered through television's live coverage that a very different picture emerged of the armed forces than the image popularized in news reports after Vietnam and in the 1980s. As *Time* magazine observed, ''[d]uring the Vietnam era, many Americans came to regard the U.S. officer class as a band of dissemblers and incompetents. As for the grunts, their ranks had long been considered a repository for society's dropouts'' (Birnbaum, 1991). But in the intervening two decades the military had changed. ''The Pentagon,'' according to defense expert Martin Binkin of the Brookings Institution, ''literally rewrote the textbook on war. It's a new ball game in every way'' (Birnbaum, 1991). As one senior air force officer observed, Desert Storm also demonstrated to the American taxpayer that the billions spent on the military since Vietnam and during the defense buildup of the 1980s ''bought a helluva lot more than $600 toilet seats'' (Robertson, 1991).

Time magazine, in an analysis immediately after the war, wrote of the ''remarkable professionalism'' of the U.S. armed forces in Desert Storm ''exemplified most visibly by the smooth TV performances of top military officers. . . .

Intelligent, frank, sometimes eloquent, these men seemed to personify a new class of American military leaders who not only have a thorough grasp of their trade but also demonstrate broad political and worldly sophistication—not to mention p.r. savvy'' (Birnbaum, 1991, p. 58). Because the U.S. armed forces performed so well, because the military men and women appeared to work so professionally, because American weapons quickly overwhelmed the world's fourth largest army, and because of good "p.r. savvy,'' the U.S. military emerged with high marks and increased credibility with the public. After the war a Gallup poll reported that almost nine out of ten Americans rated the military the most highly respected institution in the country (Gallup, 1991).

But the myth that pervaded the press and clouds the debate that still rages today seems to argue that because the military came out so well in Desert Storm, enjoyed the public's support, and seems to have so easily defeated Iraq, the press must not have been doing its job as a watchdog of government. Something had to be wrong for everything to appear to have gone so well. Press performance has been one scapegoat. Military performance has been criticized as well—not performance on the battlefield, where war was fought with bombs and bullets, but in the press pools, where the equally deadly "war of words'' was waged.

THE MYTH OF DRACONIAN PENTAGON PRESS POLICIES

One reason cited most often by members of the press and press critics to explain why the news media did not do a good job of reporting the war was the Pentagon's policies for press coverage from the front during the Gulf War. More specifically, two conditions of press coverage seem to come under frequent attack: the military's use of pools as the exclusive means of providing combat coverage and the Pentagon's requirement that news representatives be under escort when visiting units in the field. Each of these policies individually and collectively have been labeled by the press as violations of the media's right to gather and report news of the war independent of government interference. However, it is important to put these issues into both contemporary and historical perspective.

First, there was an early commitment by the Pentagon to *full coverage* of American military operations in Saudi Arabia within reasonable bounds of security. According to his testimony before a committee of the U.S. Senate examining the Pentagon's press policies in the Middle East, Williams reminded the panel that when Iraq invaded Kuwait, there were no Western reporters in Saudi Arabia. When the first U.S. forces arrived in Saudi Arabia to stop the advance of Iraq, no Western reporters accompanied them. Based on long experience, the Saudis were reluctant to permit Western reporters into their country for any reason (U.S. Senate, 1991). In the potentially volatile context of a military confrontation with a fellow Arab nation, the Saudis were even less inclined to stir the stormy situation with the injection of American reporters on scene.

However, Secretary of Defense Cheney and others were finally able to secure the Saudi government's unprecedented approval of the first of what would eventually be a stream of more than 3,500 reporters through their country. After Saudi approval, the Pentagon turned to the National Media Pool—a mechanism established after the press was excluded from the 1983 Grenada invasion—to provide an initial presence of Western reporters on scene. The National Media Pool, a group of 17 journalists, photographers, and technicians, was activated two days after the first U.S. F-15s arrived on Saudi soil; they arrived via air force transport several days later (U.S. Senate, 1991). Much has been made by the press that the United States had not forced the Saudis to accept the National Media Pool and other Western reporters as a precondition of American military support. Nevertheless, the fact is that American reporters got to Saudi Arabia to cover that part of the unfolding drama, and they arrived there before General Norman Schwarzkopf, the commander of Desert Storm. As was not the case in Grenada, as was not so even two years earlier, in Panama, the press was there because of the Pentagon, not in spite of it.

When fighting broke out and commercial airline service was suspended, the Pentagon, at the request of major news organizations, flew an additional 126 reporters direct from the United States to the war zone on board a C-141 military transport (Williams, 1991b). Before Desert Storm ended, there were more than 1,500 news reporters, producers, cameramen, and technicians supporting them in Saudi Arabia covering Operation Desert Storm. Hundreds of others were in countries surrounding the war zone—Jordan, Israel, Turkey, Bahrain. According to some accounts, there were another 3,000 to 4,000 reporters and support people awaiting visas to enter Saudi Arabia when the war broke out (Robertson, 1991).

These numbers become interesting in historical perspective. As a comparison to the press corps assembled in the Persian Gulf, consider that the largest number of reporters ever accredited to cover the Vietnam War was 637, at the height of the Tet offensive in 1968. The highest number of journalists accredited to cover the Korean War at any one time was 270. Only 461 reporters and photographers (180 of them Americans) were accredited to cover the Normandy invasion. On D-day, only 27 journalists actually went ashore with invading troops, and there were just 6 reporters at the pivotal battle of the invasion on Omaha Beach. In World War I, 90 U.S. correspondents were accredited to the American Expeditionary Forces. The French and British banned reporters from the front lines for almost a year until finally in 1915, under pressure at home and abroad, the British accredited 6 reporters to the front, assigning a driver, conducting officer (escort), and censor to each correspondent (Mathews, 1957; Knightley, 1975; Braestrup, 1985).

Because of the sheer size of the press corps there in Saudi Arabia, the logistics of moving them safely and the support and accommodations required to service them in the field, commanders and public affairs officers in country determined that the only feasible way of accommodating news coverage of combat operations was by forming pools of news media. The pool system had gotten the press to Saudi Arabia and had gotten reporters around to widely dispersed units in the desert that only the military, equipped with satellite positioning hardware and accurate maps, could locate safely and reliably. The military and the media were familiar with pools and knew they could work to get some reporters up to the front—representing the rest left behind—in position to directly observe and report on Desert Storm as it unfolded.

And the pool system did what it was supposed to do the evening the war began. When the first F-15Es took off to strike their targets deep inside Iraq, American reporters were there at their desert air bases. When the U.S. Navy fired Tomahawk cruise missiles from ships in the Persian Gulf headed toward targets in downtown Baghdad, American reporters were there as well. The military was able to place more than 130 reporters and camera crews with front line combat units when the war started (not after it had ended) because the military—and only the military—knew the time, the place, and the units, where the war would begin and how it would develop. At the height of the war there were 192 press slots in ten separate combat pools where the fighting was and in two "quick reaction" pools in the rear area to handle anything that might come up unexpectedly. And for the better part of Desert Storm—during the air campaign fought from static air bases and carrier decks—the pool system functioned reasonably well. It collapsed as a viable mechanism for reporting when the ground war began and movement of military units overwhelmed the logistical support, mobility, and communications necessary for the pools to continue to work. That is when the pool system collapsed under the weight of events, and the military was caught unprepared to substitute a more workable accommodation.

Was this the best way to handle reporting for the war? Not necessarily. But, according to Colonel Bill Mulvey, director of the Joint Information Bureau in Dhahran, "the numbers overwhelmed us. . . . We had to resort to media pools for Desert Storm because of the huge numbers. We didn't have any other choice" (Mulvey, 1991, p.4). For all its shortcomings, in the military's view the Desert Storm pool system was a workable mechanism for accommodating the press's legitimate role of providing independent coverage of the war within reasonable bounds of security, safety, and logistics. As importantly, it was a system that the military and field commanders understood and were prepared to support in the midst of fighting a rapidly unfolding air campaign and ground war to expel Saddam Hussein's forces from occupied Kuwait.

Did there need to be independent reporters in Saudi Arabia, at the front lines, eating, sleeping, and moving with combat units to tell the American people what they wanted to know, what they needed to know, about the progress and prosecution of that war; about what their sons and daughters were doing; and the sacrifices they were making in the name of their country? The answer is simple—yes! Did there need to be 1,000 or 1,200 or 1,500 reporters and supporting cast out there in the desert to do it? Probably not. However, in our system of democracy, the government is not and should not be in a position to tell news organizations, to tell editors or producers, that they cannot send a reporter to cover a war. News organizations should be able, if they have the resources to do it, and they should decide who will go. *Mirabella*, a women's fashion magazine, had the resources and sent a reporter to cover the Gulf War. Talk show host Geraldo Rivera went, on his own, as did a correspondent for *Audubon* magazine.

However, the financial ability to send a reporter or camera crew does not, in turn, obligate the government, the military, or combat unit commanders to then provide for each and every reporter or camera crew that arrives at the front with what they all seemed to demand: (1) exclusive interviews, (2) unrestricted access, (3) unlimited information, (4) food, water, and transportation to the front and the protection that comes along with it. That the First Amendment guarantees a free press in this country gets no argument from the military. "I happen to believe strongly in the freedom of the press," commented Lieutenant General Tom Kelly, director of operations for the Joint Staff, and principal briefer of the Pentagon press corps during the war. "On a day-to-day basis, the media can make you very angry—but their contribution to our democracy is unparalleled anywhere in the world" (Kelly, 1991, p. 76). However, the First Amendment does *not* guarantee the best sound bite, the best ratings share, or a Pulitzer prize for every journalist who wants to cover a war. "The First Amendment," General Kelly observed, "talks about passing laws. It does not say that you must spoon-feed every bit of information that the press would like to get" (p. 76). These "realities" of modern, mobile combat, and of covering military operations, seem to have been lost in the rhetorical fog of postwar debate.

"SECURITY REVIEW" AND THE MYTH OF CENSORSHIP

Was there "censorship" of reporter dispatches? Defense Department officials, contend that, no, there was not (Williams, 1991b).

There was government censorship of press reports during World War II and World War I, when military officers had the legal authority to examine every word that was written, every picture taken at the front and to delete anything they felt violated the ground rules (Creel, 1920; Mock, 1941; Koop, 1946). And the military did censor reporters' dispatches from the front in both world wars and most of the Korean conflict (Mathews, 1957). It is censorship when the government tells you what you can print and what you cannot and the decision is the government's, not the reporter's or the editor's, on what makes it into print or on the air. But, that's not what happened in the Persian Gulf.

The "security review" that went on in Saudi Arabia was not censorship, first, because it applied only to members of combat pools with military units at the front lines. It did not apply, as some have implied, to all reporting that took place in Saudi Arabia. Only pool reporters had their copy subjected to review by an escort officer for "security." Despite the now-famed incident of one field commander wanting to change a reporter's copy describing pilots returning from missions over Baghdad as being "giddy" to describing them, instead, as being "proud"—the fact is that most reporters in the pools did not experience the kinds of problems or delays that others apparently did with security review. At postwar military-media seminars sponsored by all the military war colleges the year after Desert Storm, correspondents who covered the war who were in attendance generally reported that they had no serious and systematic problems with security review. The numbers would seem to back that observation up. According to Pete Williams, more than 1,300 pool reports were filed by reporters with combat units during Desert Storm. Of those, only five were "flagged" by military escorts as possible violations of the security ground rules. All but one was resolved in favor of release. The single story not released was withheld by the editor—it was not ordered withheld by the Pentagon (Williams, 1991c). As with any other news story, the editor had final say, not the military.

Security review was not the onerous system of draconian censorship by the military that has often been portrayed. But myths die hard as they are told and retold again and again in the postwar debate over the military's handling of the news media during Desert Storm.

CONCLUSION

In the long history of the military-media relationship, particularly in time of war, there has never been a protracted peace between the two institutions. Underlying the relationship in peace and in war is a tension between two professions that seem antithetical to each other. Despite over 100 years of experience on which to base planning and preparations for press coverage, the military and the media continue to come equally unprepared for the demands and strains that each war places on their relationship. In the heat of battle, lessons learned from past encounters go unheeded. In the midst of war, when time and tempers are short, lessons must be relearned, to the detriment of both the military and the media. While the Persian Gulf War has added another long page to the history of this relationship, nothing resembling an armistice has been reached in its aftermath.

Both the military and the media seem to agree on one thing—the system of reporting in the Gulf War needs serious reevaluation. After more than a year of negotiations between the military and national news organizations on press restrictions for covering war, the military has finally released a set of guidelines that bridges some, but not all, of the points of difference (Department of Defense, 1992).

What the analysis finds is that the differences in the ways in which the media view their role and those in which the military views the role of the media in wartime fuel the tensions in the military-media relationship. Because the media and the military have divergent perspectives on the press's role in wartime, agreement on military restrictions on the press is unlikely. Tensions will remain in the military-media relationship. Journalists and military officers seem to be talking past one another because, as General Dwight D. Eisenhower observed almost five decades ago, the military and the media start with diverging goals for press performance when the nation is at war.

In their commentary on coverage of the Persian Gulf War, most journalists articulated libertarian philosophy to govern the press function in reporting. To maintain its independence in covering the war, the press should not have to depend on the military for transmission of journalistic products. Many journalists brought portable satellite telephones, the latest in communication technology, to the desert to facilitate the timeliness of their reporting. The military refused journalists use of their own satellite telephones because the technology stripped the military of control of the flow of information. The military took responsibility for transmission of press materials. But the military's mechanisms for getting the pool reporter pictures and copy back to Dhahran, such as drivers and beat-up ground transport, were often crudely low tech when compared to what was available.

In many military units, press pool product transmission was a low priority. Especially after the ground war began, the transmission of journalists' materials was often excruciatingly slow. Though the U.S. media were equipped to transmit materials instantaneously, the military demands for prior review of copy forced the media to return to a pony express–type courier service to get their materials back to publishers and broadcasters. Though 130 years earlier press reports of the Battle of Bull Run reached New York within 24 hours, some press reports from the front line in the Persian Gulf War took up to five days to reach the editors. Some never arrived. For a military capable of moving half a million people and millions of tons of equipment and supplies across the world in the largest logistical operation in history, the movement of words and pictures became a cumbersome ordeal. In the Persian Gulf, in the most technologically sophisticated war fought in the history of armed warfare, reporters were stripped of their own modern technology and forced to bang out stories on manual portable typewriters to accommodate the military's need for hand editing and courier transmission—a return to a bygone era.

In contrast, the U.S. military was impressing the world with its own telecommunications prowess. In their press conferences, the military invited the world to see how sophisticated its smart weaponry had become. The footage from aircraft-mounted video cameras gave the audience a close-up look, however selective, of the capabilities of modern weapons. The footage also visually reinforced the allied commanders' message that the military assaults on Iraq were precision attacks on military targets and avoided unnecessary civilian casualties and destruction.

The principles for press coverage of future U.S. military engagements, released by the Department of Defense in 1992, allow journalists to use their modern telecommunications technology, such as satellite telephones and transmitters. Perhaps in the next war the media, and not just the military, will be allowed to exploit the wizardry of modern telecommunications and technology to its fullest.

3

Image Makers of Desert Storm: Bush, Powell, and Schwarzkopf

Marion K. Pinsdorf

Reality is stronger than ideology, but not imageology.
—Milan Kundera, *Immortality*

Seeing is not believing; believing is seeing.
—Robert Pirsig, *Lila, An Inquiry into Morals*

Images during Desert Storm all seemed so clear-cut, so competent and consensus building, so deceptively easy to understand. But as books, articles, and analyses flood the public, these images evoke the mood of Haynes Johnson's *Sleepwalking Through History* (1991)—an age of illusion in which myths seem real but soon shift, where chimeras and passivity rule.

Precisely because so many individuals lacked in-depth knowledge or, worse, never sought it, wartime images now are shifting dramatically, diminishing some leaders and effectiveness of "smart" weapons. "Triumph has become ashes in the mouth of the victor" (Johnson, 1991). Benjamin C. Bradlee, former executive editor of the *Washington Post*, said during a David Frost television interview that Gulf War public relations "was the most sophisticated manipulation that ever was" (Scolino and Wines, 1992). No compliment intended. In the game terms popular during the war, the military quarterbacks studied their opponents well and ran their plays like clockwork, defeating the media in the minds of many Americans.

THE VIETNAM LEGACY

All these shifts in perception could have been anticipated. Public relations mavens know that ultimately the facts must drive the successful PR, not PR the facts. President Lyndon Johnson learned that lesson tragically in the Vietnam War. In *The Military and the Media, the U.S. Army in Vietnam* William M. Hammond (1988) critically analyzed media-military relations and their future implications. He pointed out that leaders forgot the first law of propaganda: "Even the best promotional build-up will ultimately fail to sell a questionable product" (Goodman, 1991). Or as the late John Hill, wise founder of Hill and Knowlton, taught, public relations cannot be a cosmetic, nor icing on a maggoty cake (Hill, 1975). Even when public stances and explanations contradicted facts, the Johnson administration attempted to use public relations to demonstrate South Vietnamese effectiveness, that pacification was working.

But little of this succeeded. Information officers felt caught between the president's efforts to bolster support and their own hopes to hold the military above politics. The press accused the military of trying to mislead the public (Andrews, 1991). For example, President Johnson and military leaders, who touted too many defeats as victories, suffered when the press considered the legitimate Tet victory as just more hype, soon to be discredited by the facts. Although the media took the rap for alienating the public in both Vietnam and Korea—a heritage evident in Desert Storm and among its generals—it was mounting casualties—the facts—that defeated LBJ's public relations campaign. He simply expected too much of public relations. He had his way, but at the cost of his credibility (Goulden, 1969).

The classic battle between telling all or nothing at all is both the nature of media-military relations and nothing new. As fired Air Force General Michael J. Dugan explained, the sources of tension are organic, institutional, cultural, and historical; hence the answer to any questions on improving relations are far from simple (Dugan, 1991).

Similarly, journalist Peter Andrews wrote that the media and military may never be entirely comfortable with one another. It's not in their natures: "The disciplines are too disparate. The military requires subservience of the individual to the needs of the group." The media "prizes independent initiative above all else" (1991). Elements that make good reporters make poor field commanders. Media demands disclosure. The military is driven by control, security of operations, and safety of troops. Even if the best of both sides attempt harmony, they stick and struggle at the key contention—access. In short, the military wraps itself in the flag while the media wraps itself in the First Amendment. Hence there are times when neither side listens to the other (see Andrews, 1991).

A CORPORATE TUSSLE, TOO

Such conflicting aims are not endemic to the military-media relations. With great anguish a year after the Bhopal tragedy, Warren Anderson, then Union

Carbide's CEO, lamented the same tug between his public relations people and lawyers. Many executives, military or corporate, concentrate exclusively on verbal sniping at journalists, claiming bad faith and incompetence and stonewalling. Both sides blind themselves to the common aims, risks, and demands of their jobs. When the commonality, as well as the contention, is understood, generals and the media need not be natural, everlasting adversaries (Pinsdorf, 1989). That is the hope, the ideal. The reality is still a contrast.

What made Desert Storm not only intriguing but worrisome were the dramatic changes in communication and manipulation. For example, CNN instantaneously transmitted the first bombing of Baghdad—on prime time in the eastern United States. The military's modern sophisticated media management was also of note. Alistair Cooke (audiotape, ca. 1973) illustrated how changes in communications change military strategy by applying Vietnam War–reporting techniques to the World War I battle of the Somme. Horrors of the fruitless battle, remote leadership, awesome suffering were all "brought" into British living rooms. Cooke imagined how Flanders would look to John Chancellor, David Brinkley, and Garrick Utley. Utley "reports" on trenches packed with corpses, a no-man's land strewn with bodies, and hundreds of men spiked on fences, British casualties reported at 55,000 to 60,000 but actually 250,000, all wasted against well-fortified German lines.

Cooke's conclusions were equally valid for the Somme and the Gulf War. With open reporting, with soldiers in the field saying what they think, with public protest, would the British have patriotically waved their boys off to war? Immediacy of reporting, such as CNN in Baghdad obliterated the gap between the battlefield and home front. Cooke concluded that communications alone would prevent the Battle of the Somme from being fought again (Cooke, audiotape, ca. 1973). Desert Storm politicians and the military understood this well. Aided by the relatively supine and unquestioning press, they were able to manipulate images to accomplish their objectives.

THE POLS—CONSUMMATE CRISIS MANAGERS

During the Gulf War, President George Bush publicly appeared as a consummate crisis and public relations manager. With apparent skill, he built alliances, macromanaged the military, quelled criticism so adroitly that the press seemed jingoistic and the Congress compliant. He appeared to shed the reputation of wimp for that of "resolute sheriff."

Joseph C. Goulden, in his 1969 study of illusion and reality in time of war, said that public reaction can usually be manipulated by a leader's reactions. "An unruffled president calls reporters into the Oval office and matter-of-factly reads a statement" (p. 187). Officials follow their routine schedules; briefers suggest to the press corps "that Washington isn't particularly excited about the incident" (p. 187). Result: "national calm and indifference, despite media attention" (p. 187).

Conversely, if the "president appears unexpectedly on all three television networks, solemnly informing the nation of grave danger" (p. 187), the "sight [is] calculated to grab the attention of even the most lethargic citizens. Result: a quickening of the collective national pulse; a joining of ranks to follow wherever the president chooses to lead; stirrings of chauvinism or blood lust" (p. 187).

President Bush followed Goulden's first choice—an unruffled president connoting calm and normalcy. Even his most debatable public relation choices worked. Most crisis counselors would have advised, "Return immediately to the White House. Don't look detached or seem to be enjoying yourself." But Bush stayed on vacation, confident no one would question who was running the show. When Saddam Hussein issued his call for a "holy war," Bush responded by continuing as "aerobic president." He doffed his tie and hit the links—and the waves, tennis courts, and jogging paths.

The president handled the crisis very successfully—in the short term. Granted, he enjoyed public relations and personal luck. First, Saddam Hussein attacked another Arab state, then called for popular uprisings in the region. Bush made the most of his breaks. He knew the players from long experience on the world stage. He understood the window of opportunity was small—as little as 24 hours—so he acted quickly. Unlike President Lyndon Johnson in Vietnam, he delegated effectively to top aides, military and civilian. Throughout the crisis, *Fortune* writer Ann Reilly Dowd concluded that the president maintained "balance and perspective—no easy feat" (1991).

But like much of Desert Storm, the president's vacation was not completely what it appeared. Away from the White House, he could concentrate exclusively on the Gulf. Behind Kennebunkport's deceptive surface calm, the "marathon telephone conversations" played out (Smith, 1992 p. 129.). Although World War II comparisons dominated the rhetoric (e.g., Hussein as Hitler), the president's crisis management style reflected the lessons of Vietnam. Send enough force to do the job, and don't micromanage.

Unity of message bothered two presidential aides. National Security Adviser Brent Scowcroft tried to control the whirlwind of activity—to manage and control an incredibly active president. He was out making statements, giving press conferences almost daily, up at dawn making calls, on the phone with one world leader after another, setting up meetings. Scowcroft found himself scrambling just to catch up. By December Bush lost patience with diplomacy, becoming "convinced war would be a two- to three-week solution" (Woodward, 1991, p. 307).

Robert Teeter, Bush's chief pollster, warned about sending out too many messages, with the appearance of a lack of focus. Return to fundamentals, to the strong appeals of fighting aggression and protecting lives of Americans, he counseled. But Bush pressed on, confident "he knew more than anyone about the region" (Woodward, 1991, p. 315). He had the experiences that allowed him to see all the pieces. He would put them together (p. 315). Bush's strategy, was a high-risk game. Casualties and the possibility of military defeat could resuscitate the crippling Vietnam syndrome. Bush had to win in both reality and image.

Jean Edward Smith in his *George Bush's War* (1992) analyzed the emerging disparity between a president touting consensus building while actually personalizing the war, of appearing to make coordinated decisions but actually making them almost alone, of talking of a new world order while taking his patterns and images from the World War II values of his youth. For example, Smith notes that President Bush used the "I" word as none of his predecessors ever had. They all spoke in terms of country or cause, party or people, ideas or dangers, not "I" (see Smith, 1992, pp. 1–2).

Bush's watershed "announcement that Iraq's occupation of Kuwait 'will not stand' " (Smith, p. 6) was delivered almost ad hoc while stepping off a helicopter on the White House lawn. Congress had not been consulted. The press was largely cowed by patriotism.[1] The military was not ready. The Security Council had not met. According to Smith, General Powell likened the situation to "the president . . . [with] six shooters blazing away" (Smith, p. 6).

Fired by the zeal, the president made it his war abroad and at home, revitalizing the United Nations, replacing enmity with alliances as no other world leader could. At home, few matched his enthusiasm. The State Department did not press war, nor did the military seek it. Most sought compromise or wanted to give sanctions a chance to work. The president's rhetoric became a tactical smoke screen later, obscuring the fact that Desert Storm decisively settled little (Smith, p. 11). Belatedly, the White House recognized that instability in Iraq was even more threatening to the region than the continuation of Saddam in power. Some questioned whether the unilateral authority Bush asserted and his personalization of power might have led to regrettable excess (see Smith, p. 32).

Stephen Graubard (1992) felt that George Bush knew it would be useful to craft simple arguments, to win public approval. The news on American television, though certainly believed, was, according to Graubard in fact invented, having been packaged to communicate simple, even primordial patriotic sentiments.

FLOPPING ON TV

Although President Bush got generally high marks for his public relations, the media criticized him for his derogatory pronunciation of Saddam's name, his moralistic lecturing, and his constant, seldom-appropriate World War II analogies and cultural misreadings. Although Bush did not always evince understanding of Saddam, the Iraqi leader was even more handicapped, lacking anything comparable to Bush's knowledge of the world and its leaders.

When Saddam Hussein appeared on television patting the head of a young, clearly terrified British boy, the West reacted largely with deep revulsion. In contrast, Iraq's allies, especially Jordanians, believed "He was just trying to show that children and families were safe" (Woollacott, 1991).

Nonetheless, Saddam clearly understood the importance of U.S. television and worldwide public opinion. His choice of a subdued business suit—instead of his usual military uniform with jaunty beret—to appear with British "guests" on Iraqi television was designed to convey that he was not the madman portrayed in newspaper cartoons. Also, Saddam thought he could tap into a "degree of loathing and resentment for the Al Sabah family and their fellow oil oligarchies along the Gulf littoral" (Black, 1991).

Both sides misjudged motive and talked past each other. For example, the Western habit of considering a deed good or bad in isolation is not widespread in the Middle East. There, "an action is seen within a vast context of grievances, immediate and historical, of other evils and injustices, of pain endured in the past" and to be endured in the future. Only when such "chains of consequences are calculated or imagined" (Black, 1991), can an action's total significance be weighed.

MOSTLY ABSENT ALICE

The only woman visible, but mostly invisible, during the Gulf conflict, was then–U.S. Ambassador to Iraq April Glaspie, who had served for 25 years in the Middle East. In many ways, she was an operational and symbolic anomaly. A woman ambassador in an organization where few rise that high, she became expert in a region hardly renowned for equal opportunity. In a time when appearance dominated, her performance before the Senate was startlingly out of the understated diplomatic mold. In a time of high visibility for most ambassadors, she met Saddam just once, though for what would become a key interview. She reemerged briefly when the Senate insisted on hearing her version of the Saddam interview, then disappeared into obscurity again.

Ambassador since 1988, Glaspie had no access to Saddam until, on one hour's notice, they met on July 25, 1990. In *Secret Dossier, the Hidden Agenda Behind the Gulf War*, Pierre Salinger and Eric Laurent (1991) reported in full the conversation, as well as Glaspie's contested cable report to Washington. According to Salinger and Laurent, she clearly voiced her instructions from Washington to seek better relations with Iraq,[2] which appeared to give Saddam the green light on the Iraqi-Kuwait border dispute.

She also commiserated with Saddam about press relations, particularly his ABC news profile and interview with Diane Sawyer. She applauded him for standing up to the media, noting that his appearance might increase mutual understanding.[3]

BRIDGING POLS AND MILITARY

The military was able to create for itself favorable images because of what it learned in and its changes after Vietnam. One dramatic illustration is the great contrast between Vietnam-era Pentagon spokesperson Arthur Sylvester, an old-time New Jersey newspaperman, and Pete Williams, the assistant secretary of defense for public affairs. Sylvester had the more difficult public relations challenge—a protracted, unpopular war and terrain where it was difficult to contain reporters. Williams had a very short, successful, and relatively antiseptic conflict.[4] Sylvester's hard-nosed quotes from various briefings contrast vividly with Williams's address before the National Press Club and testimony before the Senate's Committee on Governmental Affairs.

Introducing Williams, Kay Kahler, National Press Club President, noted that

although Pete Williams did his job well, many in the media are disturbed. When he artfully dodged, we winced. When he was affable, we cringed. When he seemed to divulge more, we got less. Journalists often get perturbed when someone in public office gets around us and reaches the public without our help. Pete Williams has done that. (Williams, 1991a)

But she notes something else very important was at stake: the most restrictive wartime policy on release of information ever imposed on the media by the U.S. government. Kahler did not overlook the irony of Williams's coming from a media background himself.

Williams responded with myth debunking: that the media did not cover operations well and they lacked access. To Williams (1991a), the military-media relationship is not a zero-sum game—if military credibility is up, media credibility must necessarily be down. The military emerged with heightened credibility, partly because "the press accurately reported what we did. . . . Reporters asked tough questions, challenged assumptions, exposed mistakes and held officials accountable" (p. 1). Also, Williams explained, "We waited for initial field reports to be confirmed." Even when it appeared coalition losses would be light, "we cautioned reporters about saying it would be easy" (pp. 1–2). "This is the first government operation" concerned not with spin control but with "euphoria control" (p. 2).

Williams attributed much of the public's dismay with the press to briefings, the messy making of the news, usually not seen by the public except for the rather decorous and well-managed presidential press conferences. He assumed some of the rancor was due to the normal strains of war and competition, some to the press pools. Although pools "rubbed reporters the wrong way," Williams pointed out a "rapidly moving front could not be opened" to the large numbers of reporters wanting to "roam the battlefield" (Williams, 1991a, p. 3). However, pools got reporters out to see the action, guaranteed that Americans would get reports from the scene, and accommodated a reasonable number of journalists without overwhelming fighting units.

Defending pools earlier in his Senate testimony, Williams noted they reached Saudi Arabia before General Schwarzkopf (Williams, 1991c). But many troops were deployed before Schwarzkopf, when the danger was greatest, the defense lines the thinnest. Williams conceded pools were a compromise. "The system we [had] in Operation Desert Storm—with two briefings a day in Riyadh and one in the Pentagon, pools of reporters out with the troops, a set of clear ground rules, and a procedure of ground rule appeal—was intended to permit the most open possible coverage of a new kind of warfare" (Williams, 1991c). Peter Schmeisser, in "Shooting Pool" looks at pooling quite differently: "History is filled with examples where independent reportage increases the efficiencies of the military and actually saves lives" (1991, p. 23).

The assistant secretary acknowledged some things—helping reporters in the field and dispatch of stories to the press center—could be improved. However, he dismissed questions on attempts to sanitize coverage, particularly photographs of the injured and the closing of the Dover Air Force Base mortuary to the press. He explained military personnel could be photographed if the individual gave permission. Dover's importance was downplayed as a "transit point," a "morgue," where "forensic pathologists work." There's no reason for families to go there, he explained (Williams, 1991a, b).

All very convincing, except this author remembers vividly the patriotic visibility of Dover on television following the Marine deaths in Beirut in 1983. For many evenings, the hygienic drama of flag-draped coffins, with families, seemingly chosen to represent ethnic and racial diversity, were shown on Philadelphia television. It would appear the closing of Dover had more to do with the real reasons of Vietnam—that public opinion soured on casualties, not reporting.

Testifying before the Senate, Williams explained that Desert Storm planning was done "in Macy's window." That meant "our false starts and stumbles were in full view" (1991a, p.3).

Media intentions were clear when Williams picked an officer to supervise the setting up of the Joint Information Bureau. He went with visuals and flicks. Captain Michael Sherman, USN, was a television major in college, director of navy public relations in Los Angeles (they produced the supposedly objective *Top Gun*), adviser for *The Hunt for Red October* and *Flight of the Intruder*, and experienced in flacking for the navy's latest technical gadgetry (Schmeisser, 1991, p. 23). Indeed, the network visuals of jets roaring, smart missiles firing and pumped-up pilots did seem more promotion than reality (Ibid.).

BRIEFERS IN UNIFORM

Although Generals Powell and Schwarzkopf handled the major, sensitive sessions, the multinational coalition was evident in English, French, Saudi, and other Arab briefers. Media visibility brought instant fame to the daily Pentagon spokesperson, Lieutenant General Thomas Kelly but obscured the two unheralded workhorses of Operation Desert Storm—Generals Charles Horner, who ran the air campaign, and William "Gus" Pagonis, who coped not only with the logistics of rapid deployment but also with the astonishingly successful left hook.

General Kelly served as director of operations for the Joint Chiefs under both Admiral William Crowe and General Powell. Kelly was a contradiction in images, mixing military expertise with humor, the latter often used to deflect criticisms. A tank commander by training and temperament, he was a tough-guy talker. As chief of operational traffic, Kelly lived in the world of the immediate, not images, between calamity and opportunity. He was responsible for positioning U.S. forces with proper strengths, plans, and approvals to respond to any emergency.

Doesn't sound like a general to meet and match the media. That's where the contrast comes in. A sophisticated Philadelphian, he holds a journalism degree from Temple University and is a smooth writer. Taken aback, but only temporarily, by the extent to which some reporters expected him to reveal information sensitive to troop security, he suggested they reflect on their methods. Like most other military press contacts, he was plainspoken, quietly confident, and got his job done (Woodward, 1991, pp. 99-100, 367).

Among the other prominent uniformed briefers was Marine Major General Robert B. Johnston, who had extensive communications experience, and Major General Burton R. Moore, chief of Desert Storm operations, who held a degree in radio-TV journalism (Woodward, 1991). Most controversial among active-duty peers and the media were hired military commentators, those once in uniform and even more, those who never served. Some military officers welcomed these experts as balance for reporters lacking any knowledge of weapons and combat (Pyle, 1991).

HIGHLY VISIBLE MR. INSIDE: POWELL

Aside from the "Odd Couple," messy Oscar and neatnik Felix, has there ever been a more successful linking of two very different personalities than those of Generals Powell and Schwarzkopf? Only real life, not fiction, could pair the son of poor Jamaican immigrants, an undistinguished student who entered the army through the reserve officer corps, with a second-generation West Pointer and general, who displayed his military and intellectual prowess early. Powell is a very honest professional who believes in the art of the possible. Powell played the politically sensitive Mr. Inside to Schwarzkopf's more emotional Mr. Outside very successfully (Adler, 1991). Not only did they win Desert Storm together; they became highly credible media heroes, each in his own way.

Even as Mr. Inside, Powell's visibility was high. One week in October 1990 was typical—remarks to the American Stock Exchange, a short briefing on counternarcotics programs, a memorial service, a military artwork presentation, a meeting with the military aide to the president of France, a few interviews and receptions (Woodward, 1991). According to colleagues, Powell realized very early in his career the importance of media and image in the next war and prepared himself and others for it. Powell foresaw that conflict would be televised instantly, as it was on CNN. Military operations, casualties, consequences and emotions would be seen immediately, and thus even more graphically than during Vietnam. Such coverage would vastly complicate all military operations. Powell was sure, according to Bob Woodward, that a prolonged war on television could become impossible, insupportable at home (Woodward, 1991).

Both Vietnam and the 1989 U.S. operation in Panama had shaped Powell's management style. He did not micromanage Schwarzkopf. Powell's guiding principle was to maximize fire power and troops. The stakes were high. There could not be another Vietnam. He would not be hurried into action, discounted style points. Many in the military understood Desert Storm might sour if hyped expectations resulted in lost credibility (Woodward, 1991).

Different as Powell and Schwarzkopf are, they shared the awesome realism of combat, which defined their strategies and caution. Powell, to the surprise of the unreflective, urged that sanctions be given more time, tactical patience, and any alternative to war be fully considered. Rather than a disembodied abstraction, Powell saw real men and women, faces—many of them kids' faces (Woodward, 1991). The muddy-boots combat generals urged caution, but the war proponents—whom columnist Mark Shields dubbed chickenhawks, chicken when personally vulnerable to combat—turned into hawks when able to order military power to the Gulf.

NORMAN II OF ARABIA

General Schwarzkopf's flash to celebrity intrigues more than any other personality of Desert Storm, and not only for his persona, military prowess, and cowing of the media. Not only for what his strategy reveals of the searing and changing of the military. Not only for the way he won Desert Storm. Mainly, he intrigues in how he mirrored media interests, our lust for heroes, our ephemeral attention spans.

Because we are in a thin period for heroes, our thirst and search for them are quickened. Media overkill, overexposure, the relentless attempts to find flaws in familiar faces past or current, all pique our interest with a first fresh, private individual suddenly thrust into the limelight. He reaps hype and glory, no matter how fleeting. Until Desert Storm, General Schwarzkopf was relatively unknown in public despite his prominence in C.D.B. Bryan's *Friendly Fire* (1976) and service as deputy commander of Urgent Fury (Grenada). He was just another four-star soon to retire, heading a largely paper command. But it was precisely that leap from privacy to fame, plus his own candor and humanness, that created a hero for people outside the Beltway.

Almost alone among the decision makers, Schwarzkopf had an eclectic upbringing and education; further, he knew the Gulf area well. His father served in World War II as a general in the military police and later trained the Shah's imperial police in Persia. In 1953, General H. Norman Schwarzkopf, Sr., was instrumental in the coup that overthrew Iran's Prime Minister Muhammed Mossadegh and restored the Shah to his throne. The younger Schwarzkopf, typical of army children, lived in Iran, Germany, and Italy before he was 17 years old (Bryan, 1976).

Unlike many of the press, he is deeply versed in the area. Not only is this by his residence or because of his learning Farsi and reading. Even as a commander, Schwarzkopf was studying Generals Bernard Montgomery and Erwin Rommel on desert warfare. This eclectic background showed in his successful multinational management.

Schwarzkopf's two tours of duty in Vietnam seared and shaped him in a very personal way, as Vietnam often did to both military and media. He considered war a profanity: "It's terrifying. Nobody is more antiwar than an intelligent person who's been in combat" (Bryan, 1991). Multinational management is the great crying need of business, including that of military and civilians. Schwarzkopf was confronted by a fragile and unique 33-nation coalition of Muslim and Christian, East and West, and strangeness one to the other. He sought to teach respect for Islam, that *Arab* is not a bad word. By giving each ally media visibility and credit, even if sometimes too generously, he managed nationals of many nations with a harmony that can only be the envy of corporate leaders (Bryan, 1991).

Adaptation of one's ideas may be the sincerest form of respect. For years, corporate executives have been displaying—but not necessarily reading—Karl von Clausewitz, General William Tecumseh Sherman, and General George C. Patton on management tactics. Is it any surprise that academics and corporate leaders are currently explaining a Gulf school style of management? It stresses the importance of managers mingling with the troops, motivational talks, intelligence, and surprise attacks.

Schwarzkopf's press conferences became instant manuals for managers on meeting the media. His leadership through vision and optimism contrasts with defensive managements that hide behind bureaucratic procedures and seek to avoid all risks and mistakes. From Vietnam he came to distrust a media that magnified U.S. Army failings and belittled achievements, as well as the primitive fortress mentality that soured press relations during Urgent Fury, the invasion of Grenada under the Reagan administration. In Desert Storm, these lessons produced a mediagenic general. He scheduled several weekly interviews with reporters, balancing his inclination to severely limit access with an awareness that it would only "arouse resentment" (Bryan, 1991). His candor with the media sounded like something from—or for—a public relations textbook: "I ain't no dummy when it comes to dealing with the press . . . when you try to stonewall the press . . . [they] turn ugly, and I would just as soon not have an ugly press" (Pyle, 1991, p. 103).

Schwarzkopf used every means to intimidate Saddam Hussein. Always assuming the enemy was watching, he gave the press good access to arriving equipment and men and to amphibious practice landings as well, deflecting their attention from the critically important western left hook. He gave the mother of all briefings, blitzkrieged the press with information. Schwarzkopf very simply "manipulated media coverage of the war to his advantage" (Pyle, 1991). His flair for public relations, writes Theodore Draper, "obscured the humiliation and degradation'' to which journalists were subjected by the U.S. Army in the field (Draper, 1992).

The general made mistakes—standing in the always-shifting glow of political leaders, overusing candor about personal qualms, making comments about ending the war too soon. Most serious was his helicopter policy. Even after admitting he had been ''snookered'' on the use of the helicopters, he did little when they were gunning down civilians (Draper, 1992).

OOZE AND JARGON

Words can obscure, incite, and motivate, but they seldom clarify as well as did the plain-speaking Desert Storm briefers, particularly General Schwarzkopf. One need only look to other wars and other government agencies to assess their accomplishment.

Is the debilitating weakness in most wars and most generals impenetrable jargon? Language that clarifies only for the specialists, while confusing the press, diminishes credibility. Accuracy also suffers when reporters simply do not understand what the briefers explain only in technical words. In many wars, victory has gone to the wordsmiths—Abraham Lincoln wielded a more adroit pen than did Jefferson Davis. Sherman's fierce dispatches were tocsin-shrill dispatches. And, Winston Churchill's World War II rhetoric is credited with inspiring England to stand alone.

Schwarzkopf's quotes from his Desert Storm press briefings (Pyle, 1991, pp. 155–264) illustrate the opposite, a plain style that depends on everyday experience. Just a sampling: ''A war in the desert is a war of mobility and lethality. It's not a war of straight lines drawn in the sand.'' Asked about tank maintenance, he replied, ''It's like flossing your teeth.'' Asked by a reporter about a frontal confrontation, the general replied: ''We are going to go around, over, through, on top, underneath and any other way.'' And, of course, his blunt assessment of Saddam Hussein as a military leader: ''He is neither a strategist nor is he schooled in the operational arts, nor is he a tactician, nor is he a general, nor is he a soldier. Other than that, he's a great military man.'' The general's language, rooted in realism and experience, withered questions that were not. When a reporter asked him if the minefield danger was overrated, Schwarzkopf simply asked the reporter whether he'd ever been in a minefield (Pyle, 1991).

Some verbal dodges used in warfare mean to soften, for example, ''He bought the farm,'' to mean a death. Others are designed to confuse. Urgent Fury was described as an ''invasion,'' a ''forced extraction,'' a ''predawn vertical insertion,'' a ''non permissive evacuation,'' an ''intervention,'' and a ''rescue'' (Adkin, 1989). William Safire writes how abbreviations used by airmen slipped into the briefers' language—triple A or AAA for antiaircraft artillery, SAMS for surface-to-air missiles, TOW, for tube-launched optically traced, wireguided, and SLAM for standoff land attack missile. ''Euphemism is almost as central to briefingese as acronism. Avoidance of collateral damage means 'trying not to kill civilians.' Targeting is used as a kind of euphemism for 'aiming at.' A bomb becomes 'ordnance law.' " Reporters liked the term "carpet bombing," a dysphemism for "bombing in a close pattern to destroy a large area rather than specific targets." (A dysphemism, obviously, is the opposite of a euphemism.) Hostages were called guests (Safire, 1991). But the Emmy for euphemisms must go to Marlin Fitzwater's announcement that the land war, the "liberation of Kuwait" had begun.

THE "INTENDO" GAMES

Military public relations aimed to sanitize the war, portraying it almost as a low-risk Nintendo game. That succeeded during the conflict, although grisly facts and pictures are surfacing now. Saul Landau in an article in the *Progressive* "The Real Nintendo Game" (1991) noted "the military . . . doesn't want the public to have bad news about dead and wounded Americans or malfunctioning equipment, which the public overpaid for" (p. 26). Military PR also reflects the American penchant for the upbeat, the happy endings, with a minimum of groans, blood, and deaths.

Designated network experts intoned the words of SCUDS, Patriots, Mirages, MIGS, and other high-tech wonders, and they explained new depths of evil personified by Saddam Hussein, a Central Casting–type villain. Technology was seen as a highly sophisticated video game, skillfully delivering its payloads. Cutting from the football playoff game's time-out to network news was a "vicarious pleasure" of watching big games going on in two places: "We see one team beating another in the Persian Gulf and one at Candlestick Park. A completed pass is followed by scenes of the tail flare of a Patriot missile launched to take out an incoming Scud" (Landau, 1991, p. 27).

Between these games, "we are urged to buy cars, running shoes, beer, and insurance, to feel secure in the good hands of Allstate" (Landau, 1991, p. 28). No questions asked about why we are fighting or why weapons systems must be shown publicly to prove they work or how many Iraqis died as a result of the 10,000 sorties.

Even the staid *Wall Street Journal* (1991) commented on television coverage "with all the splendor of a good football game." The pregame show featured the countdown to war. The kickoff, or announcement of the air assault, came in prime time.

Could the Pentagon have asked for a more perfect picture? "Nintendo duels, followed by many of the enemy turning themselves in. Bloodless, clean and easy" (Goldberg, 1991). Wiser generals such as Robert E. Lee and William Tecumseh Sherman thought quite differently. To them, war is terrible. And Generals Powell and Schwarzkopf are realists. Nevertheless, despite his combat experience, Powell had to remind himself constantly this was real not a game. He was watching what the public saw; an incredibly limited and antiseptic version of the war.

The war was also sanitized by spin control of potentially troubling statements. The public heard about, but didn't see, the great tank battles. Gun-camera footage showed direct hits, but errant bombs or lives obliterated were not shown. In much Desert Storm coverage, reality was left to emerge later. Only later were Iraqi soldiers shown literally being blown away, including one that jarred the image of a "clean war" by televising the wholesale destruction from the air of Iraqis fleeing north from Kuwait City. In this instance it became clear that a lot of Iraqis had indeed died (MacArthur, 1992).

Graphics, too, sanitized the war. Networks, lacking a high volume of action visuals, used sophisticated technology to produce graphics and video logos. They represented what happened but avoided the grisly. To viewers weaned on animation, it was as easy to forget as simulated reality. But graphics were effective in creating images. Viewers remembered graphics but forgot the news. The whole idea of TV graphic design was to keep it simple, fast, and varied.

Logos shared this function but also had to stay fresh and distinct while convincing viewers they really were about to see something different (MacArthur, 1992). In the "military state of Superbowl" ABC featured a "Desert Storm Showdown" logo; CBS, "America at War"; NBC, "Toward Peace in the Gulf"; and CNN, "Crisis in the Gulf." All were hyped by war music scores (Peters, 1992).

Omissions also were used to sanitize. General Powell's televised vow to isolate and kill the Iraqi army prompted a reaction from Barbara Bush to finesse it with the kids: "Be sure they're understanding what they're seeing." To Coleman McCarthy in "Not in Front of the Children" (1991, p.10) that was precisely the problem. He noted that children understood only too well since they were seeing a general, a national leader, bedecked medals and ribbons saying that killing people is America's way to solve problems.

Billy Graham blessed Bush's intervention, saying "there comes a time when we have to fight for peace." Unlike pious hawks who always omit the rest of the sentence, McCarthy finishes it by noting the method: saturation bombing, slaughtering Iraqi civilians, and further bankrupting our economy (McCarthy, 1991, p.10).

Some worried that the war coverage created a false appearance of fun. Nightly on British television there was "a bloodless sandpit to play in, and the sexy shots of Hornets and Tornados, with a camel left of frame and the sun rising over the cockpit. Cue the bagpipes: cue the British major who wants to get in there now" (Pilger, 1991).

PUBLIC RELATIONS: WINNERS AND LOSERS

Although generally the public relations of the politicians and military demonstrated public relations prowess in the Gulf, dissident voices existed then, as they do even more now. Analysts warned of long-term implications. Legislators criticized public relations firms promoting Kuwaiti interest.

Richard Zoglin, writing in *Time*, accorded the Pentagon a "masterly job of controlling the flow of information—a textbook PR campaign sure to serve as a model in future wars" (Zoglin, 1991b). Briefings were handled with extraordinary skill—filled with facts and figures and conducted by cooperative, candid briefers.

Even if the Pentagon did not actually spread disinformation, it encouraged the media's help in confusing the Iraqis. Schwarzkopf facetiously praised the press for making the initial allied buildup in Saudi Arabia seem greater than it was, thus helping to discourage an Iraqi attack. Before the ground offensive, "reporters were frequently taken to see troops near the Kuwait border to distract the Iraqis from the hidden buildup going on far to the west" (Zoglin, 1991b). Imagery dominated. The war was fought on the propaganda front as much as on the battlefield.

The PR losers were the press, which must regroup, rethink, and change. "There is probably greater public anger with the press than at any time since the end of the war in Vietnam," says First Amendment lawyer Floyd Abrams (Zoglin, 1991b). Others said the press looked like hall monitors at the senior prom too eager to accept the military's version of the war (Zoglin, 1991b). One print journalist noted that the Pentagon managed to hoodwink and embarrass the press corps at briefings by making reporters look like fools, nitpickers and egomaniacs; reporters were likened to dilettantes without military experience; dinner party commandos, slouching inquisitors, collegiate spitball artists; people who have never been in a fistfight much less combat (Sterba, 1992).

Media complaints about Pentagon censorship served to draw attention away from its own self-censorship. No federal agency forced the media to rely on the narrow range of prowar analysts who dominated the news. Nor did anyone make correspondents mouth the sanitized military lingo that routinely obscured the war's human impact.

No government edict called for the media to exult laser-guided bombs, or call the initial bombing of Iraq "a marvel," or diminish civilian casualties by noting Saddam Hussein had put them in harm's way, or forced network anchors to refer to the U.S. government as "we," thus narrowing the separation between press and state. During the war, only 1 of 878 on-air sources who appeared on nightly news represented a national peace organization. "If top editors really want to change wartime reporting, they should probe their own abdication of journalistic responsibility" (Solomon, 1991).

The military painfully learned its lessons in Vietnam and changed—a cauterizing and modernizing few corporate leaders or networks, CNN as a notable exception, have yet acted upon. The military won big because it manipulated, knew what it was doing. The press, caterwaul as it did, was caught lagging behind new technology and the military's new sophistication in media relations. CNN's instantaneous coverage, particularly from the enemy capital, a never-before event, changed the way wars will be fought and covered. If Alistair Cooke wondered whether Vietnam coverage techniques applied to the Somme would prevent the repetition of such a battle, what does CNN coverage portend for the fighting and reporting of future conflicts?

Most troubling of all the long-range issues is unquestioning acceptance—the media of military control, the public of the administration's PR messages. That uncritical hype and glory gulled us into seeing only a Nintendo, sanitized war, only what others wanted us to see. As the most visible counterforce, the public dumped on the media. But the "bottom line" of Gulf War public relations is not more control, more manipulation, but tougher, more insightful informed questions. Desert Storm tested little save military media management and advanced weaponry. The images and myths seemed so real then, but do they still now?

Would they survive the carnage of Gettysburg, an even shorter battle? In that desperate, costly, three-day conflict, more than 50,000 North and South were killed or wounded. How effective would any public relations techniques have been in explaining such sacrifices had they been in the Gulf instead of at Gettysburg?

NOTES

1. In many instances, General Schwarzkopf had the greatest and the most recent knowledge of the area. According to Smith, "If Lawrence of Arabia is alive, his name is Schwarzkopf" (1991, p. 3).

2. This text must be treated with caution, however. Theodore Draper, writing in the *New York Review of Books* (1992), explains that Glaspie "was totally unprepared to take notes," and hence the only transcript is Iraqi.

3. During a visit of Senator Alan K. Simpson and other senators on April 12, 1990, Saddam complained for an hour that Iraq was the victim of a propaganda campaign, mentioning a Voice of America commentator. Even after learning of the commentator's firing, Simpson sympathized with Saddam:

I believe your problem is with the Western media, not with the U.S. Government, because you are isolated from the media and the press. The press is spoiled and conceited. All the journalists consider themselves brilliant political scientists. They do not want to see anything succeeding or achieving its objectives. My advice to you is that you allow those bastards to come here and see things for themselves. (Quoted in Draper, 1992)

With such great media advice, it may be no wonder that Saddam flopped on TV.

4. The word *antiseptic* does not ignore Iraqi suffering, but Williams was not managing that.

Part II

Communication Practices
Unique to the Gulf War

4

High Tech Comes to War Coverage: Uses of Information and Communications Technology for Television Coverage in the Gulf War

Linda Jo Calloway

INTRODUCTION

The United States Armed Forces have engaged in three conflicts since Vietnam: Operation Urgent Fury in Grenada, Operation Just Cause in Panama, and Operation Desert Shield/Desert Storm in the Persian Gulf. Admiral Joseph Metcalf's decision to exclude media from the initial phases of the Operation Urgent Fury intervention put a limit on the use of high-tech tools developed since Vietnam for real-time war coverage. The media exclusion also marked a low in relations between the press and the military (Chiaventone, 1991). The system of press pooling put in place after Urgent Fury eased the access of media to information during Operation Just Cause in Panama.[1] The media had better access to information and began to depend on technologies based on current advances in voice communications, for example, Fax, personal computer communications, and electronic news gathering via satellite.

By the conclusion of Operation Desert Storm in the Persian Gulf, use of these information and communications technologies had matured. Gulf War television coverage relied on video, telephone, computer technologies, and radio. These are common technologies used by business, the armed forces, and the media to communicate information and to coordinate activities. In a series of interviews conducted by the author with key information officers in the four major U.S.–based networks, ABC, CBS, CNN, and NBC, in the fall of 1991, what was reported as ''new'' were new uses of existing technologies in the Persian Gulf for war coverage.

Although the technologies themselves are not ''new,'' the integration of these technologies into a set of working tools, high and low tech, routinely used by the press, the broadcast media, and military command and control under real-time battle conditions was new. These information and communications technologies used during the Gulf War changed forever the role of information for allied and enemy military forces and governments, policymakers, public observers, and the media themselves. These technologies made information immediately available worldwide. Throughout the Gulf War, satellite news gathering by the media fed real-time intelligence to both sides of the Gulf conflict. Intelligence officers used satellite news for their real-time strategy adjustments. Iraqis watched the landing of SCUD missiles in Israel and Saudi Arabia to adjust targeting while allied forces watched the same reports to target the launchers. CNN, then available in 105 countries, spawned telediplomacy (Clark, 1991).

It is clear from this new immediacy and ubiquity of media that we live in a world of just-in-time everything: just-in-time manufacturing, just-in-time news, and just-in-time business. Fast-response technologies have brought us the ability to wage a just-in-time war. A real-time war was made possible, however, mainly because President George Bush announced U.S. intentions in time to set up and configure the technologies. Following the president's lead, it became possible to ship automated data processing equipment to the Desert Storm theater within days. As a result, supplies arrived, networks were reconfigured, troops were redeployed and front-line news was gathered not only just-in-time but in real time. President Bush had brought us what William J. Small in this volume calls a "war by appointment."

This chapter examines the information and communications technologies that were used by television news crews to cover the Gulf War. It describes the information technology platform (the hardware, software, telecommunications, data, and workstations) that allowed the stakeholders in the conflict to communicate and to share information. In addition, the opportunities that the information technology platform brought to news coverage in the Gulf, the factors affecting deployment and competitive positioning, and the technologies and techniques that have been integrated into war coverage as a result of Desert Storm are discussed. Finally, this chapter discusses what we know about how the management and deployment of these technologies affected network competitive advantage and disadvantage during the war and emerging trends in information and communications that are already beginning to change media coverage of breaking news of daily events (normal news coverage).

TECHNOLOGY PLATFORMS AND INFRASTRUCTURES

Technology platforms and infrastructures and their impact on the reach and range of television coverage can be modeled. A discussion of those infrastructures available in the Gulf to the media follows and includes a model of the platform. This discussion is followed by a description of the particular technologies in terms of reach and range.

Platform Reach and Range

For an information and communications technology to be a useful part of a reporter's repertoire there has to be an infrastructure—technical as well as managerial and social. The technology platform determines the possibilities for fast news coverage. Networks with fast communication links and broad information exchange possibilities are able to gain a competitive opportunity for coverage.

The Evolution of Speed in War Coverage

In World War II, it was unusual to view newsreels that were less than a month old, and they were viewed in movie theaters. The newsreel was shot on film that was transported to the states by aircraft. Later, in Vietnam, the time lag between a firefight and the television coverage of it was shortened to 24 to 48 hours, depending on flight schedules from Southeast Asia. By contrast, "Now, in the Persian Gulf, an Iraqi SCUD missile explodes simultaneously in a Tel Aviv neighborhood and in the American living room" (Clark, 1991).

What made this change possible is today's communications infrastructure. In Vietnam, communications for video and film depended on the airlines. Today, international broadcast news depends on satellite transmission, a technology that brings coverage of events to a viewer in a quarter of a second on the airwaves.

The catalog of information and communications technologies used by the networks describes an information and communications platform. A platform is the set of services that are in use. It is described according to what parties are connected and what sorts of information can be automatically and directly exchanged. This definition of the information technology platform uses the concepts of reach and range (see Keen, 1991).

The relevant parties that can be contacted and connected to one another fast and automatically define the *reach* of the platform. The types of information and media that they can share and manipulate define the *range* of the platform. The ideal reach is to be able to connect to anyone, anywhere, just as the phone system reaches across the world. This is currently an impractical short-term target, but one that will become more realistic in the coming decade as standards allow a variety of media systems to interconnect in the way that numerous telephone systems do today.

An ideal range is one that permits, without human intervention, any computer-mediated video or audio transmission, document, message, and even telephone call to be used in any other system, regardless of hardware or software. Today in the 1990s, with widespread differences in proprietary vendor-specific technology, operating systems, and information storage and management techniques, only systems built on the same technology base can automatically and directly share messages, transmissions, and data. While this may be viewed as an advantage for a personal computer with proprietary information, it has obvious shortcomings when it is desirable to share information with disparate parties in disparate places such as coalition members in Desert Storm. (See Keen, 1991, for a detailed description of information technology platforms.)

The reach and range model can be conceptualized as a one-way or two-way configuration. For example, telegraph is one-way. Telephone technology is two-way. For purposes of this discussion, *interactive* is defined as those information and communications technologies that allow two-way transmission in real time.[2] *Real time* may be defined as communication about a process that allows a response fast enough to make a decision that affects the process (see any discussion on control theory or systems theory). Steering wheels and brakes in cars operate in real time. Monday-morning quarterbacks and most backseat drivers do not.

"High- and Low-tech" Technologies Used in Desert Storm

The information and communications technologies are described below in terms of their reach and range capabilities. Figure 4.1 consolidates the technologies used by the four television networks in Desert Storm into a platform model of their combined reach and range.

High tech is a loose term applied to computer-based technologies that seem advanced. But such tools are just those that haven't yet become members of the standard tools of the trade for users. Word processors once seemed high tech—part of the computer revolution—until users came to depend on them to get their jobs done. Many American citizens thought four-wire phones were high tech and confused them with Satellite News Gathering (commonly called SNG, or ENG, for Electronic News Gathering) technology. In fact, newspeople and the military have been using four-wire phones for decades. In news, the four-wire essentially goes back to Edward R. Murrow in London—"This is London, the bombs are falling."

All technologies that depend on transmission at a distance use some form of electromagnetic radiation for their signals. For example, AM and FM radio, microwaves, and satellites transmit signals through the air. Telephones use telephone wires. Network television normally uses the airwaves or cable (another kind of wire). Fiber-optic cables can be used to transmit electromagnetic radiation as well.

For the sake of convenience, the technologies featured in Figure 4.1 are grouped according to whether they are mainly based on FM radio, plain old telephone technology, still photography, video, computers, or multimedia. The order of their appearance is roughly by their increasing range and decreasing reach.

The figure indicates the reach and range of the U.S–based networks. The reach moves from the narrowest reach, which is people within the station newsroom, to international reaching of individuals that are external to the networks. The range of the technologies moves from voice technology, which shares voice only, through to multimedia, which potentially shares information in any digital format and is interactive. The computer technologies, as is obvious, have the

Figure 4.1
Reach and Range of the U.S.–based Network Technologies

Reach	Radio b	FM and shortwave	Voice	Satellite phone	Public access direct distance dial	Extended switchboard	Four-wire	Still Photo	FAX	Digital Photo	Frame grabbers	Video	Flyaway TV	1-way ground station TV/audio	Cable TV	2-way TV/2-way audio	Computer	E-mail	Script filing	Database access	Database text interactive	Multimedia	Graphic database interactive	Photo/graphic integration	Database interactive (multimedia)
International/External																									
Iraq				e									a												
Kuwait													c					c							
Jordan				x	x	x			x				g					x							
Saudi Arabia				x					x									x							
International bureaus and individuals				x					x									x							
International/Internal																									
Iraq				f			d											f	a	a					
Kuwait				c														c	c						
Arabia				x		x				x	x		x					x	x	x					
Overseas bureaus and individuals				x		x				x	x				x			x	x	x	x				
Domestic/External																									
External news organizations				x						x						x		x							
Realtime "wires"				x							x					x			x	x	x				
External database providers				x															x	x	x		x		
Domestic/Internal																									
Within network locations and individuals in US				x	x					x	x			x	x	x		x	x	x	x		x	x	
Network newsroom				x	x						x				x	x		x	x	x	x		x	x	x

a. CNN eventually placed a flyaway ground station in Baghdad.

b. Radio was used extensively by the military command and control, but it was not used to support television coverage.

c. After the ground war invasion of Kuwait.

d. CNN became famous for its four-wire open circuit into Baghdad, which provided the only live coverage in the United States of the initial four days of the air war.

e. ABC also got a phone call out on Britain's International Television Network (ITN) satellite phone, which was working behind Baghdad's Al-Rasheed Hotel, where the reporters were staying. Within minutes, transmission was interrupted by authorities.

f. CNN had received permission from the Iraqi government for a producer and television crew to enter the country with a satellite transmitting device that would provide live pictures from Baghdad. CBS, NBC, and ABC said they had sought permission to reenter Baghdad to report on the war in the Persian Gulf and were denied visas (Iraq to Allow CNN Satellite, 1991).

g. Twenty-four hours after the war began, Gary Shepard arrived at the Intercontinental Hotel in Amman, Jordan, with video footage of the initial air attacks.

narrowest reach and the widest range, while voice technologies have the widest reach and the narrowest range.

Radio Uses

Radio was extensively used as part of the military mobile battlefield network. The reach and range were both limited, since the objective was short-range and secure transmissions. Radio was not used by the television corps, but it was available. The military used fiber-optic cable in the field to carry their signals when it was possible; fiber is more difficult to "wiretap" into and provides a signal that degrades more slowly than wire-based or radio-based signals. Fiber was simply rolled out on the ground. Although radio is included in the reach and range table, it was not used by the television media.

Telephone Uses

Four-Wire Phone. The four-wire phones have the least reach. Although the end-to-end connection might stretch across continents, it still connects only two individual and predetermined parties. CNN used a four-wire to connect from the Al-Rasheed Hotel in Baghdad to the Philadelphia Hotel in Amman, Jordan, and used another four-wire line to connect from Amman to Atlanta. The other networks had four-wire phones, but not into Baghdad.

Just like the old army field phones, which were also four-wire, the four-wire is a plain old telephone that has a direct connection to a single destination. There is no need to provide a switching service through a local telephone switching center. The four-wire was routed through the Baghdad Poste, Telephone and Telegraph tower in Baghdad (the Iraq PTT). In the first minutes of the war, the local switching center was destroyed. However, the Baghdad PTT tower continued to function. The four-wire line is leased by the parties using it, and it is dedicated to their exclusive use. The four-wire phone voice connection between Baghdad and Atlanta (via Amman) was important in the Gulf War, because it saved CNN's coverage in Baghdad during the first days of the war. It was four days before any live television coverage was provided by the network television pools.

According to Dick Tauber, head of Satellites and Circuits at CNN-Atlanta,

Basically, getting it in place really was a product of our worldwide distribution as much or more so as our desire for it. All of the networks wanted something like that. Most of them one way or another requested some kind of circuit out of Baghdad. One initially asked for a four-wire from Baghdad to Dhahran, who were the enemies. One or two of the other networks tried to get one from Baghdad to New York. We only asked for a line between Amman [Jordan] and Baghdad. (Personal communication, fall 1991)

Jordan was a neutral party in the conflict.

Portable Satellite Flyaway Telephones. Flyaway means that the satellite phone station can be put into suitcases that can be shipped as luggage on international and domestic airline flights. Satellite phones have the largest reach of any telephone technology. They can communicate to and from almost anywhere on earth except Siberia. All the networks used flyaway phones. The flyaway is battery powered and can be set up anywhere. Flyaways used in the Gulf weighed about 65 pounds and usually took two suitcases. By the end of the war, the number of flyaway phones worldwide tripled to about 170 or 180 (Personal communication, fall 1991).

All of the networks had satellite phone access via flyaway phones in Baghdad prior to the attack on January 16. Once fighting began, ABC got one phone call out on Britain's International Television Network (ITN) satellite phone. Then within minutes, transmission was interrupted by authorities.

Public Telephones. The public phone networks, such as ATT, MCI, SPRINT, and the local telephone companies, have the next longest reach, as they can communicate to anyone with a telephone who is connected to the international phone networks. Before the air attack on January 16, reporters also had regular telephone access from the Al-Rasheed Hotel via the Baghdad Telephone Switching Center. Service was interrupted when the tower was destroyed.

Private Branch Exchange (PBX) Extensions into the Gulf. These special phone systems allowed the networks to connect from their newsrooms in the United States to their reporting sites in the Gulf with a four-digit extension number, just as they would need to contact someone in the next room at ABC, NBC, CBS, and CNN. These news organizations had the same ability to directly dial the Persian Gulf using a four-digit extension. According to NBC, phone service was so bad some places in the Gulf that ordinary public phone systems are horrible on a day-to-day basis. David Schmerler of NBC relays the story that in Cairo the network used to insulate its in-ground phone wires with paper. "Unfortunately, one day it rained . . . " Before the war, NBC offices in Cairo used to phone other Cairo offices by first dialing the United States and having offices there place a call to CBS on the other side of Cairo. Then they would conference it (Personal Communication, fall 1991).

Digital Voice. Digital voice, yet another telephone technology, has the same reach as other public phone systems, but it has the added range potential to be stored and forwarded automatically by computer. Analog phone equipment can be used to send digital information, but it first has to be converted from digital signals into analog signals by a modem. The world's phone networks are being digitized at an accelerated rate, but satellite phones, for example, remain analog for now.

Still Photo Uses

Facsimile Transmission. Facsimile has the same potential reach as voice networks, since it can connect to most phone terminals. It has more range, however, since it provides hard copy of the transmission (the Fax) and can reach "pass-along" audiences. Fax can also be digitized and stored in a computer. Fax transmissions were used in the war to move documents in Arabic to translators.

Digital Transmission of Still Photographs. Photography provides more range than Fax, as it provides color transmission. All three networks reported that they had the facilities for still transmission, but they did not have to resort to them from the field. They were deployed primarily as backup in case their television transmissions were interrupted.

Frame Capture of Video Images to Print (ABC, Various News Media). Frame capture provides the ability to capture a still picture from a video signal. The machine grabs the 525 lines from the video picture and then translates them into a signal that transmits on a voice circuit. Frame grabbers have the reach and range of digital transmission of still photographs.

ABC, for one, used frame-grabbed images for their television specials. The pencil press often published frames that were grabbed from video. Video frames are transmitted faster, and so there is more choice of pictures to print.

Video Uses

Television broadcasts have more physical information than radio or telephone broadcasts. In television, both color and sound have to be sent fast enough so that the viewer thinks nothing is missing. The television picture acts as a window into (or out of) reality. Since both pictures and sound have to be sent, the signal has to move faster. The faster a signal moves, the more information it can carry.

All the networks used the Sony "Hi-8" 8-millimeter videocameras available at retail camera stores. They provided inexpensive coverage. NBC noted that the networks used this consumer video equipment to get more equipment out in the field, to give it to more people. Also, the user can keep his head down. "A reporter with a big camera makes a nice target!" said Schmerler (Personal communication, fall 1991). ABC added that it shipped the inexpensive Hi-8s because there were fears that poison gas might contaminate equipment, and if so, they would have to be buried in the desert (Personal communication, fall 1991).

Flyaway Video Satellite Uplinks. As is the case with flyaway phones, flyaway earth stations can be packed in suitcases that travel by commercial airlines as excess baggage. The uplink station can be flown anywhere a medium-sized plane can land. The station can then be moved onto a flatbed truck that can go anywhere a truck can go. A small ground station can be packed into about ten suitcases (Personal communication, fall 1991).

The key technological breakthrough that led to flyaways was the discovery of materials that would hold their shape. The large, 8-meter satellite dishes could be disassembled, shipped, and reassembled in the field without causing distortion (Personal communication, 1991). In the Gulf, there was no two-way video from flyaways. Reporters used a voice channel to provide two-way communications.

Video from In-place Ground Stations. These stations provide less reach since they are stuck to the ground, usually in concrete, and weigh tons. More information is usually available at a ground station that doesn't move. For example, facilities that model graphics and incorporate still photographs into the video can be used. Historical footage is probably available from archives, and "studio" experts are probably closer at hand.

The first videos of the initial air attacks in Baghdad were uplinked from a permanent ground station in Jordan (the BAQA earth station). Twenty-four hours after the war began, Gary Shepard arrived in Amman, Jordan (Intercontinental Hotel) with video footage of the initial air attacks. They used a special night vision lens to get the pictures (by Fabrice Mousus), according to an ABC news cameraman.

Cable TV. Cable has a greater range available, as one notes by the myriad of channels available on cable TV. But the reach is limited to areas that are wired for cable. Cable is more vulnerable than satellite-based television, because the cables that carry the signal can be damaged. Coaxial cable, the cable used with television, can carry much more information than the twisted pair cable normally used in telephones, because it is better insulated.

Two-way Video Conferencing. Two-way video conferencing is a method for communicating used mainly in business. Current technology practice depends on using a digitized video signal that has been compressed or slowed down. The information is then sent over a telephone line that is conditioned (and insulated) well enough to move 128,000 bytes a second (KBS) or less. Although video-conferencing is sometimes used by the networks, it wasn't used in the Gulf.

Computer Uses

Electronic Mail (e-mail). E-mail via laptop or portable computer that is connected to a phone circuit has the same reach as the various voice communications channels. The range, however, is larger; simple messages can be exchanged that are stored in computers and automatically available to other computers. All four networks made extensive use of electronic mail in the field and domestically.

Another use for e-mail is access to electronic computer bulletin boards (BBs). Bulletin boards are lists of messages that users want to make available to anyone on the system about a subject. A particular bulletin board will be devoted to a certain subject. Approved users can access the bulletin board, add messages to it, or edit it. This bulletin board facility is often used by networks that choose to create a "custom wire" that keeps track of news on an ongoing story.

Access to International News-Wires and Databases. The ability to capture newswires provides more range than the ability to listen on the phone. The reach depends on the reach of the computer technology. All four networks had access through their home computers to newswires, and at least CNN had direct access to Dow Jones and other wires from the Gulf through Compuserve (a commercial service). Read-only access to commercial databases such as Lexis/Nexis or Dow-Jones provide more range than simple message exchange.

Script Filing. Script filing was done by writing directly into the home-computer memory by reporters in the field. Computer technology that let reporters file scripts as well as send messages provided a larger range of information than those whose access rights were limited to reading only.

Interactive Database Access. Any database access that allows both reading and writing updates provides the user with more range. All networks had interactive data access to information in their home computer systems.

Multimedia Uses

Computer Graphics. Computer-generated graphics are digital and can be manipulated on a computer. All networks had computer graphics in their main bureaus.

Integration of Graphics and Photos (e.g., SCITOR Computer System). A system called Photron turns graphics into television images. The SCITOR system was used to link digitized color images from satellites to graphics. ABC used the system during its television specials (e.g., "Line in the Sand") created in New York in January and February 1991 and was also the first to use the system during the 1988 Olympics (Personal communication, fall 1991). The system had virtually no reach.

Full Multimedia Integration. This is what one gets in a usual news program—graphics, stills, off-site interviews, historical footage, some live footage, sports clips, sound bites, a few commercials, a number of anchors, and a weather map.

Opportunities Presented (and Missed) by Technology in the Gulf

Amazingly enough, much of the technology brought to the Gulf by the media and the military was bought "off the shelf." An ABC spokesman put it this way: "Being frugal, we can't buy all the telecommunications facilities in advance. So everyone was trying to buy" (Personal communication, fall 1991). According to military spokesmen, equipment was purchased at local electronic shops like Radio Shack. Technologies that were described as *new* were either new to the network or new to war coverage.

The opportunities grabbed and missed in the Gulf are discussed in terms of those in which technology was used in a new way, existing uses were significantly extended by a network, and the extended technologies made their way into the everyday working tool set used by the networks for event coverage. Those tools that make their way into the working set are those tools that have become ready at hand. They are understood, available, accessible, and easy to use (see Winograd and Flores, 1986).

New Technologies. The most vivid technology that was used to cover Desert Storm was live video coverage via satellite. Satellite news gathering was integrated into the working set of tools by all the networks well before the Gulf

War. However, SNG was never extensively used before to report a war, although there was some SNG during the latter parts of Just Cause in Panama.

According to Schmerler at ABC,

The big difference was that for the first time ever, we had the first television war that was live. The picture. Here was M[artin] Fletcher in Tel Aviv sitting on a desk on camera live with a gas mask on. Similarly, the other picture is Arthur Kent in Saudi Arabia breaking into a football game saying SCUDS are coming in, and we saw a SCUD intercepted by a patriot missile. Vietnam was a film war. (Personal communication, fall 1991)

Tom Fenton of CBS and the ABC and CNN correspondents also broadcast from Tel Aviv. Only CBS specifically reported that it had used all of the technologies before the Gulf War. According to Brian Knoblock, the technologies it used were "pretty well tried and true. They were technologies that we were comfortable with using and that we'd worked with before" (Personal communication, fall 1991).

Portable up-link technology has been developing very rapidly. According to Schmerler at NBC, there are about 20 portable earth stations in the world, and at one point during Desert Storm every internationally qualified portable up-link in the world was in the gulf (Personal communication, fall 1991). ABC's Elliott Reed listed that network's use of International Marine Satellite (Inmarsat) phones as a new deployment for war coverage (Personal communication, fall 1991). CNN also reported that its use of Inmarsat phones for computer links was a first for the network.

ABC also used its SCITOR Computer system that linked graphics with satellite images for the first time during war coverage, but the system was in use at its ABC headquarters in New York before the Gulf War. During the war, it was used for television specials such as "Line in the Sand" with Peter Jennings (Personal communication, fall 1991).

Technologies Used More Extensively. Personal computers were used by nearly all reporters in the Persian Gulf theater. Many newsrooms put their news scripts onto their central computers, and these scripts, as well as headquarters newswires, were available on-line to the reporters in the field.

Advantages provided by personal computers connected to home-base newsrooms via phone line were immense. The individual reporter in the field could access newswires, news scripts, and historical data from home-based computers as well as file his or her own stories and material. Using e-mail, reporters could contact one another in the field to find out what was happening. They could have immediate access to stories their competition had filed to newspapers, network broadcasts, or wire services.

During the Vietnam conflict, reporters had either to phone Saigon or perhaps send a telex message to exchange information. Computer technology vastly enhanced the range of information available for immediate and automatic exchange among the parties reporting in the Gulf.

Permanent Members of the Tool Kit. Without a doubt, laptop computer communications, with all the added reach and range they provide in the field, are now permanent members of any reporter's kit. Without extended access to electronic networks, the reporters cannot hope to compete from the field. Almost any individual with a computer ID and access to electronic mail has the ability to report instantaneously.

One clear indicator that a technology or application has been integrated into a person's tool kit is that the person or field has adapted it into their working vocabulary. The concept of electronic bulletin boards and news wires go by the name of "custom wires" in BASYS, a computer system designed for newsrooms. NBC, for instance, has a crisis wire. One of the author's interviews at ABC occurred during the Clarence Thomas–Anita Hill hearings, and we connected to the CRISIS.THOMAS customized wire. The BASYS computer system has gotten so reliable that if it's out one minute, it's a problem for the networks (Personal communications, fall 1991).

In Desert Storm, electronic messages and electronic bulletin boards gave minute-by-minute accounts of action. Internet is one of hundreds of electronic networks that connect individuals, scholars, and research agencies worldwide. Electronic mail communications are so common that within six weeks of the Iraqi invasion of Kuwait, the U.S. Army Information Systems Command had designed, installed, and made fully operational a data communications architecture using off-the-shelf commercial products. Just as the Patriot missile became the hero of the Army's Desert Storm weapons systems, the Transmission Control Protocol/Internet Protocol became the Army's hero of Desert Storm's information systems (Weissert, 1991, pp. 40–41). TCP/IP is a standard used to communicate within the high-speed government and civilian research networks.

Satellite phones have become a permanent part of the ABC tool kit. ABC used Inmarsat flyaway phones during the Persian Gulf and by the end of the year had used them during the Russian coup and during the Madrid peace talks (Personal communication, fall 1991).

Nothing can become part of the user's tool kit that is not easily operated. Technical difficulties with the Mobile Telesystem's one-suitcase model flyaway phone cause it to blink out under certain atmospheric conditions. But nevertheless, it weighed only 65 pounds, had a dish a yard wide that opened like an umbrella, connected to a Fax or a computer, and could operate off a car battery. Leon Harris, assistant director of satellites and circuits at CNN is quoted as saying, "Peter Arnett isn't exactly known around here as a 'techno-nerd.' . . . Our guys showed him how to use it [the flyaway] in five minutes on his way out of the country" (Robichaux and Fuchsberg, 1991).

Managing the Deployment of the New Technologies

Culture, politics, and negotiation were key factors in managing the deployment of information and communications technologies in the Gulf.

Culture Issues. In Saudi Arabia, the hardest issues for reporters were getting access to key people and getting access to facilities. Before Desert Shield, the Western news media were seldom allowed free reign in Saudi Arabia. Another issue for ABC, CBS, and NBC was that they were domestic networks. "The sheiks had a dish out in the backyard where they could *see* CNN," said Schmerler (Personal communication, fall 1991).

ABC commented that there were not very many cultural issues to handle with the Arab people, because its people were so isolated from the Arab communities. The television crews were surrounded by press and military people and mainly interacted with interpreters and translators in the hotel (Personal communication, fall 1991).

According to CNN, there were disadvantages as well as advantages of being a global television network. Senior officials in the area, say in Iraq, might on occasion not like something that Wolf Blitzer or Charles Bierbaur would be reporting. "And that's certainly something that the other news networks need not concern themselves with. I mean our policy is to report everything fairly, responsibly and accurately, but on occasion that doesn't necessarily suit the desires of a government such as Iraq," said Eason Jordan of CNN (Personal communication, fall 1991).

Political Issues. One of the most visible political issues of the war coverage was whether the pool system set up by the Pentagon to provide the nation's media with words and pictures of the war resulted in wholly accurate or representative accounts. In fact, some members of the press formally charged the Department of Defense during the war with trying to "prevent, delay, hinder and obstruct access to United States bases, personnel and information" (APME News, 1991). For an excellent discussion of the media pools and censorship, see *The Media At War: The Press and the Persian Gulf Conflict* (LeMay, Fitzsimon, and Sahadi, 1991).

The United States has had a so-called "open skies" policy since 1972, which allows open entry to satellite licensing procedures and use. Many other countries are rapidly liberalizing their telecommunications, including satellite access. Nevertheless, in the Persian Gulf the local PTTs that originally controlled the postal service, telephony, and telegraph also controlled broadcast, cable, and satellite services. The monopolistic and state-owned control over receipt and transmission cost the television networks over 100 times what U.S. companies charge (Howes, 1991).

Negotiating Access Through PTTs. The issue of cost is interrelated with political issues in telecommunications worldwide. Managing and negotiating access to facilities in the Persian Gulf was frustrating as well as expensive. Permission to access any PTT facilities had to be negotiated from the local jurisdiction, and a license fee was required. According to ABC the Jordanians were the worst. "They charge you as much to use your own facilities as it would cost you to use their facilities," said Schmerler (Personal communication, fall 1991). Jordan was charging $15,000 U.S. per month for the four-wire phone.

Even using orbiting satellite facilities required permission from the country from which transmissions were sent. International satellite agreements require permission from the host country before a satellite company will relay information from the host country's soil.

CBS added that it was currently negotiating through professional groups to have immediate access anywhere for flyaway phones. "The news media only wants to move equipment into an area for a day or two; they are not destroying the host country infrastructure control forever," said Knoblock (Personal communication, fall 1991). Elliott Reed added that the one advantage to access from Kuwait was that it was free. "There was no government to negotiate with, so we asked any exiled official in London or the U.S. if we could uplink to Inmarsat. Then we had them 'sign here' " (Personal communication, fall 1991).

Permission is also required to transmit into a country. Reception is easily blocked by state-owned ground station facilities, but it was much more difficult to black out reception to private parties with satellite dishes including mobile ground stations and flyaway ground station facilities.

CNN had the advantage, however, in negotiations for using its technologies. International satellite news broadcasting from around the world, and to the world, had been part of CNN's business strategy from its beginning in the 1970s. CNN was already available in the Gulf, and the satellite dishes that received CNN are common in the wealthier areas of the Gulf. Thus the various ministries and government officials in the Gulf were accustomed to seeing CNN. This familiarity with CNN's broadcasts helped during the negotiations.

Negotiating Visas. Another difficulty was in negotiating visas. "There was lots of choreography going on with the Saudi embassy," said Reed of ABC. "We had 20 at first, then if someone would leave, we'd send another person in with the visa." This is a slightly unauthorized procedure, as a visa is supposed to be issued to a certain person.

Telediplomacy. The extended reach and range of broadcast communications in the Gulf allowed governments to access one another directly and spawned the term *telediplomacy.* Paul D. Wolfowitz, undersecretary of defense for policy in the Bush administration, said, "For Saddam Hussein, we were conscious that television was one of the few ways to get any message to him directly, not just because diplomatic channels were largely blocked, but because you couldn't have any confidence that any of his subordinates could convey a message exactly as it was conveyed to them. No one wants to spread bad news in that system" (Officials Discuss TV's Impact on Gulf War, 1991). He also noted that in his opinion, the effectiveness of the Patriot missiles as demonstrated on television played a role in Israel's decision to stay out of the war (Ibid).

Competitive Advantages and Disadvantages

Computer Reach and Range. In an arena where information was tightly controlled, or at least attempts were made to tightly control information, the reach of technology provided competitive advantage. For NBC, its advanced telephone system was an advantage. For the networks, their headquarters computer system, BASYS, which they had up and running since the mid-1980s, was also an advantage. This is a system built for newsrooms, and is used also by CNN and other networks. The BASYS platform provided e-mail, historic database access, coordinated on-line program outlining, and other services. NBC used BASYS to back-time all of its scripts and to time its news broadcasts. In BASYS, everyone could be allowed access to the basic system. Each user was given a specific profile as to what it could access—its rights and privileges (Personal communication, fall 1991). As described by NBC's Schmerler, "Computers allow you to get information to and from people better. Hundreds of people can see it. We put the scripts of news on the computer—the rundown for the nightly news." Any changes, updates, and additions could be made on-line and available in real time (Personal communication, fall 1991). CBS used the Newstar computer system, which is similar.

Live Transmission via Satellite. CBS and other networks noted that there was little competitive advantage to be had in Saudi Arabia, because of the pool structure. CBS reported a disadvantage in Israel, since there were only three satellite links out of Israel, and during the initial SCUD attacks, CBS was the network that did not have access to transmission facilities (Personal communication, fall 1991).

The ground invasion of Kuwait began on February 23 Eastern Standard Time. The ground war moved so quickly that pool rules were ignored. CBS had the initial advantage; James McKeown arrived in Kuwait City and was on the air before allied troops arrived, sending the first live report from Kuwait City. ABC's Forrest Sawyer, NBC's Bruce Willis, and CNN's Charles Jaco and Brian Jenkins came to Kuwait City within hours of McKeown (see chapter 1 in this volume). (ABC's flyaway up-link trucks were stopped by mechanical problems just outside Kuwait, causing them to arrive shortly after CBS.)

Phone Systems. NBC was the Department of Defense pool network for the invasion, and NBC felt it had the best phones. NBC had a special digitized phone system that allowed an unlimited number of people to participate on a conference call, without degradation of signal. Nevertheless, ABC and CBS also described their phone systems as competitive advantages. From the interviews, the difference appears to be that the ABC, CBS, and CNN systems were analog based.

Of course, CNN had the decisive competitive advantage during the initial four days of the war while its four-wire phone was operating alone from the Al-Rasheed Hotel in Baghdad. According to Eason Jordan, who did the original negotiating,

We did a routing with the four-wire which I guess would make it sort of a first, in that it was not a point to point service. In other words, not Baghdad to Atlanta which was what was ordered, but actually in a bit of subterfuge I guess you could say, we ordered just service from Baghdad to Amman, and separately ordered service from Amman to Atlanta. And those were tied in. We did it that way just to try to keep the Iraqis somewhat in the dark about our intentions to have a link all the way to Atlanta. (Personal communication, fall 1991)

Or, as Tauber noted, "What got us our [four-wire] circuit in the long run was the fact that they were watching CNN" (Personal communication, fall 1991).

Money. Costs were obviously a factor in competitive advantage in the Gulf War. Portable flyaway telephones were in demand and were soon out of world stock. Mobile Telesystems, a leading maker of the high tech phones had a backlog exceeding 100 units by February 1. The cost of one flyaway phone from Mobile Telesystems was $52,000 (Robichaux and Fuchsberg, 1991). It is not easy to boost output of high tech equipment. A Swiss maker of watertight cable fittings for the phones balked at boosting output, for fear the surge in orders wouldn't last, and the synthetic crystals the phones require take two months to grow and cannot be rushed (Ibid.).

Access was expensive for all of the broadcasters. Transponder space cost about $400 per hour. Licensing fees, which allowed the networks to use a county's airspace or facilities, had to be negotiated with the Postal, Telephone and Telegraph (PTT) officials of the countries. The Saudis charged $75,000 a month, and Jordan charged the standard Intelsat rate of $1,000 for the first ten minutes and $40 a minute thereafter. Israel charged $450,000 a month but provided all needed technology (Pavlik and Thalbimer, 1991).

CNN estimates it spent $25 million on the coverage of Desert Shield and Desert Storm (Personal communication, fall 1991). NBC spent between $300,000 and $700,000 a month for transponder space and the high-priced license fees charged by host countries for access to their airways (Pavlik and Thalbimer, 1991).

Ability to Negotiate Well. Connectivity is the ability to make a connection that will carry information from place to place. Working connectivity is connectivity that actually works (Howes, 1991). It has to be negotiated. CNN had the early edge in negotiating access in Iraq. Eason Jordan, CNN's managing editor for international coverage, began negotiations for the Baghdad four-wire phone connection in mid-August 1990, to keep phone communications open in case regular service failed. However, there were problems with the Iraqis that were solved (coincidentally) after CNN paid the Jordanian government $30,000 a month to operate a satellite earth station outside Amman (Personal communication, fall 1991).

The dearth of transponder space, mobile phones, and other resources in the Gulf hampered coverage regardless of negotiating leverage. At times apparently even the Department of Defense was unable to find a video transmission path directly back to the United States.

Working connectivity can also depend on social connectivity. At NBC people chat informally using e-mail with people all over the world. "I routinely chatted with people in Saudi Arabia,'' said Schmerler. At CNN, Gail Evans, who heads booking, is reported to have what has been called the biggest rolodex in the civilized world.

WHAT'S GOING TO HAPPEN IN THE FUTURE?

Certainly, the trend worldwide is for liberalized access to telecommunications facilities. CNN's Dick Tauber summarized the issue. "I shouldn't have to worry about cross-border problems with an Inmarsat phone or a cellular phone or a portable earth station in order to do my job, which is to cover the news worldwide." Broadcasters feel they shouldn't be restricted if they are using proven technologies that basically meet some standard safety rules for individual countries—and which will be gone after the coverage is finished. They do not wish to be held up for a week in customs (Personal communication, fall 1991).

Two trends are contributing the most to the accelerated ability to create reach and range in news media. Both depend on computer technology. The two trends are digital transmission and data compression of digital transmission. As Brian Knoblock at CBS described it, "The future is digital signals. Lots of work is being done with compressed video in digital. The line between video, data, and voice is just going to disappear. There will be just so many digits. This will allow us to make things even smaller and more mobile. In the analog/digital war, digital has to win because analog is not as flexible as digital is" (Personal communication, fall 1991).

The increase in digital transmission and compression is changing the dynamics of broadcasting. First, one can send more information over a narrow channel; compressed data and video can be sent over phone lines. Digital transmission techniques let all forms of information be sent as numbers. Compact disks encode sound as numbers. Digital TV encodes sound and pictures as numbers. Digital circuits on phones encode voice as numbers. A second and related point is that the cost structures are changing. Satellite transmission is massively expensive. Recall that during the Gulf War, the Saudis were charging $75,000 a month for a satellite channel.

Dick Tauber at CNN also commented on compression technology: "If we could have used a transponder and put four signals on there instead of one, we could have handled our pool responsibilities more easily. Every network, through the pool feed path could have had its own feed out instead of having to be in a line with their video" (Personal communication, fall 1991).

SUMMARY

Several lessons seem evident from this analysis of media uses of information and communications technologies for war coverage in the Gulf. First, crisis technologies are multiple in terms of type—high versus low tech—and in terms of whether they are ready at hand. Readiness at hand means that when the occasion is right, the needed tool is known, usable, and accessible. It also means the tool is not in storage. A network can't constantly have every tool ready for every chance event, but the best tools are the ones that are ready at hand and familiar, or at least easy to learn and easy to use.

The media need a coherent strategy for readiness at hand. This includes mapping of the many tools in terms of reach, range, and political practicality. One of the values of the reach and range map is to identify the mix of needs. Then, deploying the identified tools requires negotiating and contracting, making sure, for example, that crisis coverage is not damaged because there is more demand for services than supply. Had Exxon developed a comprehensive strategy for crisis response technologies prior to the Prince William Sound Spill, it would not have had, as William Small puts it, a public relations disaster when in fact it did almost everything right (1991b). The lessons from the Desert Storm news operation are in essence the same as those of the Exxon public relations fiasco (Calloway and Keen, 1992).

The air attack on Baghdad began at approximately 2:40 A.M., January 17, Baghdad time. All of the networks had phone service out of Baghdad right before the air strikes, and several, including CNN and ITN, had satellite phones. Minutes after the air strikes began, the telephone-switching center in Baghdad was hit by a cruise missile, and most of the public phone lines, including those to the hotel, were down (Shepard, 1991). CNN was not willing to use its satellite transmission phones during the first days of the war because it was concerned that the Iraqi or U.S. tracking systems or cruise bomb systems might be sophisticated enough to pick up the signals (Hamblen, 1991).

Because CNN had been successful in negotiating and contracting the "backup" four-wire phone, it had the reach and range to cover the early days of the air war in Baghdad via telephone. Lacking equivalent assets, the other networks did not.

NOTES

1. The Sidle Commission was a joint panel of military officers and retired journalists charged by the secretary of defense with examining the state of military-media relations, and provide workable solutions to the dilemma (Chiaventone, 1991).

2. For an excellent discussion of interactivity, see Everett Rogers, *Communication Technology: The New Media in Society* (Rogers, 1986).

5

Arab Audiences for Gulf War Coverage: Where Did They Turn and Why?

Douglas A. Boyd

Those interested in the topic of how people outside the Middle East, especially in Europe and North America, obtained information about the Gulf crisis have a great deal of information available to them, and more will come to light in the years ahead. Some of the studies are academic in nature (Cohen, 1990; Courtright et al., 1990; Gantz, 1991; Lewis, 1991; Wober, 1990); others were produced by journalists and media critics concerned with coverage by the United States and other multinational force countries (Dennis et al., 1991; *Witness to War*, 1991). Additionally, there are a number of Gulf conflict essays on a topic that will continue to draw the attention of the journalistic community: government/military censorship and journalistic ethics during military conflicts (Kleinwächter, 1991; Traber and Davies, 1991). Barbie Zelizer (1992) has written about CNN's role in changing journalism forms.

The Gulf conflict took place in an area with an almost unique media environment. First, with few exceptions (most of which are in Lebanon), the print and electronic media in the Arab world are either directly owned or indirectly influenced by host governments. Second, surveys since the 1960s clearly indicate that Arabs are the world's most enthusiastic consumers of both Arabic-language regional and Western international radio broadcasts. Those interested in hearing transnational radio broadcasts from other countries have an abundance of programming from which to choose on the medium- (standard broadcast) and shortwave bands; Arabic ranks just behind English as the most broadcast international language. Third, as multinational troops started arriving in the Gulf after the August 2, 1990, Iraqi invasion of Kuwait, British and U.S. military commands began broadcasting news and popular music from local FM radio stations to their troops stationed in Saudi Arabia. Fourth, for the first time, some Arab television stations in the Gulf utilized live Western news, primarily from the Cable News Network (CNN). Fifth, the amount of hardware available to receive radio and television broadcasts varies between the rich and poor Arab states. However, British Broadcasting Corporation (BBC) data indicate that Arab-world residents are well equipped with radios, television sets, and home videocassette recorders: at the end of 1990 there were an estimated 73.5 million radio receivers, 36.1 million television sets, and 10.2 million videocassette recorders in the Middle East and North Africa (British Broadcasting Corporation, 1991c).

FOREIGN RADIO LISTENING DURING THE GULF CRISIS

When Iraq invaded Kuwait early on the morning of August 2, 1990, starting what is generally known as the Gulf crisis, the habit of tuning to both neighboring and foreign radio broadcasts from the BBC, The Voice of America (VOA), and Radio Monte Carlo Middle East (RMCME) had been long established. Radio receivers were widely available; there was an interested and even eager audience. In light of this writer's experience while living in Saudi Arabia during the June 1967 war and in Egypt during the January 1977 "food riots" caused by government-increased food prices, Western radio stations were major news and information sources. Several surveys support this observation. For example, the British Broadcasting Corporation's International Broadcasting and Audience Research (IBAR) unit conducted several "crisis listening" studies after the Iraqi invasion of Kuwait. In late August 1990 the BBC contracted with an Amman, Jordan–based survey research firm to undertake surveys in Abu Dhabi, Dubai, and Sharjah, United Arab Emirates, Riyadh, Saudi Arabia; and Cairo and Alexandria, Egypt. Designed to match gender, age, and education in each location, several hundred interviews were done with respondents over 15 years of age in each city. Survey data indicate that regular audiences for the BBC more than doubled after the invasion. In the UAE, for example, a previous survey had indicated once-per-week listening at 21.5 percent of listeners; after the invasion the figure increased to 51.1 percent. Data for Cairo and Alexandria were 18.1 percent and 46.3 percent. There were increases in audiences for the BBC in Riyadh after the Gulf crisis, but they were not as large as those previously noted. Possibly because of the BBC's relatively weak medium-wave signal reaching Riyadh (compared to those of Egypt and the UAE) the postcrisis audience increase was approximately one-third (British Broadcasting Corporation, 1990a).

In November 1990 the BBC surveyed 400 adults in Amman, Jordan, and found that the BBC had twice the audience of Radio Monte Carlo Middle East. Data from the survey suggest that the attraction of regional stations such as Radio Damascus and Egyptian stations had diminished, while audiences for the BBC, RMCME, Radio Baghdad, and the VOA remained about the same as that identified in 1988. The BBC concluded after an analysis of the data from both a 1988 survey and the November 1990 survey that people in 1990 came to rely more heavily on both radio and word of mouth as their main sources of information about day-to-day events (British Broadcasting Corporation, 1990b).

The BBC did yet another survey during the Gulf crisis, this one the BBC's first in Syria. Unfortunately, unlike the previously noted studies, this one did not provide much of a basis for comparison. But the data are unique because they provide the only known radio surveys in Damascus and Aleppo. Of course, local stations had the largest audiences, but Syrians indicated that they listened to foreign radio too. Radio Monte Carlo Middle East had approximately double the total and regular audience of the BBC. The survey confirms the overall importance of radio as a news source in the Arab world. In response to the question "How did you first find out about the SCUD missile attacks on Israel?" over two-thirds said they first heard the news from radio (British Broadcasting Corporation, 1991a).

The United States Information Agency (USIA) purchased and analyzed the previously mentioned BBC "Crisis" survey data from Saudi Arabia, the United Arab Emirates, Bahrain, and Oman, concluding that radio was the medium most used by adults for day-to-day information during the crisis. The second and third most used media were television and newspapers, respectively. The report notes that foreign radio listening increased dramatically, and this was especially the case for the BBC, VOA, and RMCME. The United States Information Agency, the parent organization of the VOA, observed that the "BBC now has listening rates in all four countries that would be respectable for domestic national broadcasters" (United States Information Agency, 1991, p. 1).

Finally, as the Gulf crisis was ending, the BBC did what a few other foreign broadcasters have done: focus-group studies as a means of gaining information not available from surveys and not generalizable to the population of a country. A March 1991 study in Egypt concluded that local Egyptian radio stations during the Gulf crisis were given rather high credibility ratings by Egyptian listeners because a great deal of news heard on domestic stations was similar to that from other sources. BBC researchers summarized:

Foreign radio stations remained generally more credible than local or regional stations during the Gulf crisis. This was particularly true for the BBC and Radio Monte Carlo; increasingly, the latter's light style of presentation and its large output of Middle Eastern and Western pop music did *not* prejudice its standing as a credible source of news. The Voice of America, on the other hand, was said to lack objectivity in its reporting; most [Egyptian] respondents felt VOA was biased in support of Israel. (British Broadcasting Corporation, 1991b, p. 1)

Thus the studies indicate that in a way little changed with regard to both the attraction and importance of foreign international radio broadcasting, especially regarding news and other forms of information-oriented programming. However, the interest Arabs in the surveyed countries had in listening to foreign broadcasts increased, sometimes dramatically. This conclusion is highlighted by an Al-

Makaty, Boyd, Van Tubergen (1992) Q-study done in the western part of Saudi Arabia in late May and early June 1991. Findings indicate that the electronic media were favored over print media among the two major factor-analyzed study "types" of people because of the technological advantage radio and television enjoy over print. The constantly shifting military situation during the Gulf crisis motivated people to seek information they knew to be the most up-to-date because the broadcast media, especially local and international radio, are perceived to be more current regarding rapidly changing events in modern warfare.

While the electronic media in the Arab world were important sources of information during the Gulf crisis, follow-up questions to the Q-study underscore the importance of interpersonal communication in the Middle East: 30 respondents (75%) (N = 40) indicated that they first learned about the invasion of Kuwait from others; only 10 people (25%) heard the news directly from radio or television.

LOCAL COALITION BROADCASTS IN ENGLISH

Following the coalition's military personnel deployment in Saudi Arabia after the Iraqi invasion of Kuwait, both British and U.S. military started operating FM radio stations for their personnel in central and eastern Saudi Arabia. The British and Americans have had a policy since World War II of providing military men and women stationed outside the home country with music and news from "back home." For U.S. troops, the Armed Forces Radio and Television Service (AFRTS) constructed several stations that transmitted programming under the generic title Desert Shield Radio. Beginning in late October 1990, one station came on the air in Riyadh and more in the Eastern Province. This writer monitored several of these stations for ten days in late December 1990 and early January 1991.

In the Gulf city of Dhahran, for example, a station operated on 99.9 Mhz with the on-air motto: "This is your oasis station, FM 99.9 on the Desert Shield Network." In the Saudi capital, Riyadh, an FM station could be heard on 107 Mhz. A great deal of programming came via satellite from the Los Angeles studios of the Armed Forces Radio and Television Service. Music-oriented for the most part, with public service announcements for military personnel in Saudi Arabia, "AP Radio News on the Hour," sports, and some local DJ–type programs, the stations seem to have been popular with some, probably English-speaking, Saudis. As the new year started, a great deal of programming on these services was devoted to both live and tape-delayed American college and professional football that is traditionally aired in the United States during the holiday period. When stations were programming locally, both male and female enlisted personnel (who are used exclusively on the air on AFRTS stations) played recorded music, took requests for specific songs, and read local public service announcements, such as those noting the location where newly arrived American military could pick up gas masks.

Although no audience figures are available, the author's discussions with a number of Saudis and the sound of Western music coming from car radios and shops indicate that the popular music stereo service was a welcome change from either the conservative-oriented government radio or the numerous medium- and shortwave radio services available from neighboring or Western states. It seems that it was the Western popular music available via FM that was most attractive.

In the Eastern Province, the British operated an FM station on 103.5 Mhz. Known as British Forces Broadcasting Service (BFBS)—and with a similar format to the service provided for decades to British troops stationed in Germany—this service consisted of satellite relays of the BBC World Service English news and programming from BFBS studios in London.

TELEVISION NEWS AND PUBLIC AFFAIRS PROGRAMMING

Very little data exist concerning the role Arab world television played in the Gulf crisis. It is clear that many television systems reacted cautiously to the news of the invasion. They were generally more forthcoming about political developments prior to the actual conflict. Perhaps the slowest television system to acknowledge the Iraqi invasion of Kuwait was that of Saudi Arabia. Despite the fact that virtually everyone in Saudi Arabia knew from foreign radio broadcasts or word of mouth about the August 2, 1990, invasion of Kuwait by midday of the incident, Saudi media did not officially disseminate the information until August 5. Admittedly slow to react to any crisis news because of the intrinsically cautious nature of government-operated electronic media, the kingdom's Ministry of Information had worked since the November 1979 Mecca Mosque incident (involving the takeover of the Grand Mosque in Islam's most holy city) to be more forthcoming about news involving the kingdom. In the information age of the 1990s, ministry officials, many of whom are Western-educated, knew full well that word had spread about the invasion because it was heard on both Western and regional radio stations. However, delayed news of the invasion on television was not the only problem noted in connection with Saudi electronic media.

When Iraq began unleashing SCUD missiles at both the Dhahran area in the eastern section of the kingdom and at Riyadh, the interior capital, neither information on incoming SCUDs nor the "all-clear" was readily available from foreign radio because these stations did not always have correspondents in place who could broadcast live. Coordination difficulties—not at all uncommon in the Middle East—did not help local citizens learn much about the feared SCUDs. For example, Judith Miller, a *New York Times* reporter in Riyadh, noted that on one Sunday evening in late January 1991 "Saudi television did not interrupt its programming to announce the first air raid until after the all-clear siren had sounded. And there was no prompt Saudi announcement on television of what had hit the city or of casualties and damage" (Miller, 1991).

However, there is no doubt that Cable News Network (CNN) was a factor during the Gulf crisis, but not necessarily as one would expect. CNNI ("I" for the international service originating in Atlanta that combines features of both the "Headline News" and the regular CNN news channel) is available throughout the Middle East from a leased Russian satellite transponder. Provided by some first-class hotels in the Arab world, it is not generally viewed via home satellite dishes because the technology is either too expensive for poorer countries such as Egypt, the Sudan, or Yemen or not permitted by the government in Gulf states such as Saudi Arabia. CNN is, however, widely viewed by some Middle Eastern leaders, such as King Hussein of Jordan, Hosni Mubarak of Egypt, and Saddam Hussein and his advisers. But the major function of CNN during the Gulf crisis was its use as a video wire service by virtually all government foreign affairs and information offices. In the case of Saudi Arabia, this writer viewed breaking developments with several high-ranking government officials in the Ministry of Information and television buildings in Riyadh just prior to the January 1991 coalition-organized air attack on Iraq. In Riyadh, as well as in many other Arab world capitals, CNN is available 24 hours a day in the offices, and sometimes the homes, of major government officials. Clearly, CNN set the agenda for newsrooms because in many instances CNN was broadcasting live from, for example, the Saudi capital; the Saudis were not.

Further, there were instances when CNN coverage of some of the more dramatic Gulf crisis events appeared live on Arab television stations, but the CNN coverage was shown on a tape-delayed basis. For example, a major concern of most Arab countries was the frequent references to and live broadcasts from Israel, a country also targeted to receive Iraqi SCUDs. CNN coverage was especially good in the eastern part of Saudi Arabia, where one of Bahrain's television stations and a low-power U.S. military television transmitter located near the Dhahran Airport featured CNN coverage.

Of course, the above information about Arab information consumption patterns during the 1990–91 Gulf crisis must be understood within the context of the changing nature of both Arab world society and the mass media.

BACKGROUND TO CONTEMPORARY ARAB WORLD MEDIA ENVIRONMENT

In order to understand media consumption patterns in the contemporary Middle East, it is essential that one know something about the development of broadcasting there.[1] The present-day Middle Eastern electronic media environment and audience behavior originated in Egypt during the 1920s. During the mid- to late-1920s "broadcasting" was undertaken by both radio amateurs and a few merchants who used it for the purpose of selling merchandise (Metwally, n.d.). By 1930, most of the stations had gone off the air because broadcasters' initial enthusiasm for them had diminished. The Egyptian government was unhappy with the commercial, informal nature of radio as it was then operated. Further, there were few radio receivers in Egypt during this time; those people with radios were members of the economic upper class. Large-scale radio ownership did not come to the Middle East until the electrification of rural areas and the later arrival of the "transistor revolution" of the late 1950s and early 1960s. In the Middle East, as in other developing areas, the inexpensive battery-operated transistor radio brought the medium- to lower-income families.

With Egypt as an example, it is easy to see why radio, and later television, became both a state-run activity and a popular pastime in the Arab world. Unwilling to start a radio system on its own in the 1930s, the Egyptian government signed a contract with British Marconi Company to construct and operate a "public service" monopoly system along the lines of the British Broadcasting Corporation. The system was financed by a license fee on receivers, 60 percent of which was paid to Marconi and 40 percent to the Egyptian government to offset actual construction and costs associated with the operation of transmitters (Metwally, n.d.). Egyptian radio service began in 1934 but, despite the BBC public service model, nationalist attitudes about foreign influence fueled Egypt's dissatisfaction with Marconi's operation of the station, and the government took control. Since the government takeover, broadcasting in Egypt has been a state-run activity. With continuing political shifts in the Middle East since the end of World War II, leaders have considered the media—especially broadcasting—to be an essential communication tool.

Radio came first to the Maghreb (North African desert) countries, Egypt, Lebanon, Palestine, and Iraq—states whose European colonizers (or in the case of Egypt, "sponsors") were interested in fostering a particular kind of political communication of their own making. Britain (in Palestine) and France (in the Maghreb) found that local stations were very helpful in rebroadcasting their international radio services, so that both expatriates and local populations could hear news from Europe without having to tune to shortwave bands.

Radio gained immediate popularity in the Arab world. With the family-centered environment, high rates of illiteracy, and the tradition of an oral-based culture, those in power concluded that radio was ideal for government-to-citizen communication. Newspapers and magazines in North Africa, Syria, Egypt, and Palestine were attractive to the intellectuals, but radio became the medium of common men and women who liked the vagueness and emotional appeal of spoken Arabic. It quickly became obvious that radio was becoming a popular medium for political communication in the Arab world. Brunner (1953) mentions the coffeehouses frequented by Arab males as a place for radio listening, noting that then the coffeehouse was "a center of considerable importance, comparable to the country store of yesteryear in the United States" (p. 150).

From the beginning, radio in the Arab world was a government or quasi-government activity that those in power believed would be an essential part of government political communication. By the late 1930s Arab radio audiences became dedicated listeners to transmissions from other, especially Western, countries.

REGIONAL RADIO LISTENING

Arab radio listeners' interest in tuning to programming from neighboring states originated in Palestine in the late 1930s. It was a classic case of the colonial power—Britain—creating a radio station—the Palestine Broadcasting Service (PBS)—to provide local broadcasts to both local residents and expatriates and to retransmit what was then named the BBC Empire Service. Established on March 30, 1936, the station broadcast in three languages—Arabic, English, and Hebrew—from studios in Jerusalem and a 20-kilowatt transmitter in nearby Ramallah (*Palestine Department of Posts . . . 1935*, 1936, p. 5; *Palestine Department . . . 1936*, 1937, p. 6).

However, it was Egypt's President Gamal Abdel Nasser who set the tone for regional broadcasting when he established the Voice of the Arabs after the revolution in the early 1950s. Later, Charles Issawi accurately characterized the Voice of the Arabs' Nasser period when he observed that it had "to be heard to be believed: for sheer venom, vulgarity and indifference to truth it [had] few equals in the world" (1963, p. 217). This station made a major contribution to the high-power medium-wave transmitter construction boom in the Arab world that is still under way. Fueled by the need to protect themselves against real or imagined hostile radio attacks from regional powers, the Gulf states were especially successful in using oil wealth to create powerful stations. Saudi Arabia was especially successful in its building program, acquiring five 2,000-kilowatt (2 million watt) medium-wave transmitters for a total medium-wave transmission power of 12.8 million watts (Wood, 1991). Given that the maximum medium-wave transmission power permitted in the United States is 50,000 watts, a 2-million watt transmission from Saudi Arabia successfully competes with local stations in terms of signal strength.

TRANSNATIONAL RADIO LISTENING AMONG ARABIC-SPEAKERS

Italy was the first non-Arab country to transmit transnationally in Arabic. Rolo (1941), addressing the popularity of the Italian Arabic service in the mid-1930s, notes the type of listening pattern that is still relevant, albeit with television and videocassettes now.

When the day's work was done both the *fellaheen* (peasants) and the city dwellers would betake themselves to their favorite cafes, huddle together under a fuming oil lamp, and stolidly smoking their water pipes play game after game of backgammon until the communal loudspeakers gave forth the voice of the [Radio] Bari announcer. (Pp. 45–46)

One does not need to provide survey evidence to make the obvious point that in areas of the world where the media are government controlled, citizens tend to verify information important to them through other sources. This is the case in the Middle East with external radio.

Three countries—Britain, France, and the United States—account for the vast majority of foreign radio listening among Arabic-speakers. This is the case for three primary reasons.

1. The BBC has had a long tradition of providing objective news and public affairs programming to the Middle East. The British Broadcasting Corporation's Arabic service started in January 1938; Arabic was the first foreign language used by the external service of the British public service broadcaster (Arabic Broadcasts, 1938).

2. Although newer services, the Voice of America and Radio Monte Carlo Middle East compete for Arabic speakers seeking an alternative to news and entertainment provided by local or regional radio outlets.

3. The BBC, VOA, and RMCME are available to listeners on the medium-wave band. The BBC has medium-wave relay sites on Cyprus and Masirah Island, Oman; Rhodes is the location of the Voice of America's transmitter; and a transmitter on Cyprus relays Paris-based, French government–owned Radio Monte Carlo Middle East programming.

Although these three services attract different types of listeners, they have an advantage because they are on the medium-wave band. This does not mean that they function as surrogate stations, but they are often found on the dial near local outlets. There are, of course, other Arabic services to the Middle East, almost all reaching the area via shortwave. In fact, in 1992 there were 50 separate Arabic programmers broadcasting to the Arab world; Arabic is second only to English as the most used language for international radio broadcasting (Boyd, 1992).

The pattern for the introduction of television broadcasting in the Middle East is not as clear-cut as for radio. However, once again Egypt, while not the first country in the area to introduce television, quickly took the lead in Arabic-language productions. With its large population, thriving film industry, and intellectual environment that has produced numerous stage and film writers, Egypt dominates regional television production. As a result, it gains important hard currency from television program sales.

TRANSNATIONAL TELEVISION VIEWING IN THE ARAB WORLD

At this point, there is relatively little transnational television viewing in the Arab world. However, this will almost surely change in the coming years. Residents of North African countries can view some European television: Italian television in Tunisia and French television in Morocco and Algeria, either over the domestic channels or from satellite dishes. Residents in Jidda, Saudi Arabia, can see Egyptian television if they have a well-located outside antenna. There is some viewing of Syrian television in Jordan and Jordanian television in Syria. The Jordanian channels are also available in some parts of Israel and the West Bank. However, the most active area for international television viewing is in the Arabian Gulf states. Especially during the warm summer months, it is possible for viewers with external antennae in the Dammam/Dhahran/Al-Khobar area of eastern Saudi Arabia to see television channels from Kuwait, Bahrain, the United Arab Emirates, and Qatar.

Direct satellite reception of television in areas of the Arab world other than North Africa remains limited, but this will surely change. In poorer Arab states, most television homes cannot afford the mandatory dish and associated electronic equipment to downlink signals, and legal constraints still limit development in this area. Saudi Arabia, for example, does not permit home satellite receiver ownership, although some members of the royal family and prominent families do possess receivers. Direct broadcast satellite (DBS) transmission will become more attractive as services become more available. For example, in March 1992 the Middle East Broadcast Center—a Saudi Arabian–financed, London-based television service—started transmitting daily to the Arab world via a European satellite (Waldman, 1992). Star TV, a Hong Kong–based five-channel satellite television service reaches most countries on the Arabian peninsula (P. Schloss, General Counsel, Star TV, personal interview, June 12, 1992, Hong Kong).

MEDIA RESEARCH IN THE ARAB WORLD

It is, of course, still difficult to assess the impact of print and broadcast media on Middle Eastern societies. This is due, at least in part, to the fact that it is both difficult and expensive to do research in the Arab world. First, even in Egypt—where it is relatively easy to undertake audience research—one must secure government permission for surveys. Second, even with the low labor costs one would find in some Arab states, it is expensive to locate and train reliable interviewers. Third, it is expensive to supervise interviewers. Finally, especially in the Gulf, but most of all in Saudi Arabia, access to female respondents remains all but impossible.

Yet audience surveys are done, and they tend to be of three types. A few studies have been done by the radio and television broadcast organizations of countries such as Egypt and Jordan in order to help attract advertisers. These tend to be of questionable reliability and devoid of sophisticated analysis. Also, some advertising agencies and electronics manufacturers have surveyed viewers and listeners with the hope of learning about brand loyalty and preferences. Last, the United States Information Agency and the British Broadcasting Corporation have done regular survey work in Arab countries in order to learn about the popularity of their international broadcasting services. Such radio preference surveys started during World War II.

A foreign radio–listening survey to assess public opinion in the Middle East was funded in 1943 by the U.S. military as part of an apparent effort by those involved with psychological operations. Academics at the American University of Beirut undertook a study of radio listening in Lebanon, Syria, and Palestine; this survey included 4,427 interviews with Arabs in 15 towns in the three countries. Researchers found that the majority of listeners claimed to listen primarily for world news, followed by "serious music," and religious programs. Eighty-seven percent of the radio sets owned by respondents could receive short-, medium-, and long-wave frequencies. Data showed the BBC was both the most popular and the most credible foreign station. The most listened-to regional station was Radio Cairo (Dodd et al., 1943). Even with the passing of five decades and the introduction of new local stations, listener preferences for both Egyptian stations and the BBC remain.

An examination of over three decades of audience research done by the BBC and VOA indicates that while listening levels vary, depending on political, military, and economic events in the area, some reasonably accurate statements can be made about foreign radio–listening:

1. Previously noted is the attraction of medium-wave stations. Although a high percentage of radio receivers in the Arab world have shortwave bands, medium-wave reception is the key to attracting a sizable audience. The BBC, VOA, and Radio Monte Carlo Middle East know that shortwave is only a fill-in for those areas not served by medium-wave. Several years ago, RMCME used a shortwave relay from Morocco with the hope of reaching listeners in the southern Arabian peninsula countries that could not receive the Cyprus-based medium-wave signal during the day. Results were unsatisfactory; hence the shortwave experimental service was discontinued after only one year (J. Taquet, Director General, Radio Monte Carlo Middle East, personal interview, September 9, 1989, Paris).

2. The relative popularity of foreign stations does not mean that radio listeners do not listen to local stations. Although such stations are known to be the "voice of the government," it is important for those in the Arab world to know what the government is saying. It is the government, via local media, that sets the political, social, and economic agenda.

3. Since the 1960s, and except for times of crisis, competing domestic electronic media have tended to diminish the importance of foreign radio in Arab nations. Even in the less affluent Arab states there has been an increase in ownership of television receivers, videocassette machines, and FM radios. These, in the very broad sense, are competition for foreign radio stations.

4. Medium-wave stations operated by powerful Middle Eastern countries such as Egypt, Saudi Arabia, and Iraq (before most transmitters were destroyed in the early hours of allied air strikes) attract sizable audiences. This is a way of staying informed about what one's neighbors are doing.

5. Because of the varying reception quality of both medium- and shortwave signals, there are regional variations with regard to the popularity of foreign radio stations. To reiterate, signal strength is an important factor, especially during daylight hours, when medium-wave signal propagation diminishes. The BBC has a decided advantage over the VOA and RMCME because of its dual transmission sites—Cyprus and Masirah

Island off the coast of Oman. The BBC has both ends of the Arabian peninsula covered. RMCME's Cyprus transmitter's output is being doubled (M. Ghoneim, Director of Communication, Radio Monte Carlo Middle East, personal interview, Paris, January 7–8, 1992), but until this project comes to fruition, reception will be strong primarily in northern Egypt, Lebanon, Syria, Jordan, and Israel both during the day and at night. The VOA, broadcasting from Rhodes, has the weakest signal of the three stations, although it is strong in northern Egypt, Lebanon, and Syria. At night, the signal reaches about two-thirds of the Arabian peninsula.

6. The largest audience of the three major Western services can be claimed by RMCME, followed by the BBC, and the Voice of America. This varies primarily on a regional basis. In Egypt a United States Information Agency (USIA) survey in early 1975 indicated that the VOA was the most listened-to international station among Egyptian adults, with 8.5 percent of the adult audience listening at least once per week. Radio Monte Carlo Middle East was a close second with 8.3 percent. BBC's audience size was 6.2 percent and Deutsche Welle was 0.2 percent (United States Information Agency, 1975).

Station preferences had changed rather markedly by late 1982 when USIA did another survey, showing that the most popular stations among regular international radio listeners were RMCME (31.3%), Israeli Radio (21.4%), BBC (19.4%), and the VOA (15.0%) (United States Information Agency, 1984).

The civil war in Lebanon and its aftermath discouraged even the most motivated audience research organization. The exception is the BBC, which undertook a survey in Beirut during a civil war–fighting break. Completed in 1984, the BBC report states that residents in the western and eastern sections of Beirut had differing foreign station–listening preferences. RMCME, with just over 30 percent, ranked first among residents who "usually use" foreign radio; the BBC was the second most popular station with about 20 percent. The VOA was third with about 4 percent (Graham Mytton, Head, International Broadcasting and Audience Research, BBC External Service, personal interview, London, March 21, 1985).

Interestingly, the Gulf states' media use has been better researched since the 1970s. This is due, at least in part, to the fact that they possess such a large percentage of the world's proven oil reserves; in short, the Gulf audience is an important one for foreign broadcasters. A late-1972 USIA survey in Saudi Arabia indicated that the BBC was the most listened-to foreign radio station. Among those listening at least once a week to foreign radio, the VOA ranked second and Radio Moscow last (United States Information Agency, 1973). A survey done in Kuwait between November 1983 and March 1984 pointed out the importance of foreign stations broadcasting on medium-wave (standard broadcast): the BBC was first, with 13.5 percent of regular international radio listeners. Radio Monte Carlo Middle East was second with 7.6 percent, followed by the VOA (2.8%), and Radio Moscow (0.2%) (United States Information Agency, 1984). As noted previously, the BBC's credibility has always been high in the Gulf, but signal strength in the Gulf states because of the Masirah Island (Oman) medium-wave transmitter location provides strong signal coverage all along the eastern Arabian coast.

In May 1986 the United States Information Agency undertook audience surveys in Bahrain and the United Arab Emirates. The results show low levels of interest in the Voice of America's Arabic service—1.8 percent in Bahrain and 0.7 percent in the UAE. In Bahrain the BBC claimed 13.2 percent regular (at least once a week) listenership for Arabic, 11.7 percent in the UAE. Radio Monte Carlo Middle East did rather better in Bahrain than in the UAE, with a 4.2 percent regular listenership; in the UAE regular audience was only 2.3 percent (United States Information Agency, 1987). Once again, the data illustrate rather clearly the important role medium-wave signal strength plays in attracting Arab audiences. Even after sunset, neither the VOA medium-wave nor RMCME signals from the Mediterranean are effective in reaching beyond the middle of the Arabian peninsula (basically south of Riyadh, Saudi Arabia). On the other hand, the further south one lives, the greater the chances of receiving a reliable BBC signal from the Masirah Island, Oman, relay transmitter site just off the coast of the southern Arabian peninsula.

Some survey work done by the BBC during the Gulf crisis suggests that the audience for foreign broadcasters had increased significantly during postinvasion weeks. In Saudi Arabia and the UAE (two countries where surveys were done) foreign listening had increased; in Riyadh the BBC claimed a weekly listenership of 53 percent (British Broadcasting Corporation, 1990a).

After the invasion of Kuwait, the Voice of America increased programming hours to the Middle East by utilizing shortwave transmitters in Europe on loan from Radio Free Europe (RFE). Further, the VOA attempted to overcome the BBC and RMCME medium-wave signal advantages by successfully negotiating an agreement with the government of Bahrain that permitted the installation of a 50-kw medium-wave transmitter on that island nation located a few miles off the coat of eastern Saudi Arabia. The facility was to retransmit Arabic from VOA in Washington, D.C., to reach Kuwait, southern Iraq, and other Gulf states. Rebroadcasts of VOA English from a Bahrain-owned transmitter started in late January 1991, but because of government of Bahrain hesitation, Arabic was delayed until March, by which time the Gulf crisis was over (United States Advisory Commission on Public Diplomacy, 1991). Even a country like Bahrain that enthusiastically supported U.S. efforts during the Gulf crisis is reluctant to permit a Western country to use its soil as a location for the rebroadcasting of programming that reflects the official view of the U.S. government.

This incident highlights a major frustration of international broadcasters— negotiating with governments for frequencies and then the construction of transmission and satellite facilities. Even when such agreements are finalized, governments can pull the plug or equipment can be destroyed, as was the case during the 1990–91 Liberian civil war, when a VOA site was attacked and rendered inoperable. In the United States's quest for a suitable VOA transmitter site in or near the Gulf, the Gulf crisis may have provided an interesting opportunity;

the VOA and the U.S. State Department have been talking with the Kuwaiti government about a Kuwait-based VOA site.

The wide-ranging variations among Arab states make it difficult generally to discuss media coverage of events in the Arab world during the Gulf crisis. Although Arab countries are bound by religion, history, and language, their political and economic circumstances vary, in some cases dramatically. For example, the political, economic, and social differences between Kuwait and Yemen or the Sudan and Jordan are vast. Still, there are times when either real crisis or perceived threats from "outsiders"—the West or Israel—provide the basis for cohesiveness, albeit temporary for the most part. The Gulf crisis did not unite the Arab world, although most Arabic countries, save Jordan, the Sudan, Libya, and Yemen, joined the coalition that liberated Kuwait.

Some common media behaviors and structures among Middle Eastern states both before and after the Gulf crisis are more easily reviewed. First, during the Gulf crisis radio was the dominant medium, in part because of the long-standing practice of domestic and foreign listening but also because radio provided the most up-to-date news in a rapidly changing political and military climate. Second, there has been a long-standing reliance on radio broadcasting from other Arab states and from a few Western stations serving the area with short- and medium-wave services. However, there is a positive correlation between a strong, reliable medium-wave signal and high levels of listening to Western radio stations. Survey data indicate that foreign radio listening increased dramatically during the Gulf crisis. The BBC, Radio Monte Carlo Middle East, and the Voice of America are popular radio services in the Arab world not only because they provide a service listeners believe to be important; the stations are listened to because they can be heard on the medium-wave band. Third, television played an important role and was a valuable source of information. The visual medium is very popular in Arab countries. Although not to the same extent as in the West, television set ownership is high, and as a result people have embraced television as part of their daily routines. But the visual medium has tended to be slow to deliver information; this is due, at least in part, to the fact that most Arab television systems rely on Western, satellite-fed pictures. The American networks including CNN and the European-based services such as the European Broadcasting Union (EBU) satellite feeds as well as VISNEWS and WTN from London were the most used sources of visual material. In the Arab world, the Gulf was not the television event it was in the West. Fourth, newspapers and magazines, while important, tended to provide political commentary, espouse government positions, and provide analysis, rather than give up-to-date information about the crisis and subsequent military conflict.

In many respects, those in the Arab world continued their pre–Gulf crisis media habits; for some, media habits were merely intensified from August 1990 until after the crisis was over in the spring of 1991.

NOTE

1. For a detailed discussion of the electronic media in the Arab world, see Douglas A. Boyd, *Broadcasting in the Arab World: A Survey of Radio and Television in the Middle East* (Philadelphia: Temple University Press, 1982) or the 1993 version, published by Iowa State University Press (Ames).

6

Psychological Operations in the Gulf War: Analyzing Key Themes in Battlefield Leaflets

Jay M. Parker and Jerold L. Hale

Operations Desert Storm and Desert Shield introduced a number of powerful and devastating new weapons to the battlefield. The weapons were developed to confront the most modern products of the superpower arms race and represented the cutting edge of high technology. One weapons systems was, however, neither new nor devastating. Its power was premised not on bullets but on persuasion.

United States Psychological Operations (PSYOP) forces encouraged surrender, supported tactical deception operations, and demoralized and debilitated those remaining Iraqi soldiers who did not respond to surrender appeals. Psychological Operations forces received favorable attention from the press and, based on their successful employment in Southwest Asia, they have enjoyed significant resurgence at a time when other segments of the military are being sharply cut. To achieve all this, they methodically applied basic principles of persuasive communication and political psychology to warfare.

This chapter will address three broad issues. First, it will provide a general introduction to U.S. Psychological Operations, with particular attention paid to the Gulf War. Second, it will analyze the persuasive themes communicated in one type of PSYOP product—battlefield leaflets. The themes will be examined, using historic and contemporary examples, with a primary focus on the leaflets used in Operations Desert Storm and Desert Shield. Third, some conclusions will be drawn about the use of leaflets based upon Gulf War experiences.

Figure 6.1
Levels of PSYOP Support

STRATEGIC SUPPORT: Designed to advance broad or long-term objectives. Target audience is normally global in nature. Directed from the National Command Authority or Joint Chiefs of Staff Exploits economic, military, sociological, and political susceptibilities. Example—national programs in support of containment.

OPERATIONAL SUPPORT: Conducted to achieve midterm objectives. Target audience is regional. In support of theater operations. Units assume responsibility for strategic PSYOP in their region. Example—Desert Storm/Desert Shield.

TACTICAL SUPPORT: Planned and conducted in the operational area. Target audiences are opposing military forces as well as observers and key communicators in the target area. Supports immediate and short-term objectives in direct support of tactical commanders. Example—PSYOP integrated into the tactical plan for the "end run" to the west in Desert Storm.

CONSOLIDATION: Designed to assist in the reorientation and education of occupied areas. Target audience is the civilian population. Supports the administration and rehabilitation of the territory. Also focuses on the effects of negating the opponent's propaganda. Example—PSYOP in support of postwar administration of Germany and Japan.

INTRODUCTION TO U.S. PSYCHOLOGICAL OPERATIONS

U.S. Psychological Operations is defined as:

planned operations to convey selected information and indicators to foreign audiences to influence their emotions, motives, objective reasoning, and ultimately the behavior of foreign governments, organizations, groups and individuals. The purpose of psychological operations is to induce or reinforce foreign attitudes and behavior favorable to the originator's objectives. (U.S. Department of the Army, 1992a, p. 12)

Military PSYOP is conducted to provide support for strategic, operational, tactical, and consolidation missions (see Figure 6.1). The building blocks of PSYOP are the PSYOP Program, a carefully planned, sequential presentation of actions and/or products designed to achieve one or more specific PSYOP objectives. These objectives are statements of a "measurable response that reflects the desired attitudes or behavior change of a selected foreign target audience as a result of the psychological operations. The target audience can be any individual or group which, when influenced, can have the greatest impact on achieving the PSYOP objective" (U.S. Department of the Army, 1992a, p. 12).

The concept of psychological warfare dates back to Sun Tzu and is woven throughout the military accounts of the Old Testament. Every army has used variations of what is commonly referred to as psychological warfare. The methods may have changed and the specific motives may have differed, but in each case the effect has been to multiply the combat power and/or deterrent effect of combat forces. The modern view of PSYOP is often tainted by the association with the propaganda efforts of Adolf Hitler and Joseph Stalin or oversimplified by the crude loudspeaker taunts between battlefield soldiers.

In 1920, military historian and strategist J.F.C. Fuller went so far as to predict that combat would be "replaced by a purely psychological warfare, wherein weapons are not used or battlefields sought" (1920, p. 320). In 1946—the same year in which he wrote his famous "long telegram" outlining the basic principles of containment—George F. Kennan argued that measures short of war must include the use of economic, psychological, and political weapons. He said "it would be a mistake to consider psychological measures as anything separate from the rest of diplomacy. They consist . . . of the study and understanding of the psychological effects of anything which the modern state does in war, both internal and external" (cited in Harlow and Maerz, 1991, p. 9).

The recommendations of persons like Kennan and Fuller were followed at the strategic level. The cold war was primarily waged with PSYOP. The obvious formal PSYOP measures included U.S. institutional efforts through Voice of America and the United States Information Agency; the Soviet Union operated through similar state media outlets. In a larger sense, the concept of deterrence was itself a psychological operation designed to create and reinforce attitudes and behavior.

But despite the practice of strategic PSYOP and a long history of its effective use on the battlefield, tactical PSYOP had been a limited player in American military operations. There were some successful applications in both world wars and in Korea and Vietnam. However, the employment of U.S. PSYOP was episodic and lacked longevity. Psychological Operations units were frequently underresourced. Psychological Operations was not even institutionalized as a separate military career until the 1980s (Paddock, 1990).

Two events occurred in the late 1980s that would significantly influence the employment of PSYOP in the Gulf War. The first was the publication of the 1987 edition of U.S. Army *Field Manual (FM) 33–1: Psychological Operations*. This book updated PSYOP practices and doctrine that had not been substantially revised and reviewed since the Vietnam War. Within the next two years, the manual would undergo a significant "real-world" test.

The second was Operation Just Cause in Panama. The use of PSYOP in Panama produced important results. Psychological Operations proved to be an effective method of offering enemy forces a viable alternative to combat. Credible PSYOP programs prevented several clashes and resulted in numerous surrenders. The employment of PSYOP also demonstrated numerous weaknesses in both doctrine and PSYOP force structure as written in the 1987 manual.

Revisions to the field manual were under way when Iraq invaded Kuwait. The use of PSYOP in the Gulf War revalidated many of the ad hoc organizational measures taken in Panama. Techniques and procedures were tested in a far different environment than Central America. The importance of early and thorough integration of PSYOP into mission planning was reaffirmed. Among the

Figure 6.2
PSYOP Product Development Process

1. Analyze supported unit's mission.

2. Derive PSYOP mission.

3. Collect information and intelligence.

4. Conduct target audience analysis.

5. Assess opponent propaganda.

6. Select themes and symbols.

7. Select media and agents of action.

8. Develop product prototypes and proposed actions.

9. Pretest products and simulate proposed actions.

10. Obtain plan approval.

11. Produce products and brief agents of action.

12. Coordinate dissemination of products and programs.

13. Assess impact.

14. Modify programs as required.

final results from the employment of PSYOP in the Gulf was the institutional-ization of a methodical process for planning and implementing PSYOP.

The planning process used to develop PSYOP in the Gulf War was tested over time and was the result of both common sense and basic tenets of persuasion (see Figure 6.2). While the process shown in Figure 6.2 was not religiously followed in previous conflicts, the methodology used in the past (especially in Southwest Asia) followed the same general pattern.

Psychological Operations products can take several different forms. Because of limited open source material and incomplete postwar surveys of the target audience, an analysis of all Desert Shield/Desert Storm products and programs is not yet possible. However, one element of these PSYOP programs can be studied in some depth. Battlefield leaflets have been a staple of PSYOP and are the PSYOP products that best exemplify the process and outcome. The leaflets were dropped on Iraqi positions to induce surrender and enhance the deception plan devised by maneuver unit commanders. The leaflets demonstrate the de-velopment and dissemination of key persuasive themes that produced measurable results.

Leaflets typically include both a pictorial and a verbal message and normally convey a primary theme, with other themes noted in support of the main ar-gument. Broadly stated, four themes were communicated in Desert Storm/Shield leaflets: (1) the futility of resistance, (2) safety and fair treatment as a result of surrender, (3) the separation of enemy soldiers from their equipment, and (4) peace, unity, and family. In the Gulf War, these themes were presented and reinforced with other PSYOP products and actions. For this particular portion of the campaign, leaflets were chosen for their comparative ease of delivery, the ability to target specific leaflets to specific units, the ability to reach audiences with little or no access to other media, and their capacity for use as "safe conduct passes" for those Iraqi soldiers who chose to take advantage of the opportunity to surrender.

Psychological Operations and the Use of Leaflets

The themes communicated in the Gulf War leaflets have also been conveyed in previous PSYOP campaigns. While the focus of this discussion will be Gulf War leaflets, a fuller understanding of these contemporary products may be gained from illustrations of their historical uses. For each message theme both historic and contemporary examples will be presented.

Futility of Resistance Appeals. With the futility of resistance theme, the target audience is asked to accept the inevitability of the outcome and to avoid need-lessly prolonging the battle. To reinforce this message, leaflets have focused on the overwhelming superiority—both in numbers and technology—of the U.S. forces and their allies. Leaflets imparting this theme have been delivered to military and civilian target audiences. The messages have relied heavily on the use of fear and threat appeals and have been a cornerstone of this country's persuasive arsenal.

Historic uses of futility of resistance themes: During World War II the U.S. Air Force showered Japan and Japanese positions with leaflets communicating the futility of resistance. The following passage from one of those leaflets illustrates this theme.

These leaflets are being dropped to notify you that your city has been listed for destruction by our powerful air force. The bombing will begin in 72 hours. The advance notice will give your military authorities ample time to take defensive measures to protect you from our inevitable attack. Watch and see how powerless they are to protect you. There is nothing they can do to stop our overwhelming power and iron determination. We want you to see how powerless the military is to protect you. (Daugherty, 1958b, p. 360)

The pictorial message showed B-29 bombers dropping their payloads on unidentified targets.

Similar appeals were used versus German soldiers. One example read:

When Americans attack, they usually do so on the largest scale. They waste shells in order to save lives. They can afford that for they have the means—they have more than enough artillery, tanks, flame-throwers, tankdozers, and rocket weapons, in order to break any resistance. That is a fact. (Herz, 1958b, p. 565)

The theme was also used during the Korean War. One leaflet showed a hill strewn with the bodies of Chinese soldiers. The caption read, "These men died

Figure 6.3
Leaflet entitled "Soldier Surrounded"

The verbal message read, "Cease resistance. You are cut off."

needlessly resisting U.N. Turkish forces" (Janowitz, 1958, p. 59). A second leaflet displayed an enemy soldier crouched in the bull's-eye of a target, shielding his eyes, and glancing toward the sky (Linebarger, 1954, p. 219). A third leaflet showed an enemy soldier facing a wall containing 16 heavy guns. It read, "No soldier would attempt to fight 54 men, yet Communist China is attempting to fight 54 nations" (Linebarger, 1954, p. 305).

Leaflets expressing the futility of resistance theme typically contain common elements. The pictures usually include weapons systems or depictions of their effects, while the verbal messages emphasize the consequences of resistance. Frequently enemy soldiers and civilians are forewarned about impending attacks and even given specific timetables for the attacks to occur. The same elements recur in Desert Storm/Desert Shield leaflets.

Futility of resistance themes in the Gulf War: The Gulf War leaflets that communicated the futility of resistance theme stressed the technological and numerical superiority of coalition forces. For example, one Gulf War leaflet depicted a lone Iraqi soldier surrounded by coalition tanks (see Figure 6.3). Another leaflet depicted a single Iraqi tank on fire and under attack from coalition tanks, helicopters, and bombers. The verbal message read "Supreme firepower, long range, and lethal weapons" (see Figure 6.4).

One leaflet depicted a solid wall of clouds crushing Iraqi tanks, while coalition aircraft rode on the crest of the clouds. The verbal message read "Desert Storm Is Coming. Flee Immediately" (see Figure 6.5). Until the ground war began, this message was reinforced by the bombing campaign. The bombing provided the opportunity to further enhance the notion of the inevitability of defeat with a series of targeted leaflets.

Figure 6.4
Leaflet entitled "Fade to Black"

In addition to the visible weapons, bombs are falling from stealth bombers somewhere in the sky.

Figure 6.5
Leaflet entitled "Desert Storm Is Coming. Flee Immediately"

Note the Iraqi insignia on the demolished tanks.

Figure 6.6
Leaflet entitled "B-52 Bomber"

This leaflet was used to warn of impending bombing and then to communicate that the bombing had taken place as promised.

We made the argument earlier that PSYOP products were sequentially delivered and frequently targeted to specific audiences. One leaflet series that exemplifies the ordering and targeting of messages depicted the easily recognizable B-52 bomber as it released its bombs. The leaflet was targeted not just to Iraqi soldiers, but to the soldiers of particular units. In one instance where this leaflet was delivered, the verbal message read, "This is your first and last warning. Tomorrow the 16th Infantry Division will be bombed. Flee this location now." Following the initial leaflet delivery, the location was bombed. After the bombing a follow-up leaflet was delivered featuring the same picture but with the following caption: "We kept our promise" (see Figure 6.6).

Specific units were not always designated in Gulf War leaflets. Soldiers in positions that had been bombed sometimes received a more general leaflet telling them they had been attacked with a conventional bomb with "more explosive power than 20 SCUD missiles" (see Figure 6.7). While the appeal was less specific, the emphasis on the technological superiority of the coalition forces remained.

Some leaflets combined the futility of resistance theme with messages in support of specific deception campaigns planned and executed by maneuver units. Deception campaigns are designed to mislead the enemy so as to gain an advantage. This kind of operation required specific PSYOP assistance but created a difficult and delicate challenge for PSYOP units. By policy and doctrine, PSYOP products should not explicitly lie. That is, they should not explicitly

Figure 6.7
Leaflet entitled "Daisy Cutter"

The printing on the bomb says, "Flee and Live or Stay and Die." The message on the back of the leaflet compares the Daisy Cutter to the power of 20 SCUD missiles.

state that something has occurred or will occur if that information is false. The reasons for this are as much pragmatic as idealistic. A PSYOP program that stresses one carefully chosen truth can maintain its credibility over time. Because almost no PSYOP program can be won with a single, onetime product, a reputation for legitimacy is critical (Daugherty, 1958a; Katz, 1982).

As part of PSYOP in support of the Desert Storm deception campaign, leaflets with valid messages were printed against the background of specific unit symbols, implying that a particular type of operation might take place. For example, coalition forces released over 12,000 leaflet-stuffed bottles on the Kuwaiti coast.

Figure 6.8
Leaflet entitled "The Wave"

Note the face of the angry soldier coming out of the crest of the wave and the U.S.
Marine insignia.

The leaflets depicted a wave in the shape of a U.S. Marine's face crashing into
fleeing Iraqi soliders. These bottles drifted ashore on the very beaches where
Iraqi soldiers were preparing for a coalition landing (see Figure 6.8).

The leaflet language never said "the Marines will land." The written message
said "Cease Resistance—Be Safe." The mere implication, however, played on
Iraqi fears and led them to maintain extensive troop deployments on the Kuwaiti
shore, away from the main attack. Deception is most effective when it reinforces
perceptions, rather than when it tries to change or create perceptions.

Two related elements are critical to the success of leaflets communicating the
futility of resistance theme. First, the actual military campaign contributed to
the success of the leaflets. If the bombings or attacks had not occurred as
promised, or if Iraqi weapons had been an effective match for coalition weapons,
then these leaflets and other PSYOP products would have been rejected. Using
an illustration from World War II, some of the initial leaflets dropped on German
positions were ineffective because the war had not turned in favor of the United
States and its allies (Daugherty and Janowitz, 1958). Second, the accompanying
surrender appeals that promised safety and humane treatment were critical because they presented a clear alternative to continued fighting.

Some of the similarities between the earlier leaflets and those used in the Gulf
War are striking. While the planes differed, the leaflets depicting B-29 and B-
52 bombers are pictorially similar. In addition, both leaflets promised attacks,
and both gave specific timetables for those attacks to occur. The emphasis on

the amount and diversity of weaponry from the historic leaflets to the contemporary ones is also quite similar. Similarities between historic and contemporary leaflets are not limited to those communicating a futility of resistance theme. These likenesses run throughout most of the themes discussed in this chapter.

Surrender and Safe Treatment. Traditionally, enemy forces have not simply been demoralized by leaflets communicating the superiority of the U.S. forces and their allies. They have also received leaflets that offered specific surrender instructions and/or guarantees of humane treatment in the event of surrender. The point we made earlier bears repeating: surrender and safe treatment leaflets offer enemy soldiers a clear and viable alternative to continued hostilities. We will explicate the two elements of this theme, surrender and safe treatment, separately even though the elements are frequently combined in leaflets.

Historic uses of surrender and fair treatment themes: During the Second World War, separate surrender leaflets were targeted to different levels of the Japanese military hierarchy. The commander, the officers, and the enlisted soldiers received messages unique to their levels communicating specific surrender instructions. The following passage was taken from a leaflet dropped on Japanese positions in Okinawa where officers were the intended target audience.

A white flag of truce will be recognized as a sign of your desire to negotiate with the Americans. This opportunity is offered to all Japanese officers who wish to save the lives of their soldiers. (Vatcher, 1958, p. 404)

Across the Pacific Theater, enlisted soldiers were showered with leaflets saying "I surrender" or "I cease resistance," with instructions to hold the leaflets in a visible position while approaching U.S. forces. German soldiers received leaflets with similar instructions. Some leaflets dropped on German positions included instructions for pronouncing the words "I surrender" in English, along with instructions for displaying the leaflet when approaching Allied positions (Linebarger, 1954).

Some Korean War leaflets provided enemy soldiers with maps giving directions to U.N. positions where the soldiers could surrender (Linebarger, 1954). In addition to providing surrender instructions, the maps also fed the futility of resistance theme because the soldiers could see that their position was an untenable one. Since the maps were accurate, they bolstered the credibility of the product.

In addition to communicating specific surrender instructions, leaflets have frequently guaranteed humane treatment, food, and medical attention to surrendering soldiers. In fact, one of the earliest uses of battlefield leaflets came during the Revolutionary War, when Continental soldiers lobbed leaflets wrapped around rocks onto their British counterparts. The leaflets promised higher pay, fresh food, medical attention, and a good farm in exchange for surrender or desertion. The theme of fair treatment has been used in U.S. battlefield leaflets ever since (Linebarger, 1954; Radvanyi, 1990).

One form of leaflet guaranteeing humane treatment is a safe conduct pass. Safe conduct passes appear to be written to U.S. forces and their allies, but the actual target audience is the enemy soldier. The leaflets appear to be orders guaranteeing humane treatment to enemy soldiers who surrender. The leaflets typically bear the signature of the theater commander. Leaflets dropped on Japanese soliders during World War II, for example, contained statements such as these: "This leaflet guarantees humane treatment to any Japanese desiring to surrender. Take him immediately to your nearest commissioned officer"; "The American offer of food, medical treatment, and place of shelter in which you can safely await the end of the war is extended to each of you" (Herz, 1958a, p. 402). The leaflets included the verbal message in English and Japanese.

German soldiers faced similar appeals. For example, one safe conduct pass guaranteed "food and medical attention as required, and to be removed from the danger zone as soon as possible" (Linebarger, 1954, p. 6). The leaflets, printed in both English and German, bore the signature of General Dwight D. Eisenhower.

Safe conduct leaflets were also used extensively in Korea. One such leaflet read:

It is hereby ordered that accommodations and good treatment be given to the bearer of this certificate and his followers. They have voluntarily disarmed themselves, ceased resistance, and surrender to U.N. forces in accordance with proper procedure. (Linebarger, 1954, p. 250)

Variations of these same general strategies were utilized in Gulf War leaflets. The following section explores contemporary uses of surrender and safe treatment themes in battlefield leaflets.

Surrender and safe treatment themes in the Gulf War leaflets: Messages communicating specific surrender instructions appeared both on the reverse side of leaflets conveying other themes and in leaflets conveying only the surrender and fair treatment theme. Some surrender instructions told Iraqi soldiers to head south toward coalition positions. Nearly all of the surrender leaflets included instructions for an Iraqi soldier to remove the magazine from his weapon, place the weapon over his left shoulder with the muzzle pointing downward, place his hands over his head while proceeding slowly, and wave a white cloth or hold up the leaflet to signal his peaceful intent. The picture on the leaflets typically showed soldiers following the verbal instructions.

For armored personnel the theme remained the same, but the instructions differed to fit the weapon. Armored personnel were told to elevate their weapons to the maximum elevation, expose the tank's side to the approaching forces, and leave the hatches open. As with the other similar leaflets, the picture showed Iraqi soldiers behaving in the manner prescribed by the leaflet (see Figure 6.9).

Leaflets also promised humane treatment to Iraqi soldiers who surrendered. One leaflet depicted surrounded and defeated Iraqi soldiers leaving a building

Figure 6.9
Leaflet entitled "Tank Surrender"

Note the display of the surrender leaflets and the ways in which Iraqi soldiers are following leaflet instructions.

with their hands up and displaying "safe conduct" leaflets. The leaflet stressed that ceasing fire would lead to humane treatment, food and water, medical treatment, and shelter (see Figure 6.10).

Similar guarantees came in the form of official safe conduct passes bearing orders to coalition soldiers from the theater commander (see Figure 6.11). As with earlier versions of safe conduct passes, the implied audience was coalition soldiers, but the actual audience was the Iraqi bearing the pass. It was designed to provide security and reassurance that the promises of safety and humane treatment would be fulfilled.

The leaflets communicating surrender instructions and/or guaranteeing safe treatment were important for two reasons. First, the leaflets provided Iraqi soldiers with specific and attractive alternatives to continued hostilities. The promise of food, water, and shelter, for example, was not a random pledge. The available information on the living conditions for Iraqi soldiers indicated that basic necessities were in short supply. The leaflets sought to create a contrast in credibility. On one hand, Saddam Hussein had not taken care of his troops. On the other hand, the coalition forces, who kept all of their promises, from the pledge to bomb to the guarantee of safe conduct, made a credible commitment to provide food and water.

Second, the leaflets also countered Iraqi propaganda aimed at their own troops. The propaganda was designed to make Iraqi soldiers fearful of surrendering to coalition forces. For example, there were rumors that U.S. Marines were required to murder a member of their family in order to enlist. The PSYOP leaflet themes

Figure 6.10
Leaflet entitled "Building Surrender"

Note the display of the surrender leaflets, raised arms, and downward-pointing muzzles.

Figure 6.11
One of several safe conduct passes

The flags displayed on this, as on most of the safe conduct passes, are primarily flags from the Arab nations that joined coalition forces.

communicated that such a view was false, especially when the accuracy and consistency of the information contained in previous leaflets were considered.

The specific surrender instructions used in Operation Desert Storm were similar to those used in previous conflicts. Some of the lexical choices—for example, "I cease resistance"—directions to U.S. positions, and the instructions on how to surrender all closely resemble messages from earlier leaflets. The same is true of leaflets communicating guarantees of safe treatment. Like the battlefield leaflets from previous wars, the Desert Storm leaflets offered guarantees of food, medical attention, and shelter. The contemporary safe conduct passes shared the same implicit target audience as the earlier leaflets. The Desert Storm leaflets, like those from previous conflicts, bore the signature of the theater commander.

Separating Soldiers from Equipment. The idea of surrender followed by safe treatment has been reinforced by appeals urging soldiers to separate from their equipment. These appeals have emphasized that equipment will be destroyed and that soldiers should leave the equipment to save themselves.

Historic uses of separation themes: Leaflets communicating the need for soldiers to separate from equipment were used more extensively in the Gulf War than in previous wars. This difference in their use is largely due to technological advances in weapons systems. The theme was used against armored units in earlier wars, but more frequently armored personnel were given specific instructions about how to surrender to allied troops without separating from their equipment.

When leaflets conveying a separation theme were dropped, civilians were frequently the target audience. During World War II, leaflets were dropped on populated areas of Japan urging civilians to flee high-risk areas. They were urged to "evacuate immediately," or "at once" to avoid the destruction of Allied bombs (Daugherty, 1958b, p. 360). Similarly, leaflets dropped in Burma and Okinawa urged civilians to stay away from bridges and other areas that would be targets of U.S. bombs. Okinawans were also urged to avoid coastal areas because of impending amphibious assaults (Daugherty, 1958b).

Gulf War uses of the separation from equipment theme: Battlefield leaflets from Operation Desert Storm urged Iraqi soldiers to leave their equipment. The leaflets stated that coalition forces had no interest in killing Iraqi citizens. The principal aims of the coalition forces were to restore Kuwait's independence and to destroy Saddam Hussein's military capabilities. The simple art on these leaflets depicted the difference between remaining with the equipment and fleeing to safety. Those who stayed with their equipment would be killed, while those who left their weapons and equipment would be spared. Several leaflets echoed this theme while pictorially showing different weapons. The pictures were reinforced by a simple verbal message, for example, "Leave your equipment or defend it and die. The choice is yours" (see Figure 6.12).

The Gulf War leaflets conveying a separation theme are similar to those used in previous wars only insofar as they emphasize avoiding the risk of death or injury. The differences in the leaflets reflect the technological advances evidenced

Figure 6.12
Leaflet entitled "Burning Tank"

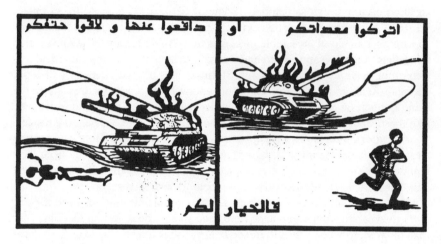

This leaflet depicts the survival of a soldier who separates from his equipment and the death of a soldier who remains with his equipment.

in the Gulf War. Coalition weapon systems systematically destroyed Iraqi equipment with accuracy and precision never before shown on the battlefield. That precision made separating soldiers from equipment a higher priority and also gave the messages added credibility.

Peace, Family, and Unity. This final subset of themes plays upon perceptions of similarity and dissimilarity. Typically leaflets expressing peace, family, and unity themes portray enemy leaders as being responsible for the conflict, self-interested, and uninterested in either soldiers or civilians. The leaflets juxtapose a soldier's attitudes and beliefs with those attributed to military and/or political leaders. The United States and its allies are portrayed as having attitudes and beliefs that are similar to those of target audience members, while the audience member's own leaders are portrayed as having disparate attitudes and beliefs from those of their troops.

Historic appeals to peace, family, and unity: Several leaflets from conflicts involving U.S. forces have emphasized appeals to peace, family, and unity. The leaflets suggested that policies pursued by the United States and its allies would restore peace and reunite families, while the pursuits of enemy leaders would lead to prolonged hostilities, death, and suffering. Leaflets dropped on Japanese soldiers during World War II suggested that military leaders did not have the best interests of their troops at heart. One leaflet read "Your worst enemies are your officers who are trying to commit you to death and separate your forever from your beloved families and homes" (Vatcher, 1958, p. 408). Another leaflet depicted a Japanese officer receiving military honors while his soldiers received a cremation box and headstone (Linebarger, 1954).

Similar appeals were made to German and North Korean soldiers. German soldiers received a leaflet suggesting their commanding officer was more interested in receiving a prestigious medal than in protecting his troops. The leaflet asked, "Can you go on following a commander who is willing to sacrifice you for his own personal glory?" (Herz, 1958a, p. 402).

A related set of leaflets stressed that the United States was at odds with a government instead of the citizens of a particular country. One World War II leaflet said, "America is not fighting the Japanese people but is fighting the military clique that has enslaved the Japanese people" (Daugherty, 1958b, p. 360). Other leaflets assailed Adolf Hitler and other Nazi leaders while urging Germans to overthrow the government.

Peace, Family, and Unity Themes in Gulf War Leaflets. Several Gulf War leaflets played on themes of peace, family, and Arab unity. This general subset of themes was depicted solely in some leaflets and as a secondary theme in other leaflets. Several leaflets stressed that the war was Saddam Hussein against the Arab world and peace. Some safe conduct passes showed the flags of nations comprising the coalition forces, with flags of Arab nations prominently displayed (as in Figure 6.11). Other safe treatment leaflets showed Iraqi soldiers surrendering to Arab brothers, sitting down to dine with them, or returning to loved ones who worried about their safe return (see Figure 6.13).

Leaflets also depicted Saddam Hussein as the cause of hostilities. One leaflet shows a caricature of Saddam on a bloodstained Iraqi flag. The brief verbal message on the front of the leaflet reads: "Saddam is the only reason for the bombing of Iraq" (see Figure 6.14). The leaflets conveyed the message that hope for individual soldiers, their families, and their country, was best fulfilled by peaceful reconciliation and cooperation. This message was powerfully communicated in a leaflet showing the silhouettes of two soldiers, one Iraqi and one Saudi, holding hands and walking into the sunset. The simple written message was "In peace, we shall always remain hand in hand" (see Figure 6.15).

Aside from illustrating the peace and unity theme, this final leaflet example illustrates the importance of careful planning and development of PSYOP. Ethnocentric Western sensibilities led to strong objections to this leaflet before it was distributed. A pretest of the leaflet was done by persons who understood the Arab culture and who realized that Mideastern men were more likely to hold hands with another man than with a woman. The leaflet was finally approved. In interviews with Iraqi soldiers who had surrendered, this leaflet was identified as the most effective. It depicted surrender not as a means of defeat at the hands of the United States of America, but rather as a means of restoring Arab unity and promoting harmony and cooperation.

Both the historic leaflets and those from the Gulf War expressed the idea that a soldier's attitudes and beliefs were discrepant from those of his commander.

Figure 6.13
Leaflet entitled "Invitation"

The back of the leaflet contained safe conduct instructions and an invitation to join "Arab brothers" in full "Arab hospitality."

Figure 6.14
Leaflet entitled "The Bloody Flag"

Note the caricature of Saddam Hussein, who is portrayed as uncaring.

Figure 6.15
Leaflet entitled "The Sunset"

It reads, "In peace we shall always remain hand in hand."

Across the range of conflicts, military and political leaders were portrayed as being self-interested. A recurring theme has been that political and military leaders selfishly keep soldiers from their homes and families. In the same way, leaflets from earlier wars and from the Gulf War stressed that World War II Allied, U.N., and coalition forces were at odds with governments and not citizens.

EVALUATIONS AND CONCLUSIONS

In reviewing and analyzing the results of the leaflet campaign, it is difficult to provide specific data that are neither too broad to be useful nor so small as to be anecdotal. However, several facts are clear, and at least eight conclusions seem warranted from these facts. First, Iraqi soldiers surrendered in large numbers, and it took far fewer troops to guard them than it would have taken to fight and defeat them. In almost every case, the surrendering soldiers produced copies of PSYOP leaflets. In some cases, the soldiers produced multiple copies of the leaflet, as if it were currency. They believed that more leaflets would ensure better treatment.

Second, certain situational and environmental realities must be factored into any evaluation. For example, a number of Iraqi units did not experience widespread desertion and surrender. They fought bravely, and those who were captured did so after putting up a serious fight. The leaflets and themes depicted in this chapter had little effect on these soldiers. In fact, these soldiers often viewed the leaflets with derision and contempt.

This is not to say that PSYOP could not be effective on this target audience.

Instead, this stresses the importance of a careful and systematic planning process. An analysis of available intelligence and a careful review of all the available target audiences must be done to determine which PSYOP product works best with each audience. In Southwest Asia, an analysis had shown that an over-whelming number of Iraqi troops facing the coalition forces were undertrained, poorly equipped, isolated from their chain of command, and running low on such essential supplies as food and water. These were not the battle-tested veterans of the Iran-Iraq War.

Third, in a similar vein, it was clear that positive messages that tapped into existing belief systems were most effective. Themes of Arab unity, family, and peace had the greatest impact. They reinforced what the target audience valued. The alternative would have been to "educate" the target audience on U.S. intentions while changing deeply held fears and resentment of Western power intervention into Middle Eastern politics.

This also relates to the reason the deception campaign was successful. It did not provide new and convincing information, but rather it played on existing beliefs about coalition intentions and provided evidence to bolster those existing beliefs. The use of a military symbol in outline form on a leaflet was sufficient to bolster the belief that an attack would originate from the Kuwaiti coast.

Fourth, the method of dissemination and distribution was also significant. At one point, the impact of continually dropping leaflets was debated. Why send the same leaflet over the same position until it literally carpeted the earth? It was determined that there was a clear value in the implied message communicated by repetitive "bombing" with paper. It further demonstrated the capabilities and comparative strength of the coalition forces. The commitment of combat aircraft to drop paper on units that could not even spare trucks to deliver water to thirsty soldiers implied at least as much as the leaflets could ever explicitly say.

Fifth, if a message is going to be effective, regardless of whether it creates, reinforces, or changes a response in the target audience, it must have an inherent credibility. Part of that credibility is internal to the production of the message. Dialogues and idioms must be correct, and graphic symbols must be accurately depicted (Janowitz, 1958). The use of Egyptian Arabic, for example, undermined the credibility of some early products aimed at Iraqi soldiers.

The inherent credibility of a message or campaign will also be enhanced by consistency. Consistency should take several forms. As noted previously, the message must have a discernible consistency with the existing attitudes and beliefs of the audience. It must also be consistent with the audience's environ-ment. A message aimed at those who are cold and hungry must respond to that need. A message of military superiority must be demonstrably accurate. The message must also be consistent with the media environment, especially when the PSYOP program uses a wide range of media. In Desert Storm, leaflet cam-paigns were reinforced by several media, including loudspeakers and radio broad-casts. The wartime setting also made it possible to ensure that the military could integrate its message with the messages presented by other coalition governments and by other U.S. government agencies.

The end result was a pattern of consistency that ought to be established in all messages. Strategic PSYOP may allow for the long-term education of an audience. In tactical PSYOP, the short-term, immediate nature of most situations militates against the creation of new attitudes and beliefs. This is especially true in the support for tactical deception operations. Arguably, the crises that most often confront occupying or liberating armies would also make this true in consolidation support. When public safety and health are immediately in danger, those themes that affirm rather than alter attitudes or beliefs appear to be the most effective.

Sixth, the message themes used in Desert Shield and Desert Storm leaflets closely mirrored those used previously. The recurring use of a finite number of persuasive message themes should not undermine the importance of PSYOP planning and development. This is true for several reasons. Psychological Operations campaigns rely on diverse media, and the careful integration of those media must be planned. Even though the message themes recur, the timing and sequence of the messages and themes must still be carefully considered. Finally, in regard to this issue, messages can take the same form but differ across contexts in their effectiveness. For example, futility of resistance messages rely heavily on fear or threat appeals. Any number of such appeals can be generated. Some of the messages will be generally more effective than others, and there may also be contextual differences in their effects (Jackson and Jacobs, 1983).

Seventh, the careful application of existing communication or psychological theory to PSYOP is hampered by the lack of high quality data. Until the complete record of everything from program planning to interviews with prisoners of war is declassified, only general observations can be made. But these observations can be tied to existing literature and ongoing research. Perhaps the most important research would be that concerning the structure and hierarchy of attitudes and belief systems.

One final conclusion can also be drawn from the Desert Storm experience. Despite the hopeful predictions of J.F.C. Fuller (1920), psychological actions in support of security goals cannot be done without an accompanying military capability. If there is a recurring lesson from PSYOP at all levels from this century, it is that PSYOP can delay, preclude, and/or mitigate military action. It cannot, however, replace military action. A credible PSYOP force must have a credible military to back up its promises and to give weight to its threats.

7

Israeli Broadcasting Media Facing the SCUD Missile Attacks

Chava E. Tidhar and Dafna Lemish

INTRODUCTION

Immediately upon the invasion of Kuwait by Iraq in the summer of 1990, the Israeli broadcasting media were faced with an unusual challenge: planning and preparing for coverage of a war that might or might not take place. Unlike the situations leading to previous wars, there were many uncertainties: Would Israel become involved in the war? If so, would it actively join the allied forces, or would it be left outside the conflict altogether?

Each alternative called for a totally different orientation and plan of action on the part of the media. Accumulated experience from previous wars focused media attention on battle zones at the frontiers. In such war situations, the media fulfilled three central functions—providing information, commentaries, and tension release (Peled and Katz, 1974).

As was not the case with past wars, this time the enemy threatened to use nonconventional weapons—such as biological, chemical, and even atomic warheads—to attack civilian populations. At the same time, there was also a possibility that Israel's neighbors would take advantage of the situation to attack Israel. Facing such a complicated and uncertain reality, the broadcast media were faced with an awesome burden and responsibility: How should a television or radio station effectively prepare itself for the unknown? The purpose of this study was to reflect on key policy dilemmas as perceived by decision makers in the broadcast media concerning preparation for the war, actual functioning during the war, and lessons derived from this experience.

A UNIQUE MEDIA SITUATION

Israel was drawn into the Gulf War in the early morning hours of January 17, 1991, with the first SCUD attack. The entire population of Israel, approximately 5 million people, was woken up by a piercing alarm. Following Civil Defense instructions, most persons entered a room prepared in advance, sealed the doorways, put on their gas masks, and listened to the radio for further instructions and information on the event taking place. As was dramatically described by a key decision maker in the media industry, "in that unusual and frightening situation, the media served as an umbilical cord to the world."

In certain respects such a situation shares some basic features with "media events" as characterized by Elihu Katz and Daniel Dayan: "live broadcasts of great events that transform individuated and stratified masses into the communities of whole societies, riveting them not just to programs in general but to the very same broadcast; transporting them not just elsewhere but to 'the center' " (1985, p. 305). Such media events interrupt the routines of people's lives as well as broadcasting schedules. The social pressure to stay at home and to participate in media events was magnified in the case of the Gulf War by military instructions to keep off the streets and to listen to radio or television at all times.

At the same time, the Sealed Room situation differed greatly from typical media events studied so far: rather than a unique, short-term and single event, this one repeated itself 18 times within a six-week period with only slight variations. In addition, viewers and listeners were not spectators and parasocial participants, but real participants in a drama that was threatening their personal lives. In this respect, the Gulf War situation can be compared to other survival crises (e.g., natural and ecological disasters) or dread risks, which are focused on time and space and are involuntary, unfamiliar, uncontrollable, acute, and unfair (Fischhoff et al., 1981).

In normal times the broadcast media in Israel consist of the Israeli Broadcasting Authority (IBA), with three radio channels and the public television station; the Military Radio Station; the Israeli Educational Television station (IETV), subordinated to the Ministry of Education; and the Second Television Channel.

Altering this diversified structure, it was decided to unify the radio stations during the Gulf War period. Moreover, during the missile alerts, TV and radio broadcasts were coordinated with information and civil defense instructions delivered solely by the army spokesman. This unification of broadcasting (to be discussed later in this chapter) served the integrative function so typical of media events (Katz, 1992) as well as of disasters (Sood, Stockdale, and Rogers, 1987).

Several additional factors enhanced the unique media context: the availability of advanced technologies that enabled instant transfer of information created a situation wherein the Israeli broadcast media were clearly operating within a global framework of media performance determined to a large degree by the U.S. government (Goren, 1992). The global framework was also characterized by the emotional emphasis in the coverage of preparation for the war and the war itself as manifested in the use of symbols rather than facts (Shinar and Stoicin, 1992).

According to Sood, Stockdale, and Rogers (1987), disaster events are times of high stress and rapid change for media organizations, as the media are forced to adapt to radically changed environmental conditions. Given these conditions, it is particularly interesting to study the perspective adopted by key policymakers inside Israeli media organizations concerning the role of the media during the Gulf War and to explore the considerations that guided their decisions and actions.

METHODOLOGY

This study is based on in-depth interviews with key decision makers in all of the radio and television stations. "Elite" interviewing as developed by Lewis Anthony Dexter was applied (1970). This type of interviewing is defined as: in-depth unstructured face-to-face conversation usually done on an individual basis.

Twelve nonstructured intensive interviews were conducted with persons who were in key policy positions when the war situation developed. Three interviewees were director-generals, four were directors of programming, four were heads of news departments and senior news editors. An additional interview was conducted with the army spokesman who, as we shall see, fulfilled a special broadcasting role during the Gulf War. Four interviewees were from the IBA, both television and radio; four were from the Second Channel; three were from IETV; and one was from the Army Radio Channel.

All interviews were conducted by the authors. In ten out of the twelve interviews both authors participated. Each interview lasted between two and half and three hours.

In order to avoid any influence of diplomatic or political considerations on the information given, the research was introduced as purely academic, and interviewees were assured that their identities would not be revealed. Without exception, all the interviewees were happy to cooperate and to have an opportunity to reflect in detail on their experiences.[1]

PREPARING FOR THE UNKNOWN

All the interviewees felt an urgent need to make some plans for the fluid situation of an unknown war. On the one hand, they shared the frustration created by the necessity to plan a detailed program of action. Yet, on the other hand, they recognized the essential need for flexibility, which would leave room for alternatives demanded by the actual circumstances. Two levels of preparation were made—structural and programming.

Structural Preparations

Two major issues were involved in structural preparations—personnel and foundations and equipment.

Personnel. Both television and radio stations prepared lists of crews to take over the studios as well as crews composed of persons to be drafted from the military reserves to cover the potential battle sites. Lists of backup substitutes were planned for in the event that it was necessary to replace key personnel called up for military duty outside their stations, as became the case in the Second Channel, for example.

Foundations and Equipment. One of the major criticisms voiced often in the interviews was the lack of advanced measures taken to secure the safety and well-being of the media employees themselves.[2]

According to the director of the IBA, this period of unclarity preceding the outbreak of the war was used to accelerate purchasing of basic equipment. Seven and a half million dollars were spent on new video cameras, editing equipment, and satellite reception plates. A confrontation with the Worker's Committee on procedures concerning new equipment was bypassed as new circumstances presented themselves.

Programming Preparations

Program directors and policy makers were clear about the need in a time of war to provide as much up-to-date information and commentary as possible. In addition, entertainment programs were considered necessary in order to provide varied outlets for the release of tension. Nonstop programming seemed to be their ideal.

Providing entertainment was the least difficult function to prepare for in advance. Rescheduling of stored programs and fervent purchasing of new programs ensured advanced planning of between three and six days of broadcasting. The assumption was that within this period each media system would be able to adjust to the new demands of the situation and to operate accordingly. Yet, as one program director noted, such organization presented the following problem:

We prepared for a nonconventional war. We had no idea what it would be like. Would anyone show up for work? So we organized ourselves to broadcast prerecorded tapes. However, it is clear that you can't have a war in the hinterland through desk-drawer broadcasting. The TV screen at home is the viewers' umbilical cord to the outside world. It can't be disconnected. You can't broadcast without production. On the other hand, how do you produce [programs] during a nonconventional war? We didn't have an answer to this problem.

It was anticipated that as in previous wars there would be a need to provide up-to-date information and commentary. Previous wars offered two models. During the 1973 Yom Kippur War, the major sources of information were produced by Israeli crews, themselves reservists, who were drafted by the military and who were allowed to join the fighting forces. All information from the battlefield was the property of the Israel Defense Forces (IDF) and was released according to political-military considerations. Issues of freedom of the press, variety of viewpoints, and the like became irrelevant. A second model was applied during the 1982 Lebanon War. Unlike the Yom Kippur War, this war did not disrupt the life of the entire country. Consequently, civilian crews were allowed to join the battle zone, and each broadcasting organization provided its own "color" and voice.

The forum of directors of the broadcasting stations in Israel and military representatives who met during the months prior to the war debated these two models. The military demanded that in the event of war in the hinterland, involving massive civilian populations, the media should face the nation through a "unified voice." Thus full cooperation with the military was necessary. On the other hand, the broadcasting organizations were eager to maintain their independence and freedom.

The result was a compromise, agreed upon in advance of the war. The crews of the television stations would be drafted and therefore would operate under the authority of the IDF spokesman. All the radio stations, the IDF as well as the IBA stations, would be united throughout the duration of the war but would operate independent of the IDF spokesman. The details of these agreements, as well as their consequences, will be discussed later.

The pressure to establish the "unified voice" was also manifest in the search for a "national spokesperson." It was clear in the discussions that were conducted that this figure was expected to be a male, with no distinct political identification, yet highly regarded and trusted by the entire population. The model for such a role was the current president of Israel, Chayim Hertzog. During the Six-Day War in 1967, Hertzog served as the key national spokesman and commentator on Israeli radio, the only electronic medium at the time. In fulfilling this role, Hertzog earned tremendous respect and admiration from all. Symbolically, he came to represent the unification of a country at a time of crisis. However, in the heated sociopolitical atmosphere of Israel in 1990, no agreement could be reached about such figure. Only in an unexpected turn of events during the war did a figure emerge who assumed this role.

In order to guarantee up-to-date information from the Arab world, closed to Israeli media, both IBA and the Second Channel made a prewar agreement with CNN. IBA television also established live lines with correspondents in Washington, and links to the European Broadcasting Union and CBS, as well as technical capability to receive information from the Arab satellite (ARABSAT).

A different type of information service that was prepared in advance was behavioral instructions for use in an emergency. Public broadcasting announcements instructing citizens in the appropriate use of such equipment as the various gas masks for different age groups and procedures for sealing rooms at home were produced. The IDF provided each station with a booklet of instructions to be read at the time of an alarm. The IDF radio station, in particular, prepared detailed procedures for releasing information in case of emergency.

Program directors were clearly aware that emergency information and reporting would have to be accompanied by commentaries and that in times of crisis, such commentary could occupy many hours of broadcasting time, especially when information is vague, unavailable, or censored. To this end, both the IBA television and IETV—who prior to the Gulf War produced the only local television news programs—prepared long lists of possible "experts" to be interviewed as necessary.

All television and radio stations in Israel were involved, to a lesser or to a greater extent, in preparation toward a possible war. What actually took place was a new and different experience for the well-experienced Israeli population at large, and for the Israeli electronic media in particular. As one policymaker said in perspective, "we were preparing for a war that never happened but were not preparing for what actually happened."

FACING REALITY

About one o'clock at night, I received a phone call from our correspondent in Washington. Immediately I called our reporter on duty and told him: "Call the Editorial Board and tell them I'm on my way!" Since the General Director of the station had approved the broadcast that was it. . . . As the equipment was warming up, our anchor man did his own makeup. It was incredible! By 2:15 A.M. we were on the air. I said: "People may be listening to foreign news. Within an hour everyone will know. The most important thing is to get on the air."

This was the beginning of the war for IBA's senior news editor. Such a response is typical in disasters when the goal of the media is to get information on the air and to the public as rapidly as possible (Sood, Skockdale, and Rogers, 1987). And, indeed, the need to broadcast at any cost, as long as possible, was common to all the Israeli media. "Most of our effort went into just staying on the air," claimed many of the interviewees. Overnight, both IBA and the Second Channel went from broadcasting the typical 5 to 7 hours daily to an 18-hour broadcast day.

All the services struggled to find their unique role in the broadcasting arena. An entire heterogeneous population was there to be attracted, each segment with its special needs: Jews and Arabs, children and adults, new immigrants who didn't understand Hebrew and deaf people who couldn't hear the news, families and lonely singles, frustrated soldiers who were not active in this war and elderly people restricted to their homes. All were dependent on the media for survival. These different populations needed to escape the fear of a catastrophe as well as to be entertained. The audience needed a constant flow of information on the unfolding of the war and concrete instructions for behavior at different times. The audience was also thirsty for explanations of the hidden meanings, contextual perspectives, implications and possible scenarios of political developments.

No wonder that the polls of listenership and viewership during the war present amazing data. During the first three weeks of the war, 43 to 49 percent of the population listened to the radio and watched television at the same time (Guttman Institute, 1991). During the first three weeks of the war, when most of the population stayed indoors, about 80 percent watched television during the afternoon and evening hours. Compared to prewar figures, listenership to the radio was significantly higher at any given hour during the war and reached over 80 percent of the population at different times (Guttman Institute, 1991). But television's performance differed significantly from that of the radio.

Television

Resisting Unification. The three television stations resisted successfully the military's pressure to broadcast in a "uniform voice." All perceived the war as an opportunity to sharpen their stations' unique public contribution. IETV, as well as the Second Channel, in particular, perceived unification as an attempt by the major IBA station to undermine competition, as well as a dangerous precedent of political intervention threatening freedom of expression. The issue was debated at an adhoc meeting of all broadcast media directors and the military spokesman, a group that became the "media high command" during the war. This internal resistance, supported by some influential politicians, allowed the three stations to maintain their independence, with one exception: The IBA station took over all TV broadcasting between the alarm and the all-clear signals.

Finding a Unique Broadcasting Format. As the most experienced station in the production of major news programs and magazines, the IBA was most prepared to provide news and information. Dependency on foreign sources, mainly CNN, during the first days of the war faded, mainly because CNN's relative advantage in terms of immediacy and exclusiveness was undermined by its shortcomings in providing contextual depth. In addition, information from the battle zone was restricted because of American policies. As a result, as the war progressed, IBA searched actively for local sources, not so much as a planned strategy, but rather as a form of "putting out fires," trying to adjust to the changing demands created by the war.

Two strategies of reporting emerged from this process. First, since very few facts were actually available, commentary assumed primary importance. A long parade of persons, most of whom were retired generals, presented commentaries on Middle East policies, military weapons, war strategies, ecology, urban planning, crisis management, stress, and so on. The experts explained and forecasted war-related activities and discussed their outcomes and implications. The pressure to fill broadcast time was enormous. Though some lists were prepared in advance, most of the experts were selected on the basis of personal acquaintance and preference. As one of IBA's top managers observed, "The reporter is also a human being—he's got his sympathies and antipathies. And, they [the experts] were eager to appear on television. We had no problem getting whomever we wanted."

The massive application of the "expert strategy" turned out to be a controversial issue. As one senior news editor explained, "If there is an enemy to proper journalism, it is the use of experts. Situational explanations are a sure recipe for screwups. . . . The experts—as talented and goodlooking as they are— took over our messages. It would have been better to just present the official government statements."

The second solution was found in the form of reporting the human side of the war. This truly brought the war to the Israeli population. Segments included stories describing the destruction and looting of homes, interviews with displaced citizens who lost their homes, and debates between residents who did or did not flee from the densely populated and heavily attacked area of Tel Aviv to safety in the periphery. Such presentations of reality from a human perspective were criticized by politicians. Television was blamed for demoralizing the citizenry. In defense, one news director argued that "we thought: these are the facts of life. It happened and we need to report it."

At IETV, a new program, called "The Open Studio," was adapted from an adolescent summer program called "Seeing 6/6." This format was flexible, multifunctional, included diverse programming, and allowed for unexpected interruptions. A young man and woman, familiar to youth, teamed to anchor the program, which, like a telethon, was broadcast continuously for many hours. The program included discussions with guests, prerecorded programs, news, entertainment, and hotline conversations. "The Open Studio" tried to provide the audience with a sense of continuity and stability. At the same time it enabled the station to adjust to the constraints forced upon it by the war. The content of the programming changed as the functions being served varied, but the frame of reference remained intact.

The proportion between the different ingredients of "The Open Studio" changed as the war progressed. At first, there was a need for simple information instructing viewers how to respond during an alarm: procedures for sealing the room, use and dangers of gas masks and antropin shots, and the storage of food and water. Viewers used "The Open Studio's" direct hotline to interact with presenters and their guests-experts. In addition, popular figures from children's programs were brought to the studio to discuss with youngsters their fears and concerns. Psychologists provided lengthy discussions of the audience's potential mental states.

As in the case of the IBA, in which a dissatisfaction with the overuse of experts was expressed, here too it was felt that there was saturation from all the psychological advice. As one program director explained, "All of them were saying the same thing, and not too cleverly. They were so busy legitimizing fear that they didn't provide effective tools to deal with it. So we gradually gave less and less of them." A similar phenomenon was mentioned by Cohen et al. (1992) in a discussion of the Israeli radio and newspaper roles during the war. These media, too, were accused of possibly creating rather than reducing mental stress, again through the obssessive legitimization of fear.

As the war progressed, IETV was faced with contradictory demands. On the one hand, there was the need to serve the entire population by providing heterogeneous programming. On the other hand, there was the need to respond to the specific demands of their sponsor and sole funding agency—the Ministry of Eduction and Culture. Since schools were closed, IETV was called upon to assist in implementation of a policy adopted by the ministry—"the flexible school." Here children were to resume schooling by gathering together in small groups in their homes. The direct implication of this policy for IETV was that the station would have to move overnight to narrowcasting of curricula-related programs targeted to specific audiences. As the station was trying to work out feasible compromises, the reality of the war changed, and schools were gradually reopened. The station was saved from the test of having to confront these conflicting demands.

Overall, "The Open Studio" earned the admiration of the other stations and the public at large. However, it presented IETV with enormous difficulties: a demand for constant flexibility, no time for planning or rehearsal, no guarantee of reliable or fixed schedules, and continuous confrontation with conflicts of interests.

IETV's regular news program—"Erev Chadash" (New Evening)—operated independently. Normally, this program was broadcast live five days a week in the early evening. A prerecorded program was broadcast on Fridays. The war created two serious dilemmas. First, there was the question of whether to maintain the familiar structure or to merge as a regular segment in "The Open Studio." Second, the station considered whether to move from an indoor, studio interview format to outdoor, location filming of hard news. Attempts to film outdoors could be perceived as a threat by the "big station," IBA. Furthermore, film production would require the intervention of the military censor, which until then had maintained a hands-off policy with the station. In the end, it was decided that "Erev Chadash" would maintain its regular format, except for the Friday magazine, which adopted a live format in order to be able to account for events that developed between recording and broadcast.

The director of "Erev Chadash" chose to use one central commentator, a journalist specializing in Middle East politics:

I took a risk, but it paid off. Normally, we provide many opinions. But suddenly, during the war, I felt it was wrong to do so. I felt that stability was needed—each day the same person, whose commentaries could be trusted, explained and criticized the developments. The audience got used to him.

The Second Channel, the youngest and smallest of the three TV stations, was characterized most of all by the voluntary spirit of its workers. As explained by an enthusiastic program director:

the sense of team spirit typical of this station was temporarily magnified. People worked very hard. They wanted to be together. A daycare center was established in the conference room. So, mothers showed up to work accompanied by their young children and their gas mask kits. It was noisy and a big mess. But it worked. . . . All we did was broadcasting.

In addition to broadcasting special children's programs, the station perceived itself as an "alternative channel for escapism." Yet, at the same time, decision makers understood that they could remain disconnected from reality, and so they looked for an opportunity to put their own mark on the broadcasting map. The result took the form of an alternative news magazine—"This Evening in the Gulf." The program consisted of CNN reports accompanied by regular commentators and guests. This program was moderated in an informal style by a woman whose previous work was as IBA sports presenter. Her special role in the broadcast news industry in Israel, as well as the almost total disappearance of other women broadcasters during the war, is discussed elsewhere (Lemish and Tidhar, 1993).

Radio

The unification of IBA's popular channels and the IDF radio channel into the Joint Channel was one of the most controversial Israeli media issues of the Gulf War. Since the final decision to unite the two authorities several hours before the outbreak of the war, the stations' representatives were involved in tiresome negotiations in search of a workable formula. Issues negotiated included whose broadcasters would be on the air and when, which crew would be assigned to field reporting, which music style would receive preference, and which linguistic style would dominate. The first few days of broadcasting were characterized by an endless number of little disagreements: "we were busy working out little quarrels of preschool nature," confessed one general director. But as time passed, the mutual teasing and yelling subsided, and the two competing staffs, so different in their broadcasting styles, learned to work in cooperation. In the end, they even enjoyed the change.

The Joint Channel provided a variety of programs during the war—news, experts' commentaries, easy listening music, and nationalistic music. However well it provided these services, it was its crucial role as purveyor of the civil defense alarm for which the radio's Joint Channel is most remembered: "We switched from being a journalistic system to being an instrument of the Civil Defense Forces—sending out alarm and all-clear signals," claimed one director bitterly. He added, "when the polls claim that there was 99 percent listenership to the radio, it is an exaggeration. What they really mean is that people were listening in anticipation of the alarm, not to our programs."

This role was completely unexpected and unplanned. It evolved as a result of the discovery that the national and local civil defense alarm system was unsatisfactory and another, coincidental turn of events. One station accidentally broadcast the secret military code "Viper," which preceded the sounding of the alarm by a second or two. The Israeli audience quickly learned the trick. By keeping their ears attuned for the code, they gained a few precious seconds to run to the prepared room before the siren even sounded. "We had a long argument with the military over this situation. I wanted clear and agreed-upon expectations. People's lives were suddenly dependent upon us. I couldn't take such a responsibility. This is not the radio's role. It was wrong," claimed one managing director. The IDF station news director agreed and added: "We were plainly a military tool. As an IDF station it was easy for us to handle, but it was a gross diversion from the proper journalistic guidelines."

Another unexpected development, quite strange in nature for any radio station, was the invention of the Quiet Channel. Many listeners who left the radio on throughout the night in order to hear the alarm found it difficult to fall asleep. A creative suggestion was brought up by the audience: broadcast silence on one channel except when there is an alarm. This way people could fall asleep peacefully and securely, knowing that they would be woken up by the alarm. It also accommodated religious people who do not operate any media systems during the Sabbath day, yet needed a trustworthy alarm system. This may be the only case in broadcast history when for many nights radio chose to broadcast "silence" and was admired for doing so!

But radio's most glorious moments were those periods between the alarm and the all-clear signals. Then, the entire population of the country listened to every single sound transmitted. The military had prepared detailed instructions for the broadcasters to read. The scripts considered all possible developments (most are still confidential in nature). An unexpected development dictated a major diversion from advanced planning. On the first night of the war, when the broadcasters were "sitting there in the studio with the booklet of instructions," the military spokesman, Nachman Shai, called the radio station and asked to go on the air. In our interview, Shai recalled how he acted: "I arrived in the city and went down into Headquarters. Everyone was busy. What was I supposed to do? So I called the radio and suggested that I be the connection with Headquarters to save time and distance between decision makers and the public. And that's how it all started."

Shai's calm style instilled trust. He provided instructions and clear, noninterpretive information. His motto—"the minute we have more information I will let you know"—turned him into a national figure overnight. An experienced journalist prior to assuming his post as army spokesman, Shai was not identified with any political party, nor was he perceived to be threatening to media decision makers. A turning point for him early in the war was a television interview in which the moderator said, "now look straight at the camera and talk directly to the audience, not as an interviewee but as a leader." As time passed, Shai realized the important role he was playing in calming down the nation at the most stressful of times. However, as citizens got used to the routine instructions—such war favorites as "you can take off your gas mask now, drink some water and relax," his airtime was shortened, and his instructions became more technical. Yet his role as the "national Valium," as he was fondly nicknamed, was greatly appreciated by all the millions locked in their sealed rooms for what may have been some of the most dreadful moments of their lives.

Overall then, facing the reality of the war, Israeli broadcasting media was characterized by both virtues and problems. It found creative and flexible solutions, made an endless number of alterations, dealt with the constant pressure to satisfy everyone, and contributed much hard work by many dedicated men and women.

BENEFITING FROM COERCION

It is in the nature of crisis situations that risks and opportunities present themselves side by side. The Lebanon War, for example, put IETV on the communication map as a current affairs broadcast medium and expanded the regular service of the station beyond educational and enrichment programs that were primarily oriented to children and youth. A daily program originally designed to provide a communication link between soldiers in the front and their families at home was accompanied by an information update segment. Later this program became a daily current affairs magazine ("Erev Chadash" mentioned earlier). The Gulf War, too, presented the broadcast media with new opportunities. And, indeed, it seems that except for the army radio station, all other broadcasting stations benefited from the Gulf War experience in some way or another.

Radio

Radio was the primary broadcast medium in the "sealed rooms" as a result of the special circumstances and the vital role that radio broadcasts played, in particular during the alarm periods. According to a news director of the IDF station, there was a spillover effect in the months that followed in terms of increase in radio audiences and positive public attitudes to the radio as an informative medium.

The temporary merging of radio channels benefited "The Voice of Israel" IBA station in two ways: it provided a unique opportunity for introducing changes in programming and opened new possibilities for hiring younger people. As the managing director of the station said, "programs which nobody dared to touch for over twenty years were put off the air and replaced by new, more innovative ones. Enforced cooperation with the Army Station during the war forced The Voice of Israel to be more open to change in terms of ideas as well as manpower."

In contrast to "The Voice of Israel," the forced merger did not benefit the Army Station. The habit of tuning to the Joint Channel, which broadcast during the war on the same wavelength as "The Voice of Israel" resulted in a loss of audience on the part of the Army Station.

Television

All three TV stations in Israel considered the Gulf War beneficial to their future aims.

New Programming. The Gulf War stimulated some breakthroughs in programming on all the stations. Programs created in response to specific needs that emerged during the war provided a springboard for new programs that have been integrated into postwar broadcasting schedules. IBA initiated and has continued its first morning news program. IETV launched its first Arabic-speaking children's program, as well as a program on Middle East countries. Both programs have become part of IETV's weekly schedule. In addition, IETV's regular current affairs program was expanded during the war to include specific items for children and youth. As the director of current affairs programming at IETV said, "this valuable experience will be utilized in IETV's long-range planning."

The most remarkable gain in programming has taken place at the Second Channel. There the war situation was seized upon as an opportunity to bypass regulations that had severely restricted its involvement in news broadcasting. As the managing director of the station said, "Our news program, 'This Evening in the Gulf,' marked the breakup of IBA's monopoly and the beginning of free competition in TV news broadcasting. The success of the program put the Second Channel on the communication map as a news and current affairs broadcaster." Indeed survey results from the first week in February 1991—late in the war period—indicate that 62 percent of those who were able to receive the Second Channel on their sets watched "This Evening in the Gulf." The program was continued as a regular part of the broadcast schedule under the new name "7:30 Around the World" and has gained a regular viewing audience.

Another program that was launched by the Second Channel during the Gulf War became one of the most popular television entertainment programs in Israel. This discussion program, now broadcast twice a week, is conducted with artists and celebrities in Israeli social and cultural affairs.

Enhanced Team Spirit. National crisis situations stemming from external threats seem to strengthen the sense of unity and cohesiveness among staff members. People demonstrate a stronger volunteer spirit. Emergency situations also call for abandoning rigid working procedures. The vital role that the media played in the Gulf War provided a unique opportunity to improve the work atmosphere so that the flexibility and enhanced team spirit could continue after the war crisis was over. Apparently this was the case at the Second Channel. However, at the more established stations—IETV and IBA TV—the spirit of volunteerism and intrateam cooperation did not last long after the war. As one of IETV program directors observed, "although 'The Open Studio' framework which IETV adopted during the war enhanced a team spirit and cooperation, when the war was over, we soon learned that what was feasible under war conditions may not be possible at other times."

Reframing Presenters. A most interesting attempt was made by the Second

Channel to take advantage of the war situation to recruit well-known television figures and to assign them different roles than the ones they used to assume. According to top management at the station, this deliberate experiment in reframing presenters' images proved to be highly beneficial. For example, a well-known presenter of sports news became a popular presenter of this channel's key current affairs program, "This Evening in the Gulf"; and an actor who was known as a playboy became a successful presenter of a popular children's program.

Improved Station Image. Decision makers in two out of the three television stations attributed to the war experience a positive contribution to the overall public image of their stations. According to its directors, IETV improved on its image as a public station that could respond to the changing needs of its target viewers. Indeed, a survey carried out in mid-February 1991 among parents (Levinsohn, 1991) indicated that over 80 percent attributed to IETV positive contributions to meeting the needs of their children, among them helping the children to overcome fear and tension, giving them a better understanding of the events taking place in their lives, providing guidance for behavior as well as giving them creative ideas for educational activities. A year later, in June 1992, IETV received a special award from the communities in the northern part of Israel in appreciation of its unique contribution to their children during the Gulf War.

The Second Channel, too, improved its public image as a reliable broadcast medium. Support of this finding was provided by an unsolicited advertisement placed in a popular weekly magazine by an anonymous viewer: "Interested in the truth? Switch to Channel Two!" In addition, broadcasting during the war contributed to the crystalization of the station's image as a nonelitist channel that cultivates an open and intimate relationship with its viewers. Indeed, the director of programming claimed that since the war he had regularly received letters from viewers addressed to him by his first name as well as phone calls to his home from wartime viewers who felt free to comment directly on a program that had just been transmitted: "Unlike IBA TV, which adopted an authoritarian, elitist style, we address the viewers at eye level. We do not look down at them, nor from the belt," he said.

Overall, then, most broadcast stations used the Gulf War as an opportunity to advance their organizational goals. However, one overriding issue remained unresolved—the dilemma of diversity versus unity, both between stations and within each station.

ADDRESSING THE DILEMMA OF PLURALISM VERSUS MONOPOLY

In the Gulf War, as in former critical media events, the Israeli broadcasting media attempted to serve multiple and diverse functions: to provide information and commentary, to assist in the release of tension, and to transmit civil defense instructions and alarms. All these functions can best be served by a pluralistic media system that adjusts itself to specific audiences' needs.

However, the need for national integration and cohesiveness at a time of crisis often advances a preference for unity so as to provide one noncontroversial source of information that can be trusted. In addition, the political system, as well as the military, would also prefer to deal with a limited number of media channels so as to ensure just "one voice." Therefore, during periods of war, democratic societies may be faced with the dilemma of media pluralism versus monopoly. This study revealed that this delimma existed in Israel during the Gulf War and was manifest in several issues.

The Controversy over the Unification of Channels

As was discussed earlier, all decision makers in the broadcast media interviewed agreed in retrospect that unification of the radio channels was unjustified. Their preference was that each channel retain its independence and unique character and so be free to serve its special audiences as it saw fit.

Alternatively, it was suggested that the media in time of war should segmentize the audience much as cable systems do. Each channel could specialize in a particular function, such as providing news around the clock or children and family programs or light programming for adults, and so on.

Both alternatives ensure the media more freedom of expression and a multiplicity of perspectives, which are crucial functions in any democratic system. However, all those interviewed agreed that during the tense period between the alarm and the release signals, all media channels should be united so as to ensure that broadcast instructions would be identical.

The Controversy over the National Spokesman

The special role played by the military spokesman was the topic of much discussion in the media in the days following the war. Familiar from studies of other disaster events, this phenomenon has been labeled by David Rubin as the "Information Czar": a person who is groomed to, but also rises to, the needs presented when the media prefer a credible, authoritative source of information with official status (Sood, Stockdale, and Rogers, 1987).

The nation's informational and emotional dependency on this authoritative figure raises serious questions over the potential functions and dysfunctions of the media in crisis situations. In retrospect, information released after the war related to civil defense procedures undermines the justification for this unconditional trust.

This information highlights the potential danger of giving up independent judgment and commentary, even as a voluntary action on the part of the broadcasters themselves. It is therefore surprising that most of the interviewees suggested that a similiar procedure be followed if the need arises again in the future.

This may be explained by the tremendous popularity of the person who performed this role in the last crisis, as well as the convenience of handing over this responsibility at critical moments of existential danger.

The Controversy over the Choice of Commentators

As it did in many other Western television venues, this war strengthened the media's preference for assigning one person the role of commentator, someone who can be identified as the station's trademark. While in Israel these person-alities have not been elevated to "star" levels, the trend was established during the war. The implicit rationale for such choices is the consistency of commentary, which engenders trust and in turn loyalty to the channel. At the same time, this strategy limits the ability of the audience to attain multiple perspectives, so needed for the formation of critical public opinion.

In conclusion of this study, the availability of modern technologies that at-tribute to the media a powerful role in times of war sharpens the debate over the relationships between information and power in a democracy. The Israeli experience during the Gulf War may serve as a unique example of broadcasting potential to serve the rapidly changing needs of society. This study reveals how media policy evolved through negotiations among decision makers, attention to audience needs, the constraints imposed by the war, and the political powers and the war situation. We can only hope that the issues confronted during the Gulf crisis will never have to be applied to another war in Israel.

NOTES

1. The authors wish to thank all interviewees for their cooperation and insightful comments.

2. Due to security considerations, we cannot go into further detail about this matter. All interviews are confidential and sources cannot be identified.

Part III

Issues and Images on Television

8

Global Pictures, Local Stories: The Beginning of Desert Storm as Constructed by Television News Around the World

David L. Swanson and Rebecca A. Carrier

No one had seen anything like it before. The beginning of a war, live, on television. First came the audio reports from television journalists in Baghdad describing the initial raid on the city by air forces of the U.N. multinational coalition in the early morning hours of January 17, 1991. Then, in live video feeds, reporters recounted the continuous roar of warplanes taking off from bases in Saudi Arabia. Soon, viewers were able to see videotape of coalition pilots taking off to begin Desert Storm and returning to the cheers of their comrades. Before long, pictures appeared of the attack on Baghdad with tracers from antiaircraft artillery lighting the night sky.

Desert Storm was a television war, the first real-time television war. Coverage was extraordinary in several respects. A new level of immediacy was achieved as same-day and live coverage from the war zone became routine. The combatants' efforts to influence public opinion through television, both before and after the fighting began, were elaborate and energetic. The drama was riveting, the audience global. Vast resources were deployed to bring the war to viewers around the world. The media rosters for the multinational coalition's Joint Information Bureaus in Riyadh and Dhahran, Saudi Arabia, for January and February 1991, list 1,563 journalists, including personnel representing 52 television services in 31 different countries, as well as international television news services (e.g., Visnews, WTN) (Committee on Governmental Affairs, 1991, 195–253). In country after country, surveys documented the large audiences who were drawn to television's coverage (e.g., Blood, 1991; Fitzsimon, 1991; Gantz, 1991; McLeod et al., 1991; Shaw and Carr-Hill, 1991).

Television coverage of the opening days of Desert Storm offers a revealing case study of what has come to be called the globalization of television news. *Globalization* refers to the process by which, increasingly, television news services around the world have become interconnected and interdependent within a global television news system. The proliferation of communication satellites, expansion of international news video services, organization of regional television news exchanges, and growth of international satellite-delivered news services such as CNN and Sky News are some of the most important elements of the global system. The system not only provides alternative information sources through transnational satellite-delivered services received directly in viewers' homes but also penetrates national systems as, routinely, coverage of events beyond one's own borders is acquired from interconnected global production and distribution systems.

Globalization raises policy questions concerning who wields the power of television news to influence public opinion and whether the creation of a global system has transferred control over the production of television news from national to international sources. Because the system's major producers and distributors are located in Western Europe and the United States, some analysts warn that the advent of a global system invites media imperialism through which Western perceptions and priorities may be imposed on news audiences throughout the world (e.g., Fisher, 1987; Tunstall, 1977). Other writers claim that national television news broadcasters routinely domesticate or adapt material acquired from the global system to their own national viewpoints and interests. According to latter analysis, charges of media imperialism reflect an inadequate and oversimplified view of how the global system works (e.g., Cohen, Adoni, and Bantz, 1990; Gurevitch, Levy, and Roeh, 1991).

In order to consider some of the policy concerns raised by globalization, we examined news coverage of the opening days of Desert Storm offered by 20 national television services around the world. Our study was limited to the content of television news and, hence, does not shed light on the equally important question of how television coverage influenced viewers. As explained below, the 20 television services were selected in order to construct a sample that was as diverse as possible along dimensions that might be expected to influence coverage of the war—patterns of media ownership and control, national sentiments favoring one or the other side in the war, degree of involvement in the conflict, and so on. In analyzing early war coverage offered by these television services, we concentrated primarily on news about events taking place in the combat zone. During this period, the U.N. coalition and the Iraqis both attempted to control television crews' access to the ongoing action and endeavored to manipulate the global television news system to their own advantage. How successful was each side at influencing initial war coverage distributed by the global system and offered by national services? In each country, was material from the global system simply passed on to viewers by their national services? Or was coverage in each country framed by domestic national viewpoints and interests? Before addressing these questions, it is helpful to consider in more detail how the global system works and how it may shape television news.

DESERT STORM AND THE GLOBAL TELEVISION NEWS SYSTEM

The global television news system consists of three main elements. The most familiar element probably is the 24-hour news services that broadcast to international audiences primarily by satellite, such as the U.S.–based Cable News Network (CNN) and Britain's Sky News. CNN's signal is beamed to more than 80 countries and "pirated by government agencies and private distributors in virtually every nation" (O'Heffernan, 1991, p. 71; see also Hester, 1991).

Visnews and Worldwide Television News (WTN), the international television news agencies based in Britain, are a second element of the global system. These organizations operate as wire services for television, supplying television news video and stories to subscribing television news services. Unlike wire services, however, these agencies not only distribute material that their own personnel have produced but also, and more typically, they distribute to members material prepared by other services, especially material produced by the major television news services that own shares in each agency. For example, WTN distributes material from Britain's Independent Television News, ABC television news in the United States, and other sources, while Visnews distributes material from the BBC, NBC television news in the United States, and other sources. Both services have a global reach. Visnews alone serves more than 200 subscribing television services in nearly 100 countries (Hester, 1991).

The third element of the global system consists of regional news exchanges through which member national services share their locally produced material with each other. The most successful exchange is the European Broadcasting Union's Eurovision News Exchange. Other active regional exchanges include Intervision, which connects national services in the former Soviet bloc, and Asiavision, which links national services in Asia through zone centers in Tokyo and Kuala Lumpur (see Wallis and Baran, 1990, for a description of regional exchanges).

The components of the global system are connected to one another, to national systems, and to the wire services in complicated ways. For example, Reuters owned 51 percent of Visnews during the Gulf War (and subsequently has moved to assume sole ownership by purchasing the shares owned by NBC and the BBC). CNN provides material directly to viewers in some countries and to national television services in other countries. It distributes both material it has produced and material it receives from national services and through regional exchanges such as Eurovision and Intervision. Some regional exchanges have their own links to other exchanges, as Asiavision receives and distributes a daily satellite feed from the Eurovision exchange, and so on. The result is that virtually every national television service now has access to roughly the same stock of material through its connections to various nodes of what has today become a global television news system.

The interconnectedness of the global network was quite evident during the opening days of Desert Storm. CNN's role in the initial days was important and highly visible, particularly its live coverage of the first bombing raids on Baghdad, and generated several controversies concerning the wisdom of live war coverage and the appropriateness of continuing to broadcast from Iraq under military censorship (for example, Corry, 1991; Mott, 1991; Rosenberg, 1991). As we shall see, CNN was a major source of material broadcast in many national television services' coverage of the outbreak of the Gulf War.

Equally important were the video news services and exchanges that provided pictures from the war zone to domestic television news services around the world. The outbreak of Desert Storm was a hugely important story worldwide. With few exceptions (for example, China's Yellow River Television Service), national television news systems endeavored to cover the story in detail. Television coverage requires video, but most national services had not the resources to send their own crews to the Gulf. Hence, video coverage of war action was available only from a handful of suppliers, and as a result, most national services were entirely dependent on the international services and exchanges for access to this material.

Through pools, restrictions on access, and in other ways, the combatants sought to control at the source the material that global television news suppliers produced. The U.N. coalition offered a steady flow of information in regular briefings and imposed a pool system that provided for security screening and sharing of video material. The Iraqis produced and broadcast a limited amount of their own material and moved quickly after the bombing began to attempt to control reports filed by journalists from Baghdad, first by imposing censorship and later by expelling all journalists during the first days of the war except CNN's Peter Arnett—and Alfonso Rojo, a reporter for *El Mundo* (a daily newspaper published in San Juan, Puerto Rico)—who evaded the Iraqis by going into hiding in Baghdad). Thus, the outbreak of Desert Storm provides a case study of how the global television news systems works in the face of determined efforts to manipulate its content. The extent to which the combatants were successful in their aims provides one measure of whether the global television news system can be made to project a single viewpoint that is imposed on viewers around the world.

GLOBAL AND LOCAL INFLUENCES ON THE PRODUCTION OF TELEVISION NEWS

In order to judge the impact of the global system on coverage of the beginning of Desert Storm offered in national newscasts, it is important to appreciate how the production of television news reflects a number of different influences that interact in complicated ways to shape the final result broadcast to viewers. Persons who work in television news are socialized within a professional culture or canon of practice that defines how the news should be selected, written, edited, and presented. Several comparative studies have found that some elements of this professional culture are shared in many different countries (e.g., Cohen, Adoni, and Bantz, 1990; Golding and Elliott, 1979; Gurevitch, Levy and Roeh, 1991; Straubhaar et al., 1992). In particular, conventions for producing television news stories and standards of news value and judgment seem to transcend national boundaries (Gurevitch, 1989; Head, 1985; Servaes, 1991; Straubhaar et al., 1992) and reflect a "transnational news-value culture" (Cohen, Adoni, and Bantz, 1990, p. 44).

One visible component of the transnational television news culture is virtually universal use of narrative structures to organize news stories. Researchers have found that across time, topic, and national borders, the narrative elements of characterization, plot, action, and resolution are employed to construct both television and print news in segments that are readily understood as "stories" (e.g., Altheide, 1976; Altheide and Snow, 1979; Hallin, 1986; Mander, 1987; Roeh, 1989; Schudson, 1982; Sperry, 1981). Other visible components of the transnational professional culture include the use of studio-based anchors or readers, preference for stories that allow television to exploit its capacity for immediacy and visual presentation, reliance on official sources of information, and preference for brief and event-focused story formats. To some extent, the development of a global television news genre is attributed to the practices of Western television systems being accepted by the rest of the world as an appropriate model (Nasser, 1983; Straubhaar et al., 1992). Because of worldwide devotion to these canons of professional practice, television news programs broadcast in every country look similar to one other.

Balanced against the forces that produce similarities between countries in television news are other forces that produce national differences. An indigenous professional culture of television journalism has developed over time within each country. This indigenous culture reflects not only global canons of television news practice but also the particular cultural, social, political, economic, and institutional context of television journalism in every country. Some national contexts have given rise to distinctive and oppositional conceptions of how journalism ought to be practiced, such as the notion of "development journalism" as a way of serving the special needs of developing nations (Martin and Chaudhary, 1983; McPhail, 1987). Thus, the professional culture that guides the production of television news in each country reflects in various ways particular compromises and combinations of indigenous and transnational conceptions of how to practice the craft.

Hence, the flow of material from the global television news system to national systems may be filtered or supplemented to reflect local interests and viewpoints. Routinely, as Michael Gurevitch, Mark Levy, and Itzhok Roeh (1991) have pointed out, international events "are shaped and reshaped by television news reporters and producers in ways that make them comprehensible and palatable for domestic audiences" (p. 214). This "domestication" process involves reporting foreign events in terms that are meaningful to domestic audiences, using culturally specific themes and frames of reference that are familiar to viewers. Thus, even with events of global importance where television news audiences in different countries all see the same pictures, "while the images may have global currency, the meanings given to them may not necessarily be shared globally" (p. 214). In addition to routine domestication, there also are more formal and official arrangements that are designed to prevent unwelcome foreign viewpoints in television news stories. For example, in some countries, officials monitor the flow of material into the country, censoring stories, deleting offensive portions of stories, and providing their own interpretations of events (Hudson and Swindel, 1988; Nasser, 1983; Ogan, 1991). Also, several Third World regional news exchanges and satellite news delivery services have been established to provide alternative viewpoints and reduce dependence on Western services (Hester, 1991; Nasser, 1983; Stephens, 1991).

In sum, existing in parallel with the international professional culture of television news are distinct national professional codes of practice that reflect both national and international interests, conventions, and viewpoints. By comparing coverage offered in various countries of the beginning of Desert Storm, it should be possible to gauge the strength and influence of some of these countervailing influences on television news. This is precisely the question that lies at the heart of policy concerns about the globalization of television news.

MANIPULATING THE GLOBAL TELEVISION NEWS SYSTEM: VIDEO FROM THE COMBAT ZONE

In order to determine how successful were the combatants' efforts to influence coverage of the outbreak of the war, we examined video recordings of nightly newscasts during the period of January 17–20, 1991, broadcast by the 20 national television services listed in Table 8.1. The sample of television services presents a fair amount of diversity along dimensions that might be expected to influence each service's overall coverage of the war and use of material taken from the global television news system. Six services represent countries who were members of the U.N. coalition (United Kingdom, France, Germany, Italy, Poland, and Spain), and seven others represent countries that provided economic, humanitarian, or other assistance to the coalition (Japan, Malaysia, South Korea, Sweden, Taiwan, Turkey, and the Soviet Union). Three countries in the sample—India, Jordan, and Malaysia—were more or less supportive of the Iraqi position, although Malaysia also provided assistance to the coalition. Other countries represent intermediate points between the opposing sides. The disproportionately procoalition cast of the sample roughly reflects the structure of support for the Gulf War, when Iraq found few allies in the face of near-global condemnation.

According to the Joint Information Bureau's media rosters for January and

Table 8.1
Nightly Newscasts Examined for Period of January 17–20, 1991

Country	Television Service	News Program
Brazil	TV Globo	Jornal Nacional
Chile	Televisión Nacional	24 Horas
France	France Regions 3 (FR3)	19/20
France	Television Française 1 (TF1)	20 Heures
Germany	Zweites Deutsches Fernsehen (ZDF)	Heute
India	Doordarshan	News (Hindi & English)
Iran	Islamic Republic of Iran Television	Evening News
Israel	Israel Broadcasting Authority	9:00 News
Italy	Radiotelevisione Italiana (RAI–UNO)	Telegiornale
Japan	Nippon Hoso Kyokai (NHK)	7:00 News
Jordan	Jordan Radio & Television	News (Arabic & English)
Malaysia	Sistem Televisyen Malaysia Berhard (TV3)	The News
Poland	Telewizja Polska	The News
South Korea	Korean Broadcasting System (KBS)	Evening News
Spain	Radiotelevision Espanola (TVE)	Telediario
Sweden	Sveriges Television AB	News
Taiwan	Taiwan TV Enterprise, Ltd. (TTV)	The News
Turkey	Turkish Radio Television Corp.	Evening News
United Kingdom	British Broadcasting Corporation	6:00 News
U.S.S.R.	Soviet Television	Vremya

February, ten of the services had representatives in Saudi Arabia during this period: ZDF (Germany), RAI (Italy), NHK (Japan), BBC (United Kingdom), FR3 and TF1 (France), TTV (Taiwan), TV Globo (Brazil), TVE (Spain), and TRT (Turkey). Also present, of course, were crews from CNN, Sky News, Eurovision, and Visnews. The 20 services reflect a mix of ownership arrangements and government control: 5 commercial systems, 8 systems operated by public corporations or agencies, 6 government-operated systems, and one system that operates under a mixed public and commercial ownership arrangement. All 20 systems are linked in various ways to the global television news system.

The January 17–20 period was chosen for analytical purposes in an effort to narrow our focus insofar as possible to coverage of the story of the beginning of the war. This was the period during which demand for video of the action was intense, but sources of such material were most limited. Thus, the period examined displays the global television system at work under conditions that maximize dependence of national systems on external sources of video material. The major events covered during January 17 through 20 were the beginning and continuation of the coalition air campaign, the initiation of Iraqi missile attacks on Israel and Saudi Arabia, the installation of U.S. Patriot antimissile systems in Israel, and the shelling of the oil refinery at Khafji by Iraqi artillery. After January 20, the story of the war rapidly became more complex with the introduction of new themes: captured coalition pilots appearing on Iraqi television on January 21, Kuwaiti oil fields being set afire beginning on January 22, a media visit to a destroyed "baby milk/chemical weapons" facility in Baghdad on January 23, and so on.

Because of space limitations, it is not possible to present here a detailed analysis of all of the coverage offered in our sample of newscasts. Instead, we offer general characterizations illustrated by some representative examples that, we hope, convey a sense of the particular aspects of the coverage that bear on information control and globalization issues.

Coalition Information Management

When the bombing campaign began, the focus of news attention shifted from diplomatic venues to the places where the action was taking place, principally coalition air bases in Saudi Arabia and Bahrain and areas under attack in Iraq and Kuwait. Its global importance was reflected in the fact that the Gulf War was the lead story in every newscast we examined during the period under study, with the single exception of the January 20 evening news from Warsaw, which opened with coverage of anti-Communist demonstrations in Moscow supporting Lithuanian independence before turning to Gulf coverage. The global importance of the war story created in every national service an appetite for information and video of the action.

Each of the major military participants in the U.N. coalition dealt with the press somewhat differently. The British military allowed reporters easier access to operations than did the U.S. military, for example. However, the U.S. Joint Information Bureaus in Riyadh and Dhahran bore primary responsibility for dealing with the vast numbers of news personnel in Saudi Arabia. The United States military public affairs managers used a pool system to restrict television crews' access to coalition air bases and aircraft carriers where strikes against Iraq and Kuwait were being launched. In each pool, a small number of reporters and camera crews were allowed to tape flight operations and interview pilots and other personnel under the supervision of an "escort officer." For example, according to the Operation Desert Storm Media Personnel Locator for February 22, Air Force Pool #4 consisted of two persons from Univision, the Spanish-language television network, and one reporter each from ABC Radio, the *Chicago Tribune*, the Associated Press, the Hearst newspapers, and the Scripps-Howard syndicate. Material produced by television crews in each pool was to be shared with other television services. In this way, a limited, daily supply of video coverage of coalition air operations was made available simultaneously to national television services, video wire services, and international news broadcasters. Because the action on the coalition side during January 17 through 20 was taking place on restricted bases and aircraft carriers, pools effectively were the only source of the action video that the story of the beginning of the war required.

In addition to pool video, television crews were able to produce their own material and to transmit it to their services via satellite, telephone (many services had reporters but not satellite uplink facilities in the Gulf, and so broadcast daily telephone reports from their correspondents), and air transport. Television crews' travel outside Riyadh and Dhahran was greatly restricted, a situation that led to many live "stand-up" reports from journalists on the roof of the Dhahran International Hotel, where most journalists in Dhahran were housed.

To supplement the material television journalists developed independently and in pools, coalition public affairs officers conducted daily briefings for the press at headquarters in Riyadh, organized as a series of briefings presented in turn by the major coalition participants. These briefings received extensive, often live, coverage, and provided a forum for the coalition to present its view of events to the world press. The Riyadh briefings' news value for television news services was enhanced by frequent use of top commanders and officials, as well as video depicting the accuracy of "smart weapons" in the early days of Desert Storm. Daily briefings at the Pentagon offered a second highly publicized forum for presenting official viewpoints and information.

Thus, the coalition strategy for managing the press during the opening days of Desert Storm recognized both the critical importance of video to television news and the enormous appetite for information about developing events. Use of the pool system gave coalition press officers a measure of control over the news video of air operations that was distributed daily throughout the global television news system. Daily briefings in Riyadh, Dhahran, and Washington provided a steady flow of information representing the U.S. and coalition viewpoint.

Notwithstanding, or perhaps confirming, journalists' strident and often-voiced objections to the restrictions of the pool system (e.g., Boot, 1991; Schmeisser, 1991; Small, 1992), the coalition press strategy was generally effective in ensuring a continuous flow to the global television news system of a relatively small collection of video images that showed coalition pilots, leaders, technology, and achievements to best advantage. All 20 of the national systems we examined used this material extensively and without regard to national sentiment in each country toward the coalition's actions. CNN was a major distributor of this material, as it carried many early pool videos in unedited form with no narration and only natural sound; it also covered coalition briefings live. Of course, the pool video and briefings offered only the coalition perspective on developing events, but CNN's early broadcasts of unedited pool video, especially, had a riveting, documentary-like quality. A number of national systems edited the pool material taken from CNN for rebroadcast on their own news programs. Alternatively, many of the systems in our sample retransmitted, in whole or in part, video from story packages that were produced by the BBC, TF1, or other major services and made use both of pool video and pictures obtained by the services' crews in the Gulf. By the time material from pool video had been edited into a story by one service, distributed throughout the global system and picked up by other services, which often did additional editing of the material and always supplied their own narration to accompany the pictures, the identity of the original service sometimes was preserved and sometimes not. In our sample, only the Iranian newscasts consistently superimposed their own graphic over the CNN logo in an apparent effort to conceal the original source of the video.

Excerpts from Riyadh and Pentagon briefings also were used by every television service we examined, although less extensively than pictures of air operations. There was greater variation among the services in use of video from the briefings than in use of scenes of coalition air operations. Elements of the briefings that received the most general coverage on our services were statements of top officials (e.g., U.S. Secretary of Defense Richard Cheney, U.S. Joint Chiefs of Staff Chairman Colin Powell, U.S. General Norman Schwarzkopf) and video of laser- and video-guided "smart weapons" in action.

During the study period, television news crews' opportunities for independent reporting from the scene of the action outside the pool system increased greatly when Iraq began launching SCUD missiles at sites in Israel and Saudi Arabia on the second day of the war. Television crews had access to missile impact sites in Israel and could watch U.S. Patriot antimissile missiles rising to intercept SCUDS over Dhahran and Riyadh. Video from these services was distributed throughout the global television news system and widely used by every national service we examined. During the study period, the SCUD attacks were television news' only opportunity to show combat action as it was happening. Dramatic live coverage from Israel during SCUD alerts was offered by a few networks and picked up and retransmitted either live or on tape by many other services in their newscasts (for example, both TF1 and FR3 carried live feeds from CNN's Jerusalem bureau during their newscasts of January 18).

Iraqi Information Management

Compared to the coalition, the Iraqis pursued a less sophisticated strategy for supporting and shaping television reports of their actions and viewpoint during the study period. Their most aggressive step was taken roughly 12 hours after the bombing began when, on January 17, Iraqi television broadcast a videotaped report showing that Iraqi President Saddam Hussein was uninjured, remained in control, continued to meet with his high command, and was receiving adulation from both his soldiers and from citizens on the streets of Baghdad. In tape shot in his office, he was shown first praying, then seated at his desk making a speech in which he denounced the coalition. This material was taped by CNN and other services and was distributed worldwide. As with early material from Saudi Arabia, every service we examined included this footage in its newscasts, although with varying degrees of editing, mostly to eliminate repetitive scenes and material.

The Iraqis had no equivalent to the daily press briefings in Riyadh and at the Pentagon that received such intense television coverage and wide distribution. Instead, the Iraqi viewpoint was presented in press releases, by announcers in radio and television newscasts, and in broadcasts of speeches by Saddam Hussein. Other than claims about large numbers of coalition aircraft that had been destroyed, these presentations generally had little of the factual content or visual qualities required to make them newsworthy, especially for television news, judged by conventional professional standards. Instead, the presentations often consisted of an Iraqi television announcer "talking head" reading a lengthy statement in which the president called for the Arab nations to support Iraq and vowed that the coalition "enemies of God" would be defeated. Lacking new and appropriate video material, the services we examined often accompanied reports of Iraqi announcements with a few seconds of video of an Iraqi television anchorman reading copy, repeated showings of President Hussein's activities on January 17, or still photographs of him.

Unlike the coalition, the Iraqis were not adept at providing information at the times and of the sort that would secure maximum exposure for their viewpoint. They provided much less information than did the coalition, and the flow of information from the Iraqis was irregular. By expelling the fewer than 30 reporters who remained in Baghdad on day four of the war, the Iraqis greatly reduced their ability to shape coverage of their side of the story. The decision to allow CNN's Peter Arnett to continue to broadcast from Baghdad was, perhaps, an effort to get the Iraqi side of the story out to the world, but reliance on a single reporter operating under widely publicized censorship restrictions amounted to a feeble effort in comparison to the outpouring of news from the coalition side. When only 16 journalists were allowed back into Iraq ten days later, the Iraqis virtually ensured that the trickle of stories from Baghdad into the global news system would be overwhelmed by the stories coming from Saudi Arabia. The reporters who returned to Baghdad faced both crude but not wholly effective censorship and difficult logistical problems, such as the fact that there were only three working civilian telephones in all of Iraq at the time (Debusmann, 1992). Accordingly, across our sample, there was generally less coverage of the Iraqi viewpoint during the study period.

The dominant images from Iraq during this period were scenes of air raids. ABC provided dramatic video of the first night's air raid on Baghdad. The ABC video was distributed throughout the global network and used by every national service. For example, on January 19, Chile's "24 Horas" newscast ran the ABC tape just as it had been broadcast on CNN. Thereafter, until January 20, when the remaining foreign news crews left Baghdad for Jordan, video of raids and destruction in Baghdad were made daily and transmitted from Baghdad and facilities across the border in Amman, Jordan. This dramatic material received general distribution and wide coverage, but it did not present the official Iraqi viewpoint on developing events.

The Global Television News System and National Differences in Coverage

The first days of Desert Storm revealed the efficiency and reach of the global television news system. Every national system we examined used more or less extensive video material from the combat zone. For many services, CNN was the major source of war video. For example, all of the externally acquired video that was identified on ZDF's "Heute" (Germany) newscasts during the first two days of the study period came from CNN. For others, the global exchange and distribution system allowed use of material from a range of major suppliers— NBC, BBC, TF1, and others. The result was that most services' coverage during the study period combined material from a variety of sources. On January 17, for example, the Israeli newscast offered material from CNN, WTN, ITN (Independent Television News in Britain), and CBS, while the Chilean newscast combined video from CNN, TVE (the Spanish television service), TF1 (the first French channel), and OTI (Organizacion de Television Iberoamericana), which supplied edited versions of pool video from Saudi Arabia.

The effectiveness of the coalition's pool system also was quite evident. The television pools provided the only available video of U.S. air operations from coalition bases, from U.S. aircraft carriers, and pictures of cruise missile launches from U.S. warships. The combat video that was available through the global production and distribution system, then, effectively was the pool pictures selected and edited in different ways by different supplier services.

Comparison of coverage from the war zone offered in the nightly newscasts of different national television services during the study period displays the relationship between global and local professional television news values and judgments. Regardless of each country's position on the war and involvement in the conflict, television newsworkers all agreed on the importance of the story. The story was covered everywhere with some effort to report actions and statements of both sides of the conflict, even when that meant resorting to talking-heads stories in the absence of more arresting video from Iraq.

Within the structure of similar patterns of news judgment and coverage, there were important national differences. For the most part, these differences reflected the national sentiment in each country toward the war and the nature of the country's involvement in the conflict, if any. For example, in nations that had little or no involvement in the war, newscasts during the opening days of Desert Storm were more likely to include some stories about matters not related to the conflict, and even sports scores and weather forecasts. Newscasts tended to be devoted entirely to war news in nations that were participating in the action. When national sentiment strongly favored one side or the other in the war, coverage of the favored side usually was somewhat more extensive than coverage of the opposing side, although this relationship was attenuated by the fact that so much more material was available from the coalition side of the conflict than from the Iraqi side. Similarly, the favored side almost invariably was covered first in each thematic story, followed by coverage of the other side. Since every national service had access to virtually the same video material, decisions about how to organize each story (which side to cover first) and how much material to use representing each side's actions and statements, rather than the content of the material, were the clearest reflections of national sentiments. Thus, both global and local elements of news cultures were evident in early war coverage. In terms of video material, every national service we examined reported essentially the same story, but in distinctive local dialects.

National Viewpoints and Constructing the Meaning of Desert Storm

Viewers of the nightly newscasts we examined encountered not merely pictures but, more important, stories with meanings. The video materials alone did not always coincide with the story being told about them. In its January 18 newscast, for example, the Iranian service paired pool video broadcast by CNN depicting air operations in Dhahran and cruise missiles being launched from the U.S.S. *Wisconsin* with narration of events taking place in Turkey. In the great majority of instances in which a newscast offered video material taken from the global distribution system, the local newscast performed at least some editing on the material and supplied its own narration to accompany the pictures. Externally obtained combat video was shaped and woven by each national television service into locally constructed narratives of what was happening, who was doing it, why, with what consequences, and toward what outcome. These narrative elements transformed individual pictures, facts, and statements into meaningful and readily understood stories. In order to understand more fully global similarities and national differences in early coverage of Desert Storm, it is necessary to go beyond the use of video materials distributed through the global system and deal with the meanings which those materials were used to convey in stories. Narrative analysis has proved to be an effective method for comparing at this level how a given story is reported by multiple news services (e.g., Entman, 1991; Nimmo and Combs, 1985).

In an effort to represent some of the differences in how different television services used common materials to construct narratives about the beginning of the war, we offer below brief sketches of the overall narratives presented in the newscasts of four services representing nations that took opposing positions on the war: Jordan, which was perhaps the closest thing to an ally that Iraq had in the war; India, which supported the U.N. resolutions but made strong gestures of support for the Palestinian cause and sympathy for Iraq's plight; Germany, a somewhat reluctant member of the coalition; and the United Kingdom, the second most active military participant in the coalition's air campaign. Space limitations allow only brief characterizations of each narrative, but it is hoped that these characterizations will reveal the general pattern of national differences in narrative construction we found in our sample and the malleable relationship between video and other materials used in news stories, on the one hand, and constructed narratives of the beginning of the war, on the other hand.[1]

Jordan. Jordan Radio and Television's 8:00 (in Arabic) and 10:00 (in English) nightly newscasts during the study period used video material from the global distribution system reflecting coalition and Iraqi viewpoints. The convention of reporting the actions of both sides in the conflict was observed, but within an overall narrative that constructed the war as a tragedy and made clear Jordanian affinity for the Iraqi cause. Both sides of the conflict were condemned for pursuing "the war option" rather than peaceful solutions. The U.N. coalition, and particularly the United States, were represented as having outraged world opinion by attacking Iraq. Extensive coverage was given to antiwar demonstrations taking place in Jordan, Pakistan, Australia, Japan, Indonesia, Bangladesh, and the United States. Local video showed protesters in Amman demanding "an end of attacks on Iraq" and cursing "the United States as the enemy of God and George Bush as a butcher of children" ("News at Ten" Jordan Radio and Television, January 22, 1991).

The coalition's military power was acknowledged, but much was made of indications that coalition bombing was less effective than first reports suggested and of Iraqi claims about civilian casualties and damage to religious sites. Patterns of sources showed comparatively less attention than most other services to statements by coalition leaders and more attention to sources who supported the Iraqi position, such as Iraq's ambassador to Japan (predicting the Americans will find that Vietnam was a "picnic" compared to the war with Iraq) and Pakistan's prime minister (who claimed that the war "benefits only Israel").

Jordanian newscasts gave especially detailed coverage to Iraq's SCUD missile attacks on Saudi Arabia and, particularly, Israel during the study period. The attacks were offered as indications that, despite the power of the coalition, the Iraqis remained formidable and dangerous. By attacking Israel, Saddam's attempts to conflate the Arab cause with his own battle were made to seem credible. Lengthy video segments combined material obtained primarily from CNN and TF1 to show in detail destruction caused by SCUD attacks in Israel, Israelis in shelters and wearing gas masks, victims being taken to hospitals, and the like. Additional lengthy segments depicted Saddam speaking, SCUD missiles in military parades, SCUD capabilities, and so on.

The plight of war refugees arriving in Jordan was also a major topic of coverage. Detailed interviews with refugees in camps on the Jordan-Iraq border depicted conditions in Iraq as the bombing continued.

India's "The News." During the study period, Doordarshan's "The News," a Hindi-language nightly newscast from New Delhi (repeated each night in English), also presented both sides of the conflict, used the standard video materials from coalition and Iraqi sources, but favored the Iraqi viewpoint. This was displayed in the order of each evening's headlines, where news favoring the Iraqis (e.g., "Second Consecutive and Serious Attack on Saudi Arabia by the Iraqis") always preceded news favoring the coalition, and within individual stories, where the Iraqi viewpoint usually preceded the coalition viewpoint (e.g., Iraqi claims about downed coalition aircraft typically preceded coalition denials). Similarly, "The News" frequently used "disdaining" or "deflating" commentary to question the credibility of coalition spokespersons whose statements it reported (e.g., U.S. officials and spokespersons were described as "conceding" and "admitting"). However, Iraqi claims, such as the claim that SCUD missiles fired on Israel and Saudi Arabia "were aimed at selected targets," were more likely to be reported at face value in Doordarshan's stories (for a description of deflating commentary, see Semetko et al., 1991, esp. pp. 71–78).

Standard video material used on every service often was narrated by Doordarshan reporters in ways that redounded to the Iraqi side. Narrating video of the first Iraqi SCUD missile attack on Israel on the newscast of Janaury 19, for example, the Doordarshan reporter noted the attack proves "that the American bombing missions have not been fully successful" and segued to a Palestinian spokesman's description of the attack as "a message for the Israelis" concerning "relieving injustice." Antiwar demonstrations in several countries were described in succeeding newscasts without mention of majority support for the coalition's actions in some of the countries where demonstrations occurred (such as the United States and Britain). In general, Doordarshan's narrative constructed the war initiated by the U.N. coalition as a tragedy fraught with potential for shortages in India and, in an unusual theme, repeatedly emphasized that Indian officials were winning world approval for the leading role they were playing in diplomatic efforts to end the hostilities. As these few examples illustrate, the wealth of video material produced not only in the combat zone but also in capitals around the world allowed Jordanian and Indian nightly newscasters, by selecting and emphasizing certain elements, to observe global conventions such as covering both sides while creating their own narratives that reflected each country's position on the war.

Germany's "Heute." "Heute," the evening newscast of ZDF, Germany's second national television network, devoted most of its attention during the study period to Desert Storm but still covered other subjects as well. About 18 minutes of the 26 1/2-minute newscasts were devoted to the war on January 18 and 19, diminishing thereafter. In every newscast, time was found for events not related to the war, including sports scores, weather forecasts, and "life-style" segments. This conforms to the global judgment of the importance of the war story while also reflecting Germany's limited participation in the coalition during the study period (Germany had a squadron of aircraft stationed at the NATO base at Incirlik, Turkey, but took no part in offensive operations).

Using standard video found on virtually all services, the "Heute" narrative of the beginning of the war strongly reflected the coalition viewpoint, presented in a matter-of-fact style. Coalition pool video, leaders, and briefers were presented at length. Iraqi spokespersons were absent except for the video from Iraqi television showing Saddam Hussein's activities on January 17, described above. Coverage of world opinion concerning the war was limited to that of the United States and the United Kingdom, where stories about antiwar demonstrations were placed carefully in the context of overwhelming majority support for the coalition's actions.

A major theme of war coverage during the study period concerned internal German reaction to the war and whether Germany might be drawn into an offensive role if NATO ally Turkey were attacked by Iraq. Large antiwar demonstrations took place daily within Germany and received extensive nightly coverage on "Heute." Each such story was followed by statements from government officials and political leaders condemning the protesters as misguided and uninformed. Simultaneously, debate about what role Germany ought to play in the coalition was heated and also received detailed coverage. On average, "Heute's" war coverage during the study period was about evenly divided between coverage of these war-related events taking place at home and events occurring in the Gulf.

Thus, "Heute's" narrative mirrored Germany's position on the war not only in its valence, which was slanted decisively to the coalition side, but also in its degree of elaboration. Desert Storm was the top story, but sports competitions, weather, and other subjects continued to receive attention from "Heute." ZDF's nightly newscast, in short, offered the narrative of an indecisive supporter who wished to avoid becoming a participant.

BBC's "Six O'Clock News." The BBC's early evening newscast from London wove lengthy segments of coalition pool video into a romantic narrative of heroism in the face of villainy. In evocative narration to accompany pool video of air operations, BBC reporters described how "Iraq trembled under the hammer blows of Tomahawk cruise missiles, . . . precision weapons of the twenty-first century" and, on January 17, opined that the "stunning results" of the coalition's "lethal aerial armada" had given rise to hope "that the allies could triumph without a war of attrition between the massed armies in the desert." A number of interviews with British and American airmen taken from early pool video displayed the heroism and determination of coalition personnel.

The "Six O'Clock News" constructed the beginning of the war as a morality play, with the enemy personified in the iniquitous figure of Saddam Hussein. Iraqi video of Saddam's activities on the day after the bombing, video that Jordanian and Indian newscasters had pointed to as evidence of the Iraqi leader's resolve and popularity, was dismissed by BBC broadcasters as amateurish propaganda. President Hussein's "long and rambling" televised speech received this review: "Although he castigates America for attacking him, the general reaction around the world has been to blame Saddam Hussein personally for forcing an unwanted war."

Consistent with the developing narrative, "Six O'Clock News" offered numerous coalition leaders and spokespersons, quoted and pictured at length, and relatively few Iraqi spokespersons. Nevertheless, statements from both sides were dutifully reported, although in ways that supported the BBC's morality-play narrative of the war.

"Six O'Clock News" took particular care to construct the role of British leaders and forces in the Gulf vis-à-vis their U.S. counterparts. It was clear that the Americans were in charge, but Prime Minister John Major's continuous consultation with President Bush was invoked as evidence that the British were the unquestioned number-two member of the coalition. Excerpts from pool video that depicted British operations in Bahrain and briefings in Riyadh were used more extensively than on other services, although American operations received the most time in newscasts during the study period. In this way, too, the theme of the importance of British participation as second only to that of the Americans was sustained.

Thus, both the British and German newscasts during the study period reflected the extent of each country's participation in the war. Many of the video materials that were used in the Jordanian and Indian newscasts also appeared in "Heute" and the "Six O'Clock News," but the narratives offered by the latter differed markedly from those of the former. Indeed, the magnitude of the differences among all four narratives provided an indication of the importance of individual national viewpoints and sentiments as a counterpoint to the global professional culture in constructing television news.

CONCLUSION

The findings of our necessarily brief characterization of a large sample of newscasts confirm that television news has indeed become a global system, thanks to satellite technology and the development of a complex network of connections linking together national and international television systems and services. In the opening days of Desert Storm, the efficiency and reach of the global system were well displayed as, worldwide, viewers saw the same pictures of the developing conflict.

Our findings also illustrate how the global television news value culture and individual national sentiments combine to differentiate news narratives in each country. In each service we examined, a more or less common stock of material was woven into a distinctive narrative that both observed global professional conventions (e.g., primacy of video material, need to report both sides of the conflict) and elaborated national sentiments and involvement in the Gulf War. Rather than imposing a single view on national television news services, it seems to be the case that a global culture of television news practice exists side by side with particular national professional cultures, and this combination produced a set of nationally specific narratives of the opening days of Desert Storm that were similar in structure and quite different in substance.

NOTES

An Arnold O. Beckman Research Award to David Swanson from the Research Board of the University of Illinois at Urbana–Champaign funded translation costs, research assistance, and other expenses of this study.

1. For a more detailed analysis of narratives offered by these and other services during the first week of the war, see Swanson and Smith (1993).

9

CNN's Americanization of the Gulf War: An Analysis of Media, Technology, and Storytelling

Lynda Lee Kaid, Roger Myrick, Mike Chanslor, Cynthia Roper, Mark Hovind, and Nikos Trivoulidis

Again I want to emphasize that the study of propaganda must be conducted within the context of the technological society. Propaganda is called upon to solve problems created by technology, to play on maladjustments, and to integrate the individual into a technological world.
—J. Ellul, *Propaganda: The Formation of Men's Attitudes*

The recent Gulf War presents the communication scholar with a unique situation for study for three reasons: (1) it was a relatively self-contained news spectacle, lasting 45 days; (2) it was the first international war story to receive extensive coverage by CNN, the all-news network; and (3) it has been represented as the most technologically advanced war to date. The purpose of this study is to examine how CNN used technology to tell the story of the war, and how it must use technology, given the current historical context, in order to create credibility for itself as a network. The consequence was a war story with a decided bias.

THE TELEVISION NEWS DRAMA

In this chapter we attempt to understand the way in which CNN framed its reporting of the Gulf War. Toward that end, the study provides a detailed content analysis of CNN's nightly report during the Gulf War, with a particular emphasis on changes in coverage during the 45 days of the event. The primary conclusions of this analysis suggest that CNN presented an American view that often focused on the media players and offered disproportionate coverage to telecommunications and military technology.

This study relied on perspectives that focused on dramatistic elements and the construction of meaning in the text of television network news. The dramatistic literature offers a theoretical and methodological account of the storytelling approach network newscasts use to represent the news to an audience by focusing on the elements of topic/theme, character, and conflict. Some studies have limited their focus to individual elements within the news drama, emphasizing (1) the actor/character within the drama (Berkowitz, 1987; Carragee, 1990; Marlier, 1989; Smith, 1989; Zettl, 1989), (2) the way conflict is used to familiarize the audience with a particular perspective (Andersen, 1988; Barton, 1988; Greenberg et al., 1989; Larson, 1986; Lee, 1989; McCormack, 1989; Weaver, 1990), and (3) the representation of topic or theme (Atwater, 1987; Farrell, 1989; Graber, 1990).

Related work has focused on the importance of structural and technological elements of network news as narrative structures that contribute to the way we understand news. Gary Gumpert and Robert Cathcart (1985) maintained that codes and conventions used in television orient viewers to view the "external" world as meaningful only through television structures. For example, media's use of a certain visual grammar to report the news invites the audience to understand the world in visual terms that are often presented without context. D. L. Altheide (1976, 1985; Altheide and Johnson, 1980; Altheide and Snow, 1979) has also contributed to this approach by looking at the ways news becomes news in network broadcasts. To understand this process, Altheide identified a media logic in newscasts that determines what news is included for broadcast. Altheide's "media logic" notion may be exemplified by the media's emphasis on stories that can be told with videotaped visuals, limiting stories to areas where networks have reporters in place. His work represented a pivotal move in the history of dramatistic analysis of network news: the notion that television news constructs a vision of the world that constitutes and is constituted by elements of storytelling, or drama.

The work of E. G. Bormann (1972, 1982; Bormann et al., 1984), which also focused on political visions, can be classified as a predominantly dramatistic approach that relies on concerns similar to Altheide's. Through fantasy theme analysis, Bormann looked at dramatistic and linguistic elements in political texts and identified rhetorical visions common to the media and the audience and the ways these visions come to represent "reality." For example, any news story depends for its meaning on other news stories and audiences' previous experiences. In a similar vein, Dan Nimmo and James E. Combs (1985) provide a systematic and comprehensive examination of dramatistic analysis at work in television news coverage of crisis events. Using both quantitative and qualitative methods, these researchers examined dramatistic elements at work in network coverage of crisis events. They concluded that each network emphasized a particular journalistic style that constituted a mediated vision of reality used by that network. Examples include the differing perspectives of the various networks in their reporting of Jim Jones and the Guyana tragedy in 1978 or the finding that in reporting the 1979 Three Mile Island crisis CBS followed a more "elitist/

factual'' style, while ABC's coverage style was more readily characterized as "populist/ sensationalist" (p. 85).

In this study, dramatistic elements provide the viewer with at least two significant foundational points for our analysis of the Gulf War spectacle: dramatistic elements are used by the media, and they simultaneously *constitute* the media to provide audiences with mediated visions of reality.

MEDIA AND TECHNOLOGY

The relationship between media and technology is of pivotal importance to the Gulf War story. Whereas Vernon R. Wiehe (1986) explored the lack of human concern found in general discussions of technology as it relates to medicine, energy, and communication, many scholars claim that technology in U.S. media implicitly emphasizes a particular worldview or ideology, which explicitly emphasizes technology as universally scientific, progressive, objective, and, therefore, "right" (Bruck and Allen, 1987; Mattelart, 1977). Further, this pervasive view of technology tends to bias the subject matter and content it deals with.

Other analyses that tend to support this finding focus on the audience's experience of technology in the newscast. For example, Ray Funkhouser and Eugene F. Shaw (1990) have explored how technology and television introduce a new experience to the viewer that equates "synthetic" experience with "real" experience. Arthur Kroker (1985) claims that technology and television embody the "real" experience of postmodern culture, alienation, consumption, and diversion from human issues. This literature asserts that not only is technology grounded in an ideological perspective, it identifies itself as a presentation of "real," unmediated and lived experience, when actually the experience exists largely because of technology. In these instances, technology is uncritically transparented to audience assessment; the implication is that such a free ride for technology is to the detriment of audiences' understanding.

Academic assessments of Gulf War reporting have examined the consequences of framing and credibility through technological capability. Jeff Zorn (1991) asserted that certain technological techniques used in reporting the Gulf War story worked to demonize the enemy. Similarly, Barbie Zelizer (1992) focused on the way CNN used technology to assert itself as a credible news source. Tamar Liebes (1992) argued that news sources framed the war with mechanisms favoring the U.S. version of the war story. Finally, Rebecca Carrier and David Swanson (1991) examined the domestication of the war through technology. All concluded that technology strengthened the credibility of media sources and presented the war from an American perspective. How CNN technology may have aided and abetted this outcome is the guiding question of this chapter.

In order to unravel CNN's vision of the Gulf War drama (if indeed there was such a techno-bias), our own research focused on the story as it was told through the dramatistic elements of topic/theme, character, and conflict. Whether these elements acted as a paradigm to make the war understandable, palatable, and ultimately "American" for the audience is explored. When used in conjunction with a technological emphasis, how was CNN able to exceed its role as a disseminator of information and emerge as an active participant in the event? To what extent was the consequence of coverage not information about the war, but a mediated vision of the war?

METHOD

This chapter reports a content analysis of 45 days of CNN coverage of the war in the Gulf. CNN was chosen because it received international attention for its reporting of the war. Specifically, data were videotaped copies of CNN's network coverage of the war in the Gulf beginning with the first official day of the war, January 16, 1991, and ending with the last official day of war, March 1, 1991. Analysis was limited to the 5:00–6:00 P.M. (EST) newscast because CNN used this hour as a summary of the day's events. Consequently, the bulk of information contained during this hour, at least for the time period studied, focused on coverage of the war. CNN provided the videotapes directly to the researchers.

Categories

To facilitate the examination of dramatistic elements, the researchers developed broad, investigative categories that identified storytelling elements at work within the newscasts. Categories included topics, characters, and conflicts. These categories required open-ended responses.

Units of analysis for this research were individual news segments. Researchers defined the news segment as that portion within each newscast which was introduced and concluded by the network anchor (usually in Atlanta or Washington).

Descriptions of the three categories are: (1) *topic* category identified the primary focus of the news segment (for example, "U.S. response to SCUD missile attacks on Israel"); (2) *character* category identified the primary people present and/or talked about in the news segment, including reporters and anchors; and (3) *conflict* category identified opposing ideas, disagreements, or interests present within the news segments (for example, conflict between U.S. media and administration, conflict between advocates for war and advocates for peace).

Coders also categorized the following information: the presence of discussions of media or military technology, the mention or discussion by the media of their presence or participation in the war, and the tone (either negative, positive, or neutral) of the central issues and characters covered in CNN's broadcasts. Researchers coded and timed specifically for source of broadcast, video technology used, and amount of bomber footage.

Coding Procedure

A sample of the coverage was coded to establish intercoder reliability. Using Ole Holsti's formula (Robert North et al., 1963) for intercoder reliability, the overall reliability across all categories averaged +0.81. Intercoder reliability for individual categories ranged from 0.70 for tone of coverage, to 0.85 for mention or discussion by the media of their presence or participation in the war, to 0.90 for discussion of military or telecommunications technology.

Researchers also condensed open-ended data into brief abstracts identifying patterns and themes in the coverage that worked to construct the drama of the war. These abstracts were used to explore whether dramatistic elements telling the story of the war were being used within the newscast. Frequency counts of the open-ended data were used to determine the most predominant categories within the divisions of topic, character, and conflict. Once these categories were established, open-ended data were transferred into them. Based on the categories that emerged, open-ended data were transferred to the categories of topic, character, and conflict. Intercoder reliability for the coding of the topic, conflict, and character categories averaged +0.86.

RESULTS

The content analysis of the 45 days of Gulf War coverage on CNN yielded 636 news segments which dealt with the Gulf War during the 5:00 P.M. daily news. The total amount of time devoted to the Gulf War by CNN during these 45 one-hour time blocs was 105,730 seconds (or over 29.3 hours). The following results concentrate on a description of the topics, characters, conflict, technology, and tone of these 636 segments.

Topics

The main topics of coverage were established by identifying the dominant theme of each news segment. As Table 9.1 shows, "Reactions to the War" was the dominant theme in more segments than any other topic since 17.3 percent of the segments concentrated on this topic. "Reactions to the War" was a category into which coders placed all stories that had as their primary focus citizens' and political elites' responses to the war. An example would be President George Bush's reaction on January 27 to the approaching ground war. The second most frequently covered topic was "Military Action/War Updates" (15.6%). This category included reports on military activities such as troop movements, allied military strength, and weaponry. An example would be war updates given by the anchor on the half hour, covering the day's major military activities. Other recurring topics included "Allied Bombing" (i.e., number of sorties flown); "Diplomacy/Peace Negotiations" (i.e., reports on Soviet peace initiative); and Israel (i.e., SCUD attacks on Israeli targets).

Table 9.1
Dominant Topics in CNN Coverage

Topic	Percentage
Reaction to War	17.3
War Updates/Military Activities	15.6
Diplomacy/Peace Negotiations	11.8
Allied Bombing	11.6
Israel	9.3
Iraq	7.7
Ground War	5.5
Kuwait	5.2
Saudi Arabia	3.1
Allied POWs	2.2
Other	10.7

Characters

As CNN told the story of the war via the topics above, the most dominant characters were the anchors and reporters who were present to cover stories. Over the course of the 636 news segments, there were 648 recurrences of anchors. This high occurrence of anchors indicates that on a number of occasions, both anchors were involved in the reporting of a story. Reporters were equally omnipresent, appearing 544 times. There were 328 military personnel, 224 world leaders, and 133 U.S. officials. World leaders were defined as heads of state, including U.S. and Iraqi presidents, and any non-American government officials, such as ambassadors. U.S. officials included nonmilitary, government representatives, such as Secretary of Defense Dick Cheney. Interestingly, private citizens (203) were more frequently used for CNN than were experts/analysts (118). Experts/analysts were defined as all spokespersons independent of military or government ties.

Conflicts

A critical aspect of dramatistic storytelling is the emphasis on conflicts that are played out during the event being covered. Conflict was defined as the adversarial relationships (opposing ideas or interests) within a news segment.

Table 9.2
Conflicts Present in CNN Coverage (N = 636)

Conflicts	Percentage
Iraq vs. U.N. coalition	24.2
Iraq vs. United States	15.9
Iraq vs. Israel	9.6
Press vs. Censorship	7.7
U. N. Peace Proposal vs. Soviet Peace Proposal	5.3
Disinformation	5.2
Protestors vs. Proponents	4.6
Saddam vs. World Leaders	3.5
Terrorism	3.5
Iraq vs. Environment	3.3
Iraq vs. Kuwait	3.0
Saddam vs. Iraqi People	2.2
Jordan vs. U. N. coalition	1.7
Other	17.0

Conceivably, a single news segment could contain more than one conflict. In CNN's coverage, several types of conflict were apparent. As Table 9.2 shows, the most frequent of these conflicts was, of course, the conflict between Iraq and the allies which was present in 24.2 percent of the news segments. The conflict between Iraq and the United States was present in 15.9 percent of the segments.

Uses of Technology

A key aspect of the CNN coverage was its use of technology to convey the Gulf War story. Over one-fourth of all the news segments (25.6%) discussed some type of military technology. Segments providing detailed information about war technology, its performance, its capabilities, and potential uses were coded under this category. Some examples include a segment on January 21 when, during bomber footage, anchorperson Donna Kelly informed the audience that SLAM stands for "standoff land attack missile." Similarly, on January 28 a computer graphic was used to provide detailed information on the Harriar jet. Another example occurred on February 5, when a discussion of chemical weapons was offered.

Additional emphasis on technology was given to the telecommunications technology used to cover and execute the war. Discussion of such technology was included in 12.3 percent of the segments.

Particularly important was the way in which technology allowed the media themselves to be direct players in the war effort. CNN discussed or mentioned the importance of its own presence on the scene or its role in covering the war story 254 times. For example, the first day of coverage was dominated by audio reports from reporters Bernard Shaw, Peter Arnett, and John Holliman. The hour of coverage included 21 mentions of media presence or participation. An additional example of media participation included mentions of governmental censorship. One example of this occurred on February 11, when before a segment from Arnett, viewers were reminded that he was working under "constraints by Iraqi government officials." A particularly rich source of media insertion in the war was provided via a series of "Press Goes to War" programs that were aired sporadically, usually during the last half of the hour on weekends. These programs featured journalists in question-and-answer discussion formats examining the war and the role of the media in it. The very existence of such programming was a clear indication of the importance the media, and particularly CNN, placed on their own participation in the war.

There was frequent showing of video footage from actual bombing attacks. Such video presentations were present in 47 different segments over the course of the 45 days of CNN coverage.

Although CNN and other news media constantly complained about being forced to rely on the military for information and video "opportunity," the majority of the actual video coverage on CNN during this time span relied on live or taped footage from CNN's own files (1,619 minutes). Much less emphasis was given to "pool video," which came from the media pool established and supervised by the U.S. military in Saudi Arabia (48.5 minutes) or directly from military footage (31.3 minutes). CNN did use 62 minutes of video provided by other sources, including the controversial footage provided by Iraq on U.S. prisoners of war.

Another distinctive aspect of the CNN coverage was the reliance on computer graphics in the CNN program. A total of 409 of the 636 individual news segments made use of such technological devices to supplement and visualize coverage. Such uses of computer technology in these instances included maps highlighting war areas; combinations of graphics and photographs to illustrate such items as quotes from officials; and the use of special graphic boxes to frame anchors, reporters, and interviewees during discussion sessions.

Table 9.3
Tone of CNN Coverage

Subjects	Positive	Negative	Neutral
Iraq (n=457)*	9%	66%	25%
U.S. Military (n=358)*	66	9	25
U.S. Government (n=285)*	54	16	30
Technology (n=218)*	58	12	30
Saudi Arabia (n=140)*	22	14	64
Israel (n=128)*	33	18	49

*Chi-square tests indicated significant difference in tone at $p < 0.000$.

Tone

A final consideration given to the CNN coverage in this project concerned the tone of the coverage of various players and aspects of the war. Table 9.3 provides a summary of the tone (positive, negative, neutral) of the coverage of several major players and war aspects in the various news segments.

It is not surprising that the only topic to receive overwhelmingly negative coverage was Iraq; 66 percent of coverage about Iraq had a negative tone. Israel and Saudi Arabia both received more positive and neutral coverage, although both were treated to some negative commentary. The most positive treatment went to the U.S. military, which received a resoundingly positive treatment (66%) with only a small amount (9%) of negative commentary. The U.S. government was presented almost as well, receiving 54 percent positive treatment, although 16 percent of the segments about the government were negative.

Finally, the CNN coverage gave a substantially positive endorsement of technology itself. When it was mentioned, 58 percent of the mentions about technology were positive, with only 12 percent being negative. Chi-square analyses indicated that the differences in tone were statistically significant for every coverage category examined.

DISCUSSION

Overall the results indicate CNN's coverage of the war was dominated by the characters of anchors and reporters in ways that solidified media involvement and uses of technology and also gave an American view of the conflict. The CNN coverage was particularly consistent in presenting a positive slant on American involvement (militarily, governmentally, and technologically) while vilifying the opposition.

These data provided a descriptive grounding for our dramatistic interpretation of the CNN war coverage which included these basic stories: (1) initiation of the war, (2) SCUD attacks, (3) media coverage, and (4) the ground war. Within each of these phases, three narrative moves, or constructs, were used by CNN to tell the war's story: the Americanization of the war, the media's role in the war, and the use of military and telecommunication technologies in the coverage. The remainder of this discussion will examine how these three constructs worked together to represent a vision of the war.

Initiation of the War: Early Coverage

On January 16 and 17, 1991, the reporting of the war began with a focus on the allied bombing of Iraq and an immediate attempt by CNN to Americanize the war. On these two initial days coders observed the main topic as the allied bombing of Iraq in 21.2 percent of the segments and various responses to the attack in 24.2 percent of the segments.

The majority of responses reported came from the U.S. administration and Israel, who espoused varying degrees of confidence in the U.S. effort. Only one response, from Jordan, came from the opposition to the U.S. attack. Consequently, the responses to the United States's initial bombing were presented as being primarily positive, illustrated by the sheer bulk of time devoted to pro-American response. In fact, coders rated the overall tone of reporting on these first two days as highly pro-American. For instance, as Table 9.4 shows, on these two days coders identified 68 percent of all segments that dealt with Iraq as incorporating a negative tone toward that country, while the American government and the American military were rated as positive 76.2 percent and 81.8 percent, respectively. The journalists, thereby, narratively succeeded in legitimizing the U.S. actions and participated in the construction of a good and evil dichotomy, a dichotomy that recurs and frames subsequent reporting of the war (Liebes, 1992).

A curious move can be detected during the first days of coverage. Within the segments on allied bombings, the most recurring topic present was the journalists' role in the war. CNN and its technology became the primary source of information on the war and, in effect, became the expert on the war. For example, out of the 18 stories coded on January 16, only four of the characters who were identified were not journalists. While some of this self-reflexive focus is understandable, given the fact that CNN had three reporters trapped in Baghdad during the initial allied attack, this intense involvement allowed CNN to establish itself as a significant player in the drama.

Segments featuring CNN's participation in the war included such stories as

Table 9.4
Selected Key Elements During Phases* of CNN Gulf War Coverage

	Initiation Jan.16-17 (n=33)	SCUD Attacks Jan.18-24 (n-103)	Media Coverage Jan.25-29 (n=68)	Ground War Feb.22-Mar. 1 (n=127)
Topics				
Allied Bombing	21.2%	17.5%	11.8%	3.1%
Diplomacy	9.1	3.9	5.9	18.9
Reactions to War	24.2	15.5	30.9	15.0
War Updates	24.2	9.7	11.8	17.3
Characters				
Reporters	81.8	70.9	63.2	59.0
Military Personnel	6.1	31.1	23.5	22.8
World Leaders	18.2	29.1	23.5	17.3
Tone**				
Iraq	(n=25)	(n=75)	(n=46)	(n=96)
Positive	8.0	0.0	13.0	15.6
Negative	68.0	82.7	69.6	58.3
Neutral	24.0	17.3	17.4	26.1
U.S. Military	(n=22)	(n=53)	(n=34)	(n=69)
Positive	72.7	81.2	64.7	66.7
Negative	4.6	5.6	8.8	5.8
Neutral	22.7	13.2	26.5	27.5
U.S. Govt.	(n=22)	(n=57)	(n=30)	(n=58)
Positive	81.8	46.8	56.7	56.9
Negative	4.6	10.6	16.7	20.7
Neutral	13.6	42.6	26.6	20.7
Technology	(n=13)	(n=48)	(n=25)	(n=24)
Positive	69.2	56.2	60.0	50.0
Negative	15.4	16.7	0.0	16.7
Neutral	15.4	27.1	40.0	33.3

*Only news segments which fell into these identified phases are included in this table.
**The n-sizes differ for each variable because the coding for tone was based only on segments in which the particular entity was mentioned.

the dangers faced by journalists in the field, the lack of information available to the press because of military and administrative restrictions, and the assurance of correspondents' safety to relatives. The consequence of this self-reflexive focus on journalists and their technological ability to deliver the war to the audience served to entrench the journalists within the event. More specifically, CNN reporters created roles for themselves as narrators, participants, and experts with respect to the events, referring to themselves or discussing their own presence or participation in covering the war in 48.5 percent of the segments during the initial phases of the conflict.

Finally, either military or telecommunication technology was discussed in 45.4 percent of the segments during CNN's initial coverage. In these technology related stories, 69.2 percent were presented with a positive tone (see Table 9.4). CNN set the stage for its subsequent coverage with a positive spin on technology and with its reporters as integral parts of the story.

Coverage of SCUD Attacks

January 18 through 24 were days grouped together because of the heavy emphasis on SCUD attacks, particularly those aimed at Israel. The media's attempts to Americanize the story of the SCUD attacks became immediately evident. Journalists were supplemented by a barrage of officials. During the early coverage, the military was identified as a central character in 6 percent of the segments; while in the SCUD attack period, the percentage rose to 31 percent (Table 9.4). The percentage for world leaders rose from 18.2 percent to 29.2 percent. While this change occurred early in the coverage of the war, the use of characters here can possibly be interpreted as a dramatic reaction to the SCUD attacks on Israel. The media and the administration seemed to have made use of highly authoritative personae and technology in the segments possibly to solidify the U.S. position as strong and capable, a position that may have been necessary, both in order to pacify Israel and to present an indestructible position domestically and internationally. This strategy also lent further credibility to the media's position.

The images of Iraq and Saddam Hussein, established during the initial coverage of the war, also became reinforced. For instance, when describing the SCUD, CNN claimed that Saddam was using SCUDs against civilian targets. This story carried with it the implication that Saddam was a vengeful murderer. The story segments carried a negative tone toward Iraq 82.7 percent of the time during this second phase of war coverage (Table 9.4).

Coverage of the Media

A dramatic change in focus occurred on January 25. While the efforts to Americanize the war story remained prevalent, CNN now entered with the force of a cavalry. Although the main topics on this day were war updates and reactions to the war, accounting for 43 percent of all stories, the most telling story was CNN's technological reporting of and involvement in the war. The day began with a report on the battle between the press and censors, ranging from Iraqi to U.S. restrictions. By identifying censorship as a central topic, the reporters attempted to maintain their perceived impartial personae and subtly influence or negate the effects of the censorship. For instance, CNN reporter Richard Blystone said, "we want to remind you that an Israeli official was on the scene monitoring everything the reporter said." By so doing, he somewhat undercut the credibility of the information, retained CNN's technological capability, and thus subverted the effects of censorship.

Further evidence of the media's centrality can be seen at the end of this news day during an interview, made possible via satellite, between Bernard Shaw and Iraqi ambassador Al-Shewaish. Shaw took it upon himself to challenge the ambassador's words. The implication was that Shaw was now a U.S. diplomat challenging the Iraqi ambassador's various pronouncements. At this point, CNN's role as participant changed, as it became involved in the war at an administrative level.

After a return to the focus on SCUD attacks on January 26 and 27, CNN switched its emphasis to worldwide responses to Iraqi actions on January 28 and 29, further emphasizing the American perspective. In addition, the mention of telecommunication technology rose from 21.1 percent on January 26 and 27 to 32.4 percent on January 28 and 29, reinforcing the technological capabilities of the media. One of the more interesting events in the media's involvement in the war occurred on January 28, when Peter Arnett interviewed Saddam Hussein. The media's self-entrenchment in the war story was obvious here, but a curious element was added. CNN used the interview as a major story on two successive days of reporting and included in this report the U.S. administration's response to the interview. This event cemented CNN's participant role in the war story. Not only was Arnett interacting with Hussein, something the U.S. administration had difficulty doing, but Arnett's interview was an event significant enough to warrant response from the Pentagon. The interview and the network were treated as war news, rather than a report of the news about the war.

In sum, the findings of this section on CNN's coverage reinforced the previous emphasis on the Americanization of the war. However, with such a strong emphasis on the media and technology during this period, CNN was able to solidify its position as a key player in the war drama and maintain its credibility as a narrator of the war story. As mentioned at the beginning of this chapter, the media must insert themselves as characters in the dramatistic rendering of the war because it is this dramatization that makes the war meaningful for viewers. Moreover, since this was a technological war militarily, CNN's insertion into the war story was also dependent on its ability to represent itself technologically.

Coverage of the Ground War

As the ground war approached, the media used two techniques to reinvent the war story as American. First, there was a heavy emphasis on the general success to date of the allied forces. Second, the media spent a great deal of time discussing the strength of U.S. military technology, with multiple stories on the effectiveness of specific defensive weapons. Reports on technical superiority began to supplant human interest stories (there are few stories about the human element during this period). Perhaps this served to help raise support for a ground war that might have been unpopular if too much emphasis had been placed on the human suffering caused by the war. However, much support can be rallied for a ground war if technology, both military and media, is in place to ensure success.

The final phase of the war spectacle began with the initiation of the allied ground war on February 24, 1991. The ground war signified a crucial and strategic period. Curiously, it was also during this period that the media tended to cut themselves out of the war events: during the early coverage, reporters appeared in 81.8 percent of the segments; during the SCUD phase, the percentage drops to 70.9; and during this final phase, the percentage dropped to 59 (Table 9.4).

The day after the ground war began, the media immediately began to report on U.S. success, Iraqi POWs, and Iraqi withdrawal. The dominant characters were once again anchors and reporters. Since the war's outcome was essentially decided by this time, it appeared safe for the media to once again involve themselves in the war story. Diplomacy became, for the first time, a major topic of coverage, appearing in 18.9 percent of the story segments (Table 9.4). Possibly the "new world order," made possible with Iraqi defeat, must be explained to the viewers and justified as ultimately humanistic. Good (the allies led by the United States) had prevailed and the evil Saddam Hussein had been taught a lesson. This conclusion to the war story has the consequence of creating a sense of catharsis for the media, the U.S. government, and the viewing audience. The dramatistic structure thus allowed for both identification and justification as a consequence of the war story.

CONCLUSION

Ultimately, the media's role in this war was not to question the events "objectively" but, rather, to present those events in such a way that made them understandable, palatable, and ultimately inevitable for the viewing audience. The consequence was a story of the war that asserted American superiority and the indispensability of the media and their technology.

NOTE

The authors would like to express their appreciation to Cindy Chanslor and Agena Farmer for their assistance in the completion of this project.

10

The Persian Gulf War Debate in the U.S. Congress on C-SPAN: An Analysis of Political Communication in a Global Setting

Leonard Shyles and Robert M. Fischbach

That man is . . . a political animal . . . is evident . . . [since] man is the only animal . . . endowed with the gift of speech. And whereas mere voice is but an indication of pleasure or pain, and is therefore found in other animals, . . . the power of speech is intended to set forth the expedient and inexpedient, . . . the just and unjust, . . . and the association of living beings who have this sense makes a family and a state.

—Jowett, *The Politics of Aristotle* (pp. 54–55)

INTRODUCTION AND RATIONALE

As Max Lerner writes, one implication of a still-relevant master idea that emerges from Aristotle's *Politics* is that at each stage in the political development of a nation, there is room for human action and will. "The political material contains . . . the potentials to be made into actuality, but that material must . . . be acted on. If maturity can be hastened and helped, then decay can be foreseen and prevented" (Jowett, 1943, p. 21).

If one adopts Lerner's perspective and combines it with Aristotle's views about the powers of speech to delineate the expedient and the inexpedient, then one presumes that through rational debate of relevant issues and material conditions, it is possible for a nation to forge beneficial policies that can influence its future and enhance its general welfare; that through debate, a nation finds its best means of guiding the ship of state; that through deliberation, a state can determine best what is in its best interest.

This preference for depending on rational deliberation over sheer luck or a talisman in coping with a nation's destiny is perhaps analogous to the preference a passenger aboard ship might have for a captain who uses his glass to avoid rocks and storms on the horizon, thereby preparing a safer course for his vessel, over one who neglects to assess foreseeable conditions and thereby needlessly risks losing his ship to dangers that might otherwise be avoided.

American classic democratic political theory is clearly premised on the view that policies of national interest are best forged not by luck or fate or the edict of a single individual, but by selecting a preferred policy after hearing many voices. A decision on a course of action is reached after open debate and rational analysis of those salient and important issues that can reasonably be brought to light. In theory, at least, America's self-governance is presumed to be significantly enhanced by such activity; her political destiny is believed to be better shaped when guided by broad democratic participation and open consideration of varying viewpoints.

In the United States, and in the rest of the world, possibilities for political participation in the 1990s have been dramatically increased by the recent proliferation and maturation of newly integrated mass communication technologies. Through radio and television, cable and global satellite video transmission, in concert with upgraded telephone and computer services and interfaces (i.e., Fax machines and modems), such technologies have enabled the world's political animals to gain access to a plethora of communication channels featuring news of the political choices of American citizens and of transnational publics.

It is today possible for any household with access to a satellite dish or cable service to watch sessions of the Congress and Senate of the United States on television. Current media configurations permit not only observation of these deliberative bodies but extend access to include interactive capabilities. This means that audience members with a telephone can call public affairs programs to question elected officials and political candidates directly. By so doing, the polity can engage in political dialogue with their leaders and representatives.

In a recent application of such media capabilities, political participation went beyond talk to include direct campaign finance. For example, in the 1992 American presidential primary campaign, former U.S. Governor of California, Jerry Brown, featured an "800" toll-free telephone number for citizens and supporters of Brown's candidacy to call to make campaign contributions. Using this method, Brown was able to carry on a national political campaign for an entire primary season, and found his war chest in the black at the conclusion of his ground-breaking, novel, unique, and remarkable bid.

In addition to cable and satellite television and the new use of telephones in political campaigns, Fax machines and modems have also found increasingly powerful new political applications. For example, these newly integrated fledgling technologies were used to inform global audiences of the events going on inside China during the 1989 Tiananmen Square massacre. In this instance, Fax machines were instrumental in delivering news of political hard-line repression of student street demonstrations to publics that might otherwise have remained in the dark regarding these developments. A domestic instance of the innovative use of new video technology (the camcorder) with powerful political effects was evident in the video of the 1991 beating of Rodney King in Los Angeles which reached worldwide audiences and was widely believed, particularly after the 1992 trial of the assailants, to be a significant contributing factor precipitating the worst case of rioting and civil unrest in U.S. history.

From the perspective of America's political ideology and heritage, the growth of possibilities for political awareness and participation via new telecommunication channels should be welcomed and celebrated. But it is also a cause for concern and deep reflection. The telecommunications technologies throughout the world increase the ability to energize citizens' political participation and fuel growth of democratic political development, as well as growth in awareness of political events generally. But at the same time caution is required as the unintended effects such innovations can bring begin to emerge.

Political information is transmitted to the citizenry via channels that can also be received by global publics, and insofar as U.S. domestic deliberations may be received by unintended audiences, including adversaries, there is a need to consider how such global and instantaneous transmission of political information might affect the content of U.S. domestic political debate about momentous and sensitive issues carried by these new media configurations. And while American citizens increasingly come to depend on mediated telecommunications to stay informed about vital political issues, there is a need also to consider how such publicity shapes the content of political discourse. How aware of ''other publics'' (including adversaries) are U.S. political leaders when they communicate with one another via new media channels about vital political issues? Do political representatives cast their remarks, intended for domestic consumption, for international audiences when it is also known that such speech will be instantaneously transmitted globally? In short, how does carriage impact content? While such issues are nothing new in a free society, the pervasiveness, immediacy, and power of the current telecommunications environment underscore and emphasize these concerns as never before.

The specific interest of this research was the televised deliberation by the Congress and Senate of the resolution to grant President George Bush the right to use military force in the Persian Gulf for the purpose of ejecting Iraq from Kuwait after January 16, 1991. Part of this debate was carried on C-SPAN (Cable–Satellite Public Affairs Network) and featured the political speeches of over 60 senators and representatives.

This chapter provides an analysis of the political communication content of the C-SPAN televised war debate in Congress. There were two objectives: first, to describe the political appeals used to justify each vote in Congress either to oppose or support a military response to Iraq's invasion by the January 16 deadline set by the United Nations; second, to describe the attention paid during the debate to communication concerns by each speaker regarding other publics, media channels, and so on that might have been able to receive the debate on television both inside and outside the United States. Description of these aspects of the debate offered the opportunity to learn which issues were most salient to partisan groups of representatives; it also offered a means of discerning which appeals, if any, were most frequently given in favor of a vote for or against war, as well as a means of identifying those appeals thought to be most persuasive for guiding the ship of state through the dangerous shoals of war. Such analysis should aid in understanding the influence of televised coverage on political deliberations of national and international importance.

RESEARCH QUESTIONS

The questions that guided this research were:

1. What kinds of appeals were used by speakers in the congressional and Senate debates televised on C-SPAN to justify voting either for or against permitting President George Bush to use military force in the Persian Gulf after January 16, 1991?
2. What was the relative emphasis of the appeals in the speeches?
3. What differences in emphasis, if any, were there in the appeals used by speakers favoring versus opposing the use of force? What differences in emphasis, if any, were evident in arguments used by Republicans versus Democrats?
4. What relevant communication channels, audiences, and sources were mentioned most frequently? What differences with regard to these communication variables emerged between Republicans and Democrats, or between those voting for versus against the use of force?

In succeeding analyses, the data in this study were treated not as a sample but as a census.

METHODS

Acquisition and Description of C-SPAN Debate Transcripts

Transcripts of the televised Senate and congressional Gulf War debate on C-SPAN were purchased from the Purdue University Public Affairs Video Archive in December 1991. The study was based on 53 speeches, 41 delivered by Democrats and 12 by Republicans.[1] All Republicans and 6 of the Democrats spoke in favor of supporting the resolution granting the president the authority to use force after the January 16, 1991, deadline. Hence, 18 speakers supported the use of force, and 35 were opposed (all Democrats).

Word count. For this study a word count of each speech was obtained so that fair comparisons could be made among speeches in terms of how frequently different speakers offered arguments and reasons to justify their votes. Since some speeches varied in length (some were only a couple of hundred words; others were several thousand words), raw frequencies were transformed into a rate per thousand words of text.

DEVELOPMENT OF POLITICAL APPEALS CATEGORIES

Upon receipt of the transcripts from the Purdue Archive, speakers' names and party affiliations were masked in all speeches in order to focus on the specific nature of the arguments advanced. In a few instances, the text of a speech contained an occasional reference to the speaker's identity (e.g., "My constituents in Ohio will be watching me as their senior senator") but overall, for the purposes of this analysis, the sources of the arguments were not known to the coders.

OPERATIONAL DEFINITIONS

Political appeals were operationally defined for each speech as the total number of words and phrases *used in the speeches themselves* that constituted explicitly stated and separate reasons given by each speaker to support or oppose the use of force. Communication references were operationally defined as the total number of words and phrases *used in the speeches themselves* that had as their primary focus either *sources*, including individuals, groups, and/or organizations cited by speakers as offering relevant information and testimony about the Persian Gulf crisis; mediated communication *channels*, including telecommunication, broadcast, and print media mentioned as outlets speakers had come to rely on for their deliberations; and potential *audiences*, including explicit mentions of individuals and/or groups from both inside and outside the United States, able to receive live coverage of the congressional war debate. This type of coding is a form of thematic content analysis (Holsti, 1969, p. 116). While this approach is an extremely rich and an almost indispensable method of analysis in research on political discourse, it proved to be an arduous and time-consuming task.

CODING AND RELIABILITY ISSUES

In order to maximize reliability during coding, each of the two investigators independently read a 10 percent subsample of speeches and isolated what each believed to be all discrete reasons favoring or opposing the use of force.[2] This procedure yielded nine political appeals categories that defined and guided the direction of the remainder of this study. It is important to recognize that while subsequent analyses are quantitative in format, a real interest remained to characterize the congressional war debate qualitatively, using the quantitative findings as a guide back to the substantive appeals used by the speakers.

Nine political appeals categories were defined as follows.

CONSTITUENCIES AND NATIONAL INTEREST. In this category went terms with primary focus on the real or perceived nonmilitary interest, concern, and welfare of the American people, including nonmilitary references to economic and social issues, and the well-being of existing alliances (or lack of same).

FAIRNESS IN BURDEN SHARING. Herein went references concerning equitable contribution by all agents of the coalition in meeting coalition objectives (or lack of same).

GLOBAL GOVERNANCE AND ORDER. International and global issues of peace, rule of law, and world order (or lack of same).

GOAL ATTAINMENT. All of the specifically stated objectives set by the coalition and the U.N.–approved resolutions (i.e., reversing Iraq's occupation of Kuwait, depriving Iraq weapons of mass destruction, diminishing Iraq's military capability and threat to the region, etc.) or the failure of such measures.

HISTORICAL PRECEDENCE. Past events, trouble spots, and individuals used to draw distinctions and/or analogies to the Persian Gulf crisis.

HUMAN RIGHTS AND SANCTITY OF LIFE. Justice and fairness in the treatment of nationalities and ethnic groups (or violations of same) and/or references to the intrinsic value of all human life and the moral commitment to preserve it.

LEGAL PRECEDENCE. References to lawful documents and those invoked as such that indicate requirements, procedures, and obligations to be followed by legislative bodies and the president.

NATIONAL SECURITY. References with primary focus on the safety of the nation and its people from aggression (military, terrorist, or other physical threats) by potential enemies or adversaries.

PRUDENCE AND TEMPORAL EXIGENCY. References with primary focus on caution, discretion, choosing a sensible course, commitment to safety, maintenance of flexible options, and references to time constraints, timeliness, and the importance of time as a factor in taking advantage of opportunities.

The final set of communication categories included eight audience categories, five channel categories, and 10 source categories as follows:

Audiences

1. Congressional colleagues

2. Citizens, voters, and constituents

3. Saddam or Iraq

4. Other coalition partners

5. Foreign neutral powers

6. Domestic political elites, excluding the executive branch

7. President Bush and the current administration

8. U.S. troops

Channels

1. Radio, television, or video transmissions
2. Newspapers, magazines, newsletters
3. Postal and telegrams
4. Polls and surveys
5. Other

Sources

1. Prior Senate and congressional speakers
2. Experts and elites, excluding the executive branch
3. Constituents and citizens
4. Troops (U.S. only)
5. President Bush and the executive branch
6. Coalition partners
7. Arab elites outside the coalition, excluding Saddam and Iraq
8. Israel
9. Saddam or Iraq
10. Other

THE RELIABILITY OF CODER JUDGMENTS

Both unitizing and category reliabilities were computed for the two coders' independent judgments during a pilot test using a 15 percent random subsample of speeches following Holsti's recommendations (see Holsti, 1969, p. 140). For unit reliability on the appeals categories the ratio of coding agreements to the total number of coding decisions was 73 percent. Category reliability on the same data was computed to be 0.60 using Scott's pi (Scott, 1955).[3]

RESULTS AND DISCUSSION

The first two research questions dealt with the frequency and emphasis of the appeals in the U.S. congressional debate on the Gulf War as carried on C-SPAN. To answer these questions, the frequencies and rates of political appeals mentioned per thousand words of text were compared for all speeches for all categories and are summarized in Table 10.1. Inspection of Table 10.1 reveals that the most frequently used arguments by all speakers focused on references to prudence and temporal exigencies (22 percent of all arguments). After the prudence category, the categories of goal attainment, concerns of constituents, and references to historical precedence accounted almost equally for an additional

Table 10.1
Distribution of Political Appeals (%) and Rates per Thousand Words of Text (R) by Totality, Party, and Stand for Congressional Gulf War Debate on C-SPAN

	TOTAL	PARTY		STAND	
		Republican	Democrat	For	Against
No. of speeches	53	12	41	18	35
Total word count	77,910	15,767	62,143	21,349	56,561
Overall frequency	1,160	240	920	349	816
Overall rate	14.89	15.22	14.80	16.11	14.43

Categories

	%	R	%	R	%	R	%	R	%	R
Constituencies	15	(2.22)	19	(2.92)	14	(2.04)	15	(2.44)	15	(2.14)

Fairness in burden sharing	6	(0.91)	0	(0.06)	8	(1.13)	1	(0.14)	8	(1.20)
Global governance and order	7	(1.01)	13	(1.90)	5	(0.79)	11	(1.78)	5	(0.72)
Goal attainment	15	(2.23)	23	(3.49)	13	(1.91)	23	(3.70)	12	(1.68)
Historical precedence	14	(2.10)	10	(1.46)	15	(2.27)	14	(2.25)	14	(2.15)
Human rights/ sanctity of life	4	(0.54)	5	(0.76)	3	(0.48)	5	(0.75)	3	(0.46)
Legal precedence	10	(1.54)	1	(0.19)	13	(1.87)	2	(0.23)	14	(2.02)
National security	7	(1.04)	10	(1.59)	6	(0.90)	11	(1.73)	5	(0.78)
Prudence/Temporal Exigency	22	(3.30)	19	(2.85)	23	(3.41)	19	(3.09)	23	(3.38)

44 percent of all arguments. The category of legal precedence was the only other category to account for more than 10 percent of all arguments coded. Table 10.1 also shows that the overall rate of presenting arguments or reasons to support a vote either for or against the use of force was about 15 reasons per thousand words of text.

NATURE OF POLITICAL APPEALS

In general, prudence arguments dealt with the substantive question of whether sanctions were preferable to an early resort to war. Some speakers had not yet become convinced that all nonmilitary options had been tried; they believed diplomacy needed a fuller opportunity to work. Among those favoring sanctions were Senator Bill Bradley (D., N.J.) who articulated his position this way:

A unified sense of national purpose, a strong international coalition, economic sanctions unprecedented in their breadth and impact, enough military force to hold Saddam back, and firm, patient pressure, these were the tools the administration developed to get the Iraqis out of Kuwait. I believe they can work. . . .

I prefer now to strangle Saddam Hussein with economic sanctions which cost less in terms of American lives and dollars than would a massive military invasion that [would] cost thousands of American lives, billions of additional taxpayer dollars, and endangers our long-term vital interests in the region. (January 10, 1991)

In terms of goal attainment, similar concerns revolved around whether sanctions could ultimately convince Saddam to leave Kuwait. Some asserted the view that sanctions had a reasonable chance to succeed, that Saddam had in fact been stopped, and that no one believed Saddam would go farther. Others felt that no matter how powerful, successful, and effective sanctions were, they would never achieve the goal of ejecting Saddam from Kuwait. Eventually, cheating would undermine the embargo; black markets would develop. A smuggling trade through Jordan would foil the coalition. Saddam would then have the time and resources needed to launch a full-scale political propaganda campaign that would quickly undermine the coalition by fomenting Arab hatred against the infidel occupiers from the West. Hence, from this view, letting sanctions work was simply not realistic; therefore a defensive posture would never be enough to achieve policy goals.

Perhaps the most thoroughgoing polemic against the wisdom of extending sanctions was offered by Utah's Senator Orrin Hatch, a conservative Republican, who, in a speech several thousand words long, offered the following rationale in defense of an early resort to force:

Now, have the sanctions failed? Number one, after six months, sanctions have had their day in court, but it's time to recognize the fact that sanctions alone will not force Saddam Hussein to withdraw from Kuwait. They can impoverish Iraq, but they cannot break Hussein's will. Number two, what have the U.N.–sponsored sanctions achieved? They have dealt a serious blow to Iraq. They have cut off 90 to 95 percent of its imports and exports. They have starved Iraq of the hard currency needed to pay for even those goods that can be smuggled into the country. . . .

But what have the sanctions not achieved? They have not at all weakened the Iraqi military forces. Hussein's military has stockpiled spare parts that make up . . . the bulk of the force immune to the effects of sanctions. . . . They are ready for the long haul. But most important, the sanctions have not changed Hussein's mind. A man who accepted the loss of over one million Iraqi troops in a decade of war with Iran will not cave in as a result of higher consumer prices.

[The argument to] give sanctions more time to work I think is fatally flawed. None of its advocates explain how much time. . . . If we wait, we may very well find . . . that the loss of time means even more casualties . . .

If we wait . . . the cost in . . . lives will escalate dramatically. [It] will give Iraq's forces more time to build up the greatest fortified work . . . minefields, fire ditches, dug-in armor, infantry positions with overlapping fields of fire—all designed to channel attacking forces into pre-planned killing zones. . . .

Those who urge us to wait . . . foolishly believe that things can only get worse for Hussein and better for us, but that's not the case. There are any number of scenarios that could undercut the position of the United States, without a shot being fired. We could see sanction-evading foreign firms . . . devise better ways to smuggle the goods that Baghdad wants. . . . We're seeing it now through Iran, through Syria, through Jordan. . . .

. . . more time for sanctions to work, also carries risk. What looks like the safe course of action could quickly become most perilous. (January 10, 1991)

Concern for constituents and national interest was expressed in questions about whether the war option had won the support of the American people, as well as with assessing the additional strain a war with Iraq might have on an already shaky domestic economy (standard of living, budget, job market, tax burden, oil prices, and the obviously creaky overburdened health care system). The cost of war was regarded by many speakers as far worse than the cost of a defensive posture. In short, constituency and national interest concerns were about consensus and cost.

But such concerns also dealt with global credibility. The United States's reputation was on the line all over the world. It stood to lose out if goals were not achieved. If Iraq's aggression were allowed to stand, the United States's global leverage and prestige would falter significantly. Hence, a close connection was drawn between U.S. national interest and world credibility in the debate. Further, it was pointedly argued that the domestic economic survival of the United States was directly tied to the free flow of oil; therefore, denying control of the oil life blood jugular to Saddam was viewed as essential.

From the historical perspective, arguments about what to do often drew from the lessons of past U.S. conflicts, among them the war in Vietnam, Korea, the two world wars, and even the recently ended cold war. Specifically, the lessons of Vietnam underscored the needs to "commit the nation before we commit the troops" and to supply enough force to win if force were to become necessary. Other historical arguments compared Saddam to Hitler. (Saddam had been responsible for gassing his own citizens and had recently fought a long war with Iran that had resulted in over 1 million dead.) The argument was also expressed that the country had adhered to a cold war policy of containment of communism for over four decades; certainly sticking to a policy of sanctions with Iraq for another six months was not unreasonable.

POLITICAL ARGUMENTS: REPUBLICANS VERSUS DEMOCRATS

The third research question concerned how political arguments varied by party and by stand. To determine this, the proportions of the various categories by party and by stand for or against force were computed (see Table 10.1). As Table 10.1 shows, the leading category of appeals for Republicans was that of goal attainment, with 23 percent of all arguments coded, followed by concerns for constituents and temporal exigencies, both with 19 percent of the appeals. These outcomes were lower than those scored for all speeches. The most prominent appeals for Democrats were in the category of temporal and prudence arguments (23 percent of all Democratic appeals). Moreover, Republicans were more concerned with issues of global governance than were Democrats; Republican speakers exceeded that of the population by almost two to one (13 percent of all items coded for Republicans versus only 7 percent for all speeches, and only 5 percent of such appeals for Democrats).

POLITICAL ARGUMENTS: SUPPORTERS VERSUS NONSUPPORTERS

While a great deal of concern for prudence and timing was evident on both sides in dealing with the Persian Gulf crisis, the magnitude of concern does not by itself reflect the substantive difference in the way opposing speakers used such arguments to justify their positions. In general, for those favoring force, the prudence arguments followed several lines: some expressed the view that it was the duty of Congress to back the president (e.g., now is the time to rally 'round the chief; if we abandon the president, we erode his credibility; since the president has already assembled a coalition force behind a spate of U.N. resolutions, there is no turning back; a vote now against force would dismantle what the president has set in motion; now is not the time to change the foreign policy of the U.S. government). Another line took the view that the longer the coalition waited for sanctions to bite, the more time Saddam would have to dig into Kuwait, to fortify his defenses, and erode unanimity and troop strength within the coalition—in short, time was on Saddam's side (e.g., waiting will punish allied troop readiness and morale and will weaken the coalition; the earlier we use force, the fewer the casualties; the longer we wait, the greater the opportunity for Saddam to break apart the delicate coalition; backing down now means we face worse aggression later). Yet another prudence appeal made in favor of force advocated the need to send the proper signal to the enemy (without a deadline, we telegraph that we don't mean what we say; a vote permitting force is the best way to induce Saddam to withdraw, thereby avoiding force altogether; supporting sanctions alone does not realistically consider the mind of Saddam; a vote "for" sounds a certain trumpet). Still other proforce prudence arguments took on a philosophical tone (patience and delay are not always virtues; waiting is historically a bad response to threats; waiting is wishful thinking; sometimes you simply must do what's right; there is no turning back). Finally, some favoring force simply declared that enough was enough (further patience is a copout; the United States and the United Nations have tried all other avenues; without a deadline, nothing will happen; the time is now, not six months from now; the president has gone the extra mile to avoid force; sanctions have had their day in court; force is the only remaining alternative).

By contrast, speakers opposed to force advocated allowing sanctions more time to work to weaken Saddam and the Iraqi army, to soften them up for an easier kill. They reasoned that if force eventually were to become necessary, the coalition would face a weaker enemy who could be ejected from Kuwait more easily after letting sanctions take their toll. Among the most salient of these arguments were those asserting the need to turn to war only as a last resort (we have not yet exhausted all other remedies; other alternatives still exist; we can't yet say we've tried everything; one six-hour meeting of our diplomats with Iraq is by no means exhaustive; U.N. diplomats believe Saddam may be ready to accept a settlement; no one has yet declared that the current strategy has failed; war in just four days is too soon; it is not worth it to sacrifice lives on the altar of impatience; a prowar vote would be justified only after all other means fail; there is no clear rationale for war now; war now would leave the effectiveness of sanctions untested; we have not yet given peace enough chance; a rush to war is imprudent; there is strength in patience; experts said sanctions would take a long time).

Yet another rationale from the perspective of prudence to vote against force entailed the view that time was on the coalition's side (we are in control of events; we have the luxury of time; we face better odds with a weakened enemy— waiting will weaken Saddam). Another line of argument questioned the prudence of the president's shift in policy from a defensive to an offensive posture (from "shield" to "storm"), characterizing the policy change as a fatal, serious mistake, a foolish policy, one that advocated war without contingency plans for the aftermath that might lead to a serious power vacuum in the region. Some called the policy shift premature and unnecessary, one fraught with danger and liabilities far more troublesome than the problems brought by extending sanctions; among the most critical of these speakers were Senator Edward M. Kennedy (D., Mass.), and his nephew, Rep. Joseph P. Kennedy (D., Mass.). In his speech before Congress, Senator Kennedy urged Congress to exercise its responsibility to ensure that "all peaceful options [be] . . . exhausted before resort to war." Said the senator:

There is broad support in Congress for the goals of the United Nations resolution . . . the world has not gone the last mile for peace and we have not reached the last resort of war.

The Secretary General of the United Nations, Perez de Cuellar, will meet with Saddam Hussein on Saturday. President Bush, France, the European Community, Algeria and other Arab nations are still testing avenues for peace. No one knows whether any of these efforts can succeed. No one can predict what moves the unpredictable Saddam Hussein will make. I reject the "good cop/bad cop" theory that the more belligerently the United States threatens war the more likely these other diplomatic initiatives will succeed. In fact, I believe it represents the worst kind of brinksmanship that only makes war more likely. (January 10, 1991)

In a similar vein, the elder Kennedy's nephew concurred with these remarks before the House:

We are told in recent days that now the CIA Director has changed his testimony, that he is now saying that sanctions will work, but they won't force Iraq out of Kuwait. But you know, we heard Secretary Baker and we heard Secretary Cheney the other day tell us that when General Waller told us that the troops would not be ready to fight on January 15th that they were making a mistake—that he was making a mistake because it was his first time before the press, that in fact he was a rooky. In other words, he was telling the truth.

And I would maintain that the CIA Director was telling the truth just three weeks ago when he testified that sanctions would work. Better to achieve our goals by reducing the flow of goods, not increasing the flow of blood, and better to keep talking than start shooting.

There's a misguided machismo mentality in America that says somehow or another this is the John Wayne aspect, this is the way we ought to conduct foreign policy. We ought to be the bully boys. We ought to get out there and be the policeman of the world.

Well, the fact is, folks, if we want to take that battle to every single conflict around this world, this country will not be morally bankrupt, but will be—will be bankrupt economically as well within six months. And it's time for us to question the fundamental policies that George Bush has articulated that mean that he is asking the members of this chamber to commit themselves to war in just four days. (January 11, 1991)

Finally, some invoked the image of the American GI serving in the Gulf in order to stave off votes favoring force (a vote against will show that we are not casual about life; we owe it to our soldiers to support sanctions and show them we won't rush to war; this crisis is not enough reason to die yet).

From the foregoing, it is clear that speakers on both sides were adept at appealing to prudence and temporal arguments in order to justify their votes and that while each side used such appeals extensively, each did so with diametrically opposed objectives. For this reason, it is important to focus not only on the quantitative data but on the content underlying them in order to appreciate the substance of the Gulf War debate. Hence, as was stated earlier, this is one analysis where quantitative results are best used chiefly as a guide back to the content that generated them.

Specifically, legal references were overwhelmingly tied to the constitutional responsibility of Congress to act as a balance or counterweight to the president in executing war policy. Some members of Congress spoke at length about the constitutional provisions designating Congress as the sole legitimate agency of government to declare war. This was because the Bush administration had, only a few days earlier, claimed that it did not need Congress' approval in order to initiate military action. In response to this, Senator Joseph Biden (D., Del., and Chairman of the Senate Judiciary Committee), argued that Congress alone had the legitimate authority to declare war, calling arguments to the contrary by the administration "profoundly misguided and deeply undemocratic" (January 10, 1991). Other such pronouncements included the view that it was not required that the Congress support the president, that U.N. resolutions favoring force had no effect on the constitutional calculus, that the U.N. charter could not grant the president authority to go to war, that only the U.S. Congress could take the United States to war, that President Bush's position on such military authority was "dead wrong," that the Constitution could not be ignored, and that to give the president total discretion would evade constitutional responsibility. In light of this review of constitutional law, the administration's contrary spoken views regarding these matters, and its immediate goal to execute the invasion of Kuwait, it is therefore not surprising that most of the legal arguments articulated were initiated by those opposed to granting President Bush the right to use force.

BURDEN SHARING

Burden-sharing arguments strongly differentiated speakers favoring force from those opposed. Those in favor rarely raised such issues; by contrast, those opposed made much of the fact that Americans stood to shoulder most of the economic and military risk while other nations (especially those with the greatest vital interests in the region) were content to stay on the sidelines and "hold our coats." Angrily, some members of Congress pointed out that if war ensued, 90 percent of the casualties would likely be American. Further, it was argued, American taxpayers would pay for it. In addition, half of our Arab allies had already announced that they would not attack Iraq. Representative Barbara Boxer (D., Calif.) pointedly articulated the burden-sharing issues with a factual report delivered in a direct rhetorical style. Said Boxer:

Let's see if it's the world versus Saddam Hussein. The Netherlands gets 100 percent of its oil from the Persian Gulf, no ground troops; Japan, 63 percent of its oil from the Persian Gulf, no ground troops; Spain, 59 percent of its oil from the Persian Gulf, no ground troops; France, 38 percent . . . 8,400 ground troops; Italy, 36 percent of its oil from there, no ground troops; Australia, 22 percent of its oil, no ground troops; the United Kingdom, 16 percent, 24,000 ground troops; Germany, 11 percent, no ground troops; the US of A, 11 percent of its oil, 300,000 ground troops and a lot of our treasure in budget. Now, are we, as my friend George Miller would say, Uncle Sam or Uncle Sucker? . . . This is wrong for America.

What about our Arab allies? I was in the Persian Gulf. They told me not one of our Arab allies would fight side-by-side with our people in Iraq. Is that fair? Is that right? (January 11, 1991)

Others who were opposed to war argued that we could no longer afford to be the world's policeman; under these conditions, the new world order was more a slogan than real. As Representative William H. Gray III (D., Pa.) questioned aloud, "What about the new coalition? Don't we have partners? Only if we mistake words for deeds. All our combined allies have paid is $4.3 billion toward the $30-billion cost of Desert Shield" (January 11, 1991). It was apparent that the world was "willing to fight to the last American" (January 11, 1991). Most insulting of all, some noted, Saudi and Kuwaiti princes vacationed in seaside resort casinos while American GIs were gambling their lives, hunkered down in the desert. Finally, it was speculated by some that 95 percent of Arab enmity would be directed against the United States and that the economic contribution by our allies (mainly Germany and Japan) to Desert Shield had been "penurious." By contrast, the few speakers favoring force who responded to the burden-sharing issues did so mainly to reassure their opponents. For example, Rep. Ike Skelton (D., Mo.) noted, "there are countries who are benefitting from our efforts who have not given their full measure of support. . . . Should . . . one American be harmed as a result of this crisis, the American people will long remember who stood with us shoulder to shoulder and who was absent" (January 11, 1991).

In summary, the areas of greatest difference between those in favor versus those opposed to force were in the arguments concerning goal attainment (those voting for granting the president the right to use force devoted 23 percent of their arguments to this category versus only 12 percent for those voting against), legal precedence (those in favor of force devoted only 2 percent of all references to issues of legal precedence versus 14 percent for those opposed), and issues of fairness in burden sharing (those in favor of force used this category less than 1 percent of the time, while those opposed invoked such issues in their arguments 8 percent of the time).

Democrats and Republicans also differed in the arguments they made concerning historical precedence and goal attainment. Democrats' speeches devoted 15 percent of their arguments to historical issues, compared to only 10 percent for Republicans'. By contrast, in the area of goal attainment, Republicans outpaced Democrats by a margin of almost two to one. Party differences were also clearly reflected in arguments concerning legal precedence. Republicans expressed arguments in favor of the use of force from the legal perspective only 1 percent of the time, while Democrats voiced legal concerns over 12 percent of the time. In most instances references to legal precedence in Democratic speeches concerned commitment to the view that Congress alone has the legitimate right to issue a declaration of war.

COMMUNICATION VARIABLES

Research question four sought to discern what potential audiences were invoked by U.S. senators and representatives during the C-SPAN war debate, as well as to identify the media channels and sources of information explicitly mentioned by speakers. In coding communication variables, explicit references to: (1) individual sources, (2) mass-media channels, and (3) audience members who could potentially receive the C-SPAN debate were identified.

For unit reliability of the communication categories, the ratio of coding agreements to the total number of coding decisions was 71 percent. Category reliability on the same data was 0.61, using Scott's pi. As with the political construct, after coding, the analysts resolved all remaining discrepancies via discussion, debate, and mutual agreement. This additional step was deemed necessary in order to ensure that a thorough and acceptable analysis was performed for all speeches.

AUDIENCES

As Table 10.2 shows, within the communication component of audiences, the greatest share of such references was devoted to colleagues; (speakers mentioned colleagues 47 percent of the time).[4] Most often, audience references to colleagues were as follows: "the gentleman from California"; "I arise in support of my colleague from Indiana, to whom I say"; "I suggest each and every one of us"; "you who advocate that course"; "my friend"; "those in the minority"; "I say to the leadership on both sides"; "I urge my colleagues"; "as the Senator will recall." The next greatest share of audience references was to Saddam Hussein (22 percent), followed by references to President Bush, with 12 percent (these included references like "the message we send to the White House"; "the President's staff").

It is interesting that while most of the explicit audience references were to other senators and representatives (indicating that people in Congress do a lot of talking to themselves), the next most salient (intended) audience for these speakers was that of the enemy himself, Saddam Hussein. These references repeatedly included phrases like the following: "Our vote will send a clear message to Saddam"; "Saddam will understand that we mean business"; "This vote lets him know"; "The primary message coming from the Congress today is to Saddam Hussein." One speaker, Senator John Glenn (D., Ohio), warned Saddam not to misinterpret the bipartisan debate in Congress, with these words: "We're told that Saddam Hussein quite often watches American television, so perhaps our remarks here today should be tailored directly to the camera and hope that it gets on the international TV and sends a message directly to Saddam Hussein: do not misread this debate" (January 11, 1991). This suggests that members of the C-SPAN–televised Congress are aware of being available to transnational publics, a condition that opens the possibility that they tailor their

Table 10.2

Distribution of Communication References (%) and Rates per Thousand Words of Text (R) for Three Components of Communication by Totality, Party, and Stand for Congressional Gulf War Debate on C-SPAN

	TOTAL	PARTY		STAND	
		Republican	Democrat	For	Against
Number of speeches	53	12	41	18	35
WordCount	77,910	15,767	62,143	21,349	56,561
Overall communication (reference frequency,rate)	422(5.42)	94(5.96)	328(5.28)	110(5.15)	312(5.52)
Audience Component					
Reference Frequency/Rate	117(1.50)	41(2.60)	76(1.22)	51(2.39)	66(1.17)
Percentage of Overall	28	44	23	46	21

Categories	%	R	%	R	%	R	%	R	%	R
Colleagues	47	(.71)	42	(1.08)	50	(.61)	37	(.89)	55	(.64)
Citizens/voters/constituents	8	(.12)	2	(.06)	11	(.13)	4	(.09)	11	(.12)
Saddam/Iraq	22	(.33)	29	(.76)	18	(.23)	33	(.80)	14	(.16)
Coalition partners	5	(.08)	0	(0)	8	(.10)	2	(.05)	8	(.09)
Neutral foreign audiences	1	(0)	2	(.06)	0	(0)	2	(.05)	0	(0)
Political elites (excluding executive branch)	2	(.03)	2	(.06)	1	(.02)	2	(.05)	2	(.02)
Bush administration	12	(.18)	20	(.51)	8	(.10)	16	(.37)	9	(.11)
U.S. troops	3	(.05)	2	(.06)	4	(.05)	4	(.09)	3	(.04)

Table 10.2 (continued)

179

Table 10.2 (continued)

<u>Channel Component</u> (Reference frequency,rate)	42 (.05)		6 (.38)		36 (.58)		8 (.37)		34 (.60)	
Percentage of Overall	10		6		11		7		11	
Categories	%	R	%	R	%	R	%	R	%	R
Radio/TV/Video	33	(.18)	50	(.19)	31	(.18)	50	(.19)	29	(.18)
Newspapers/magazines/ newsletters	12	(.06)	17	(.06)	11	(.06)	13	(.05)	12	(.07)
Postal/Telegram	29	(.15)	17	(.06)	31	(.18)	25	(.09)	29	(.18)
Polls/Surveys	14	(.08)	17	(.06)	14	(.08)	13	(.05)	15	(.09)
Other	12	(.06)	0	(0)	14	(.08)	0	(0)	15	(.09)
<u>Source Component</u> (Reference frequency,rate)	263	(3.38)	47	(2.98)	216	(3.48)	51	(2.39)	212	(3.75)

Percentage of Overall	62		50		66		46		68	
Categories	%	R	%	R	%	R	%	R	%	R
Colleagues	31	(1.04)	43	(1.27)	28	(.98)	45	(1.08)	27	(1.03)
Experts (excluding executive branch)	26	(.86)	23	(.70)	26	(.90)	22	(.51)	26	(.99)
Constituents	7	(.24)	4	(.13)	8	(.27)	6	(.14)	8	(.28)
U.S. troops	4	(.24)	9	(.26)	3	(.11)	8	(.19)	3	(.12)
Bush administration	21	(.69)	11	(.32)	23	(.79)	10	(.23)	23	(.87)
Coalition partners	5	(.18)	2	(.06)	6	(.21)	2	(.05)	6	(.23)
Neutral Arab Nations	1	(.04)	0	(0)	1	(.05)	0	(0)	1	(.05)
Saddam/Iraq	1	(.04)	0	(0)	1	(.05)	0	(0)	1	(.05)
Israel	1	(.03)	2	(.06)	1	(.02)	2	(.05)	1	(.05)
Other	3	(.10)	6	(.19)	2	(.08)	6	(.14)	2	(.09)

remarks to such audiences. In fact, the proportion of mentions of Saddam as an audience member was far greater than that scored for citizens (voters, constituents), and coalition partners combined (8 percent and 5 percent respectively, versus 22 percent for Saddam). Such an outcome is striking because it accrues from speakers' references both about, as well as to, Saddam, indicating their awareness (or desire) that Saddam might receive their statements as they were being uttered.

CHANNELS

As for the communication component devoted to channels, one-third of all such references were to radio, television, and other video transmissions, while an additional 29 percent referred to postal services. This outcome suggests that letters, postcards, and telegrams still seem to be a popular way for constituents to communicate with members of Congress.

References to polls and surveys accounted for 14 percent of all channel references by these elected representatives. The categories of newspapers and other print media, and "other" each accounted for 12 percent of mentions.[5]

SOURCES

As for the source component, Table 10.2 shows that over 30 percent of the time, speakers cited one another (i.e., "subcommittee findings") when presenting reasons to support their votes, while over a quarter of all source references were to experts outside the Bush administration (i.e., seven of eight former secretaries of state, the Congressional Budget Office, the Government Accounting Office, a foreign official, the Pentagon, eminent Constitutional scholars, former secretaries of defense, former national security advisors, the CIA director). Further, just over a fifth of all source references were to the president's office (the president himself, or members of the president's cabinet, e.g., the secretary of state). Constituents were cited as sources of information or influence only 7 percent of the time, and coalition partners were cited only 5 percent of the time. It is important to recognize that overall, senators and congressmen in these debates cited sources far more frequently than they did audiences or channels in articulating their views. As a percentage of all communication references, source variables accounted for 62 percent of all mentions, while channels received only 10 percent, and audiences received 28 percent. This finding suggests that even though senators and representatives were aware that they were carried live via satellite television (perhaps globally) and were potentially being received beyond their colleagues and constituents by international audiences, including enemies, they still devoted most of their attention to justifying their positions and citing authoritative and relevant sources to support their views rather than to acknowledging the diverse audiences they may have been reaching.

In summary, the most salient communication components included audiences of congressional colleagues, Saddam Hussein, and President Bush and his admin-istration; further, the channels mentioned most frequently included those of the broadcast media and the postal services, while the most salient sources included colleagues, experts outside the Bush administration, and the president and other members of his administration. Finally, in comparing the results of Table 10.2 with those of Table 10.1, the overall rate of mentioning communication channels, audiences, or sources was only 5.4 times per 1,000 words of text, or about one-third as often as the rate that accrued for presenting arguments either supporting or opposing force. This outcome suggests that even when congressional speakers were aware that they were being televised, they still focused most of their attention on the substantive issues at hand rather than being inordinately attracted by the presence of the media or the audiences the media might reach.

COMMUNICATION COMPONENTS BY PARTY AND STAND

An additional concern of this research was to determine whether Republicans and Democrats communicated differently during these debates. Did those voting for versus against the use of force communicate differently?

AUDIENCES

Both Republicans and Democrats directed the greatest proportion of their audience references to their own colleagues (Democrats, 50 percent and Repub-licans, 42 percent). Republicans focused 29 percent of their audience references to Saddam and Iraq, while Democrats devoted 18 percent. A stark contrast between Republicans and Democrats was observed in the audience category of President Bush and the administration. Republicans devoted one-fifth of all references to the president, while Democrats referred to the president only 8 percent of the time. This suggests that Republican speakers may have been more attentive to the administration's wishes regarding the outcome of the debate than were Democrats among all C-SPAN speakers—either that or Republicans were simply invoking their leader. On the other hand, there seemed to have been a greater acknowledgment by Democrats than Republicans of the audiences of citizens, voters, constituents, and coalition partners during the debate (11 percent and 8 percent for Democrats' references to citizens and partners versus 2 percent and 0 percent by Republicans, respectively).

Among speakers in favor of force, 30 percent of all audience references were to Saddam, while only 14 percent of such references were made by speakers opposed. Among speakers opposed, 55 percent of all audience references were to colleagues, with another 11 percent devoted to citizens. By contrast, among speakers favoring force, attention to citizens was relatively low. In summary, speakers in favor of force addressed the potential audience of Saddam and President Bush noticeably more than did those opposed, who were more attentive to coalition partners, citizens, and colleagues.

CHANNELS

With respect to channel references, differences between Republicans and Democrats and between those in favor versus those opposed to force were observed. The biggest differences appeared to be within the category of radio and video transmissions (50 percent of all references in Republican speeches versus only 31 percent for Democrats). On the other hand, Democrats seemed to be more involved with receiving postal messages from constituents than were Republicans (references to mail channels were recorded for Democrats over 30 percent of the time versus only 17 percent for Republicans). Of course, this disparity diminishes when postal references are compared between those in favor versus those opposed to force; however the small raw frequency of channel references for Republicans must temper these results.

SOURCES

For both Republicans and Democrats, the greatest share of source references was to colleagues; 43 percent of all sources cited in Republican speeches were to colleagues, while only 28 percent of such references were found in the speeches delivered by Democrats. By contrast, Republicans and Democrats tended to invoke experts outside the executive branch of government about equally. But with respect to sources within the administration, Democrats cited the president and others in the executive branch 23 percent of the time, while Republicans invoked such sources less than half as often (only 11 percent of the time). This outcome is interesting because it seems counterintuitive—that is, one might expect that since the president was asking for permission to use force, it would be natural for his partisans to cite him more often than his opponents would. Why then did the reverse occur? This may be explained by the fact that much of the president's own rhetoric and actions immediately prior to the adoption of a war policy (i.e., doubling troop strength to 430,000 U.S. troops to mount a credible military threat while clearing the way to use it through lobbying the United Nations to pass the necessary resolutions) were explicitly committed to a desert shield policy of sanctions, international embargo, and containment of Saddam. When Democrats cited the president, it was in order to highlight his own commitment to a defensive strategy, the purpose of which was to defend Saudi Arabia and to isolate Saddam Hussein. Hence, what the speakers opposed to force were doing was throwing the president's own "shield" rhetoric back in his face in order to postpone the transition to war. This outcome suggests that the Persian Gulf war debate in Congress was partisan even when it invoked the president's own language.

Those favoring force invoked colleagues 45 percent of the time, while those opposed mentioned colleagues just over 25 percent of the time. It is again apparent that a great disparity in citing the president and the executive branch exists between those favoring versus those opposing the use of force (23 percent among those against force versus 10 percent among those in favor). This outcome further underscores the rhetorical strategy among members of Congress opposed to war who used the president's own language favoring an embargo and sanctions to force Saddam to withdraw from Kuwait, in order to press for a nonmilitary solution to the Persian Gulf crisis.

CONCLUDING REMARKS, LIMITATIONS, AND FUTURE DIRECTIONS

The complexity and scope of the Gulf War debate in Congress televised on C-SPAN challenges even the most astute observer of political communication to assess the forces and motives that shaped it from multiple perspectives. This research offered a unique opportunity to begin studying mass-mediated war deliberations in a systematic way. One objective accomplished by this analysis was to provide a condensed but detailed picture of the debate itself; such description constitutes an essential step toward understanding the reasons that featured speakers voted the way they did.

It was interesting that speakers with diametrically opposed viewpoints appealed roughly equally to time and prudence arguments in order to support their votes, thus demonstrating how the same arguments may be used to support contrary policies in matters of war and peace, life and death. However, while both sides frequently used similar appeals for contrary purposes, some appeals were unique to a particular side. Speakers opposed to force invoked the most burden-sharing arguments, angrily accusing coalition partners of shirking their responsibilities. By contrast, speakers favoring force refrained from criticizing allies, opting instead to treat them with relative decorum, diplomacy, and respect, placidly ignoring disparities among coalition members in shouldering economic and military burdens. Further, those favoring force tended to direct more of their speech toward Saddam and Iraq, while those favoring sanctions seemed more attentive to coalition partners and constituents.

The complexities of the Gulf War debate make it difficult for an analysis such as this to exhaust the full significance of all the issues. The limitations of the present study stem from both the breadth of the subject and the methods employed to study it. For example, relying solely on explicit mentions of particular audience members in order to arrive at an accurate measure of speakers' intentions regarding them is by itself not valid—what must be considered in tandem with such measures is the context of those references within the overall debate and other situational factors (both historical and immediate) that gave them meaning. In short, motives that shape language are not necessarily reflected in language. Further, the total number of mentions of some audiences, sources, and channels was at times small, and that made inference difficult.

From a substantive standpoint, this study did not compare other war deliberations with those of the Persian Gulf crisis. Such analysis is warranted, however, from a number of perspectives, and the current study could serve as a baseline and reference point for such research. Future research might also look at the influence of speakers' party, age, years in elective office, and other factors, on the decision to vote for war. A review of the vote overall by party reveals that among Republicans, 204 voted in favor of force and 4 voted against, while among Democrats, 96 voted in favor of force, and 224 voted against (Barone and Ujifusa, 1991, pp. 1477–1483). Clearly the votes, as well as the debate, were highly partisan; hence it is not surprising that C-SPAN speakers often warned Saddam against taking comfort in any discord he might have witnessed on television. It is also noteworthy that most of the Democrats who voted with Republicans in favor of force were from southern states—such findings raise interesting questions for follow-up studies. The present study, in attempting to place rational order on political judgment, underscores the Persian Gulf war debate as a prime source for communication scholars and others interested in discovering more about how language interacts with global media to influence human behavior. As a topic, the Persian Gulf War will likely remain a dynamic tapestry of richly textured material worthy of research and political analysis well into the twenty-first century.

NOTES

1. The original data set included 63 speeches, from which a 10 percent random sub-sample was used for category development of the key political and communication variables of interest in this study. These 6 speeches were subsequently dropped from the analysis. In addition, 2 speeches were not identified with respect to who delivered them, and data from 2 others were lost during the coding process. This resulted in a data set consisting of nearly 80,000 words of text.

2. The procedures followed the principles that if either coder had any doubts about including an item, it was better at this stage to include the term for further consideration rather than to reject it.

After discussion and debate between the researchers, following the coding, a set of nine purportedly mutually exclusive and exhaustive political appeals categories was created. These categories were then pilot tested on a new 15 percent random subsample of speeches to assure that they did indeed adequately exhaust the various reasons offered to support or oppose the use of force. The communication variables were treated in a like manner.

3. Here it is worth noting that, theoretically, for nine categories used with equal frequency, the proportion of agreement between two coders by pure chance alone would be about 0.11. Scott's pi is a conservative index of reliability in that it corrects not only for the number of categories in a category set but also for the probable frequency with which each is used. It was decided that coding for all documents could go forward, but that after the initial stage of independent coding, the coders would then meet to resolve all remaining discrepancies by discussion, debate, and mutual agreement. This second step was deemed necessary in order to ensure that a thorough and acceptable analysis was performed for all speeches.

4. It was agreed that these references would not include protocol mentions of the type

"Thank you, Mr. Speaker" during opening remarks but would include such references later in a speech.

5. "Other" was used to code channel references that were not specifically identified. With regard to polls and surveys, it is acknowledged that while they may have come to the attention of a senator or representative via separate media channels (and therefore may not in themselves be considered traditional "channels" per se), it was not always clear from the speeches how such information was acquired—hence, these results should be tempered accordingly.

Bibliography

Abend zeitung. (1991, January 19). München, Germany.

Adkin, M. (1989). *Urgent fury, the battle for Grenada*. Lexington, MA: Lexington Books.

Adler, B. (1991). *The generals, the new American heroes*. New York: Avon Books.

Akher Saa. (1991, January 23). Cairo, Egypt.

Alter, J. (1991, February 11). Does bloody footage lose wars? *Newsweek*, p. 38.

Altheide, D. L. (1976). *Creating reality: How TV news distorts events*. Beverly Hills: Sage.

Altheide, D. L. (1985). *Media power*. Beverly Hills: Sage.

Altheide, D. L., and Johnson, J. M. (1980). *Bureaucratic propaganda*. Boston: Allyn and Bacon.

Altheide, D. L., and Snow, R. P. (1979). *Media logic*. Beverly Hills: Sage.

Andersen, R. (1988). Visions of instability: U.S. television's law and order news of El Salvador. *Media, Culture, and Society, 10*, pp. 239–264.

Anderson, D. A. (1983). The origins of the press clause. *UCLA Law Review, 30*, pp. 455–541.

Andrews, P. (1991, July/August). The media and the military. *American Heritage, 24*(4), p. 82.

al-Anwar. (1991, January 21). Beirut, Lebanon.

Apple, R. W., Jr. (1991, February 4). Press and military, old suspicions. *New York Times*.

Arabic broadcasts from London. (1938, January 13). *Great Britain and the East*.

Atwater, T. (1987). Network evening news coverage of the TWA hostage crisis. *Journalism Quarterly, 64*, pp. 520–525.

Back up the bombing boasts. (1991, January 23). *New York Times*, p. A18.

Baker, B. (1991, August). Last One in the Pool. . . . *U.S. Naval Institute Proceedings*, pp. 71–72.

Barone, M., and Ujifusa, G. (Eds.). (1991). *The almanac of American politics, 1992*. Washington, DC: National Journal.

Barton, R. L. (1988). Television news and the language of the acid rain in Canadian-American relations. *Political Communication and Persuasion, 5* (1), pp. 49–65.

Berelson, B. (1948). Communications and public opinion. In S. Schramm (Ed.), *Communications in modern society*. Urbana: University of Illinois Press.

Berkowitz, D. (1987). Television news sources and news channels: A study in agenda building. *Journalism Quarterly, 64*, pp. 508–513.

Birnbaum, J. (1991, March 11). A new breed of brass. *Time*, p. 58.

Black, I. (1991, September 2). The border of decision. *Guardian Weekly*, p. 8.

Blasi, V. (1977). The checking value in first amendment theory. *American Bar Foundation Research*, pp. 521–558.

Blood, R. W. (1991, May). *Public reaction in Australia to the media and the war*. Paper presented at the annual meeting of the International Communication Association, Chicago.

Boot, W. (1991, March/April). Covering the Gulf war: The press stands alone. *Columbia Journalism Review*, pp. 23–24.

Bormann, E. G. (1972). Fantasy and rhetorical vision: The rhetorical criticism of social reality. *Quarterly Journal of Speech, 58*, pp. 396–407.

Bormann, E. G. (1982). Fantasy and rhetorical vision: Ten years later. *Quarterly Journal of Speech, 68*, pp. 288–305.

Bormann, E. G., Kroll, B. S., Watters, K., and McFarland, D. (1984). Rhetorical visions of committed voters: Fantasy theme analysis of a large sample survey. *Critical Studies in Mass Communication, 1*, pp. 287–310.

Boyd, D. A. (1982). *Broadcasting in the Arab world: A survey of radio and television in the Middle East*. Philadelphia: Temple University Press.

Boyd, D. A. (1992, March). *International broadcasting to the Middle East in Arabic: A survey of broadcasters, motivators, and audiences*. Paper presented at the Challenge for International Broadcasting and Audience Research II, Quebec City, Canada.

Braestrup, P. (1985). *Battle lines*. New York: Priority Press.

Braestrop, P. (1991, February 11). Censored. *The New Republic*, pp. 16–17.

British Broadcasting Corporation. (1990a). *Crisis listening in the UAE & Egypt*. London: International Broadcasting and Audience Research.

British Broadcasting Corporation. (1990b). *Crisis listening in Amman*. London: International Broadcasting and Audience Research.

British Broadcasting Corporation. (1991a, February). *The BBC in Syria: Survey in Damascus & Aleppo during the Gulf war*. London: International Broadcasting and Audience Research.

British Broadcasting Corporation. (1991b). *The BBC in Egypt: Group discussions in Cairo*. London: International Broadcasting and Audience Research.

British Broadcasting Corporation. (1991c, June). *World radio & television receivers*. London: International Broadcasting and Audience Research.

Bruck, P., and Allan, S. (1987). The commodification of social relations: Television news and social intervention. *Journal of Communication Inquiry, 11*, pp. 79–86.

Brunner, E. deS. (1953). Rural communications behavior and attitudes in the Middle East. *Rural Sociology, 18*, pp. 149–155.

Bryan, C.D.B. (1976). *Friendly fire*. New York: G. P. Putnam & Sons.

Bryan, C.D.B. (1991, March 11). Operation desert Norm, getting to know the general. *New Republic*, p. 24.

Calling a truce. (1991, April 1). *Newsweek*.

Calloway, C. J., and Kenn, P. (1992, September). Organizing for fast response. Fordham University Graduate School of Business Administration Working Paper.

Carragee, K. M. (1990). Defining solidarity: Themes and omissions in coverage of the Solidarity Trade Union movement by ABC news. *Journalism Monographs*, p. 119.

Carrier, R., and Swanson, D. (1991). *International television coverage of the Gulf war: Some preliminary observations*. Paper presented at the meeting of the Speech Communication Association, Atlanta.

Censoring for political security. (1991, March). *Washington Journalism Review*.

Chancellor, J. (1991, February 1). Censorship doesn't honor our dead. *Newsday*, p. 17.

Chiaventone, F. J. (1991, August). Ethics and responsibility in broadcasting. *Military Review: The Professional Journal of the United States Army*.

Clark, K. R. (1991, October 7). A gift of satellite technology: Instant war. *Broadcast News*.

Cohen, A. (1990). *Between news and reality: Differential perceptions of the war*. Paper presented at the meeting of the International Communication Association, Chicago.

Cohen, A. A., Adoni, H., and Bantz, C. R. (1990). *Social conflict and television news*. Newbury Park, CA: Sage.

Cohen, A. A., Brog, A., Cheffer, C., Paz, U., Raviv, T., and Witztum, E. (1992, Spring). *Israelis in the sealed rooms: Mental health and the mass media during the Gulf war*. Paper presented at the ICA conference, Miami.

Coleman, T. L., Jr. (1989). *The news media: Should they play a role in crisis management?* Carlisle Barracks, PA: U.S. Army War College.

Collins, T. (1991, September 30). Envying despots who control the media. *Newsday*.

Commission on the Freedom of the Press. (1947). *A free and responsible press*. Chicago: University of Chicago Press.

Committee on Governmental Affairs. (1991, February 20). Hearing on *Pentagon rules on media access to the Persian Gulf war*. U.S. Senate, 102nd Congress, 1st sess.

Cooke, A. (Circa 1973). Letters from America. A personal choice by Cooke from a weekly BBC broadcast, audiotape; from author's collection.

Correspondents protest pool system. (1991, February 12). *New York Times*.

Corry, J. (1991). TV news & the neutrality principle. *Commentary*, *91* (5), pp. 24–27.

Courtright, J., McLeod, D., Perse, E., and Signorielli, N. (1990, Spring). *The role of the media in the Persian Gulf war*. Paper presented at the meeting of the International Communication Association, Chicago.

Creel, George. (1920). *How we advertised America*. New York: Harper & Row.

La Croix. (1991, January 26). Paris, France.

La Crónica de León. (1991, January 18). León, Spain.

Daugherty, W. E. (1958a). The creed of a modern propagandist. In W. E. Daugherty and M. Janowitz (Eds.), *A psychological warfare casebook* (pp. 35–46). Baltimore, MD: Johns Hopkins University Press.

Daugherty, W. E. (1958b). Bomb warnings to friendly and enemy civilian targets. In

W. E. Daugherty and M. Janowitz (Eds.), *A psychological warfare casebook* (pp. 359–362). Baltimore, MD: Johns Hopkins University Press.

Daugherty, W. E., and Janowitz, M. (1958c). *A psychological warfare casebook*. Baltimore, MD: Johns Hopkins University Press.

Debusmann, B. (1992, August 6). *Problems of information in time of war*. Lecture presented at *The present and future of political communication*, seminar sponsored by the Universidad Completense de Madrid, El Escorial, Spain.

Dennis, E., et al. (1991). *The media at war: The press and the Persian Gulf conflict*. New York: Gannett Foundation Media Center.

Department of Defense. (1991). *Conduct of the Persian Gulf conflict: An interim report to Congress* (pp. 19–23). Washington DC: Department of Defense.

Department of Defense. (1992, May 21). *Pentagon adopts combat coverage principles*. News Release No. 241–92. Washington, DC: Office of the Assistant Secretary of Defense (Public Affairs).

Dexter, L. A. (1970). *Elite and specialized interviewing*. Evanston, IL: Northwestern University Press.

Diamond, E. (1991a). CNN's Triumph. *New York*, January 28.

Diamond, E. (1991b). How CNN does it. *New York*, February 11.

Diehl, J. G. (1989). *Lights! Camera! Action! The operational commander and the media*. Fort Leavenworth, KS: U.S. Army Command and General Staff College.

Dodd, K., Rustum, J., Badr, N., and Haddad, G. (1943, September). *A pioneer radio poll in Lebanon, Syria, and Palestine*. Beirut, Lebanon: American University of Beirut.

Does bloody footage lose wars? (1991, Feb. 11), *Newsweek*, p. 38.

Dowd, A. (1991, September 10). George Bush as a crisis manager. *Fortune*, p. 55.

Draper, T. (1992, January). The Gulf war reconsidered. *New York Book Review*, p. 52.

Draper, T. (1992, January 30). The true history of the Gulf war. *New York Review of Books*, p. 43.

Dugan, M. J. (1991, May 29). General vs. journalists, cont. *New York Times*, p. 31.

Editors of Major News Organizations. Letter to Secretary of Defense Dick Cheney (1991, April 29). Washington, DC.

Ellul, J. (1965). *Propaganda: The formation of men's attitudes*. New York: Random House.

Entman, R. M. (1991). Framing U.S. coverage of international news: Contrasts in narratives of the KAL and Iran Air incidents. *Journal of Communication, 41*(4), pp. 6–27.

Ethiel, N. (Ed.). (1992). *Reporting the next war*. Chicago: Robert R. McCormick Tribune Foundation.

Farrell, T. B. (1989). Media rhetoric as social drama: The winter olympics of 1984. *Critical Studies in Mass Communication, 6*, pp. 138–182.

Fischhoff, B., Lichtenstein, P., Slovic, S., Derby, L., and Keeney, R. L. (1981). *Acceptable risk*. Cambridge, MA: Harvard University Press.

Fisher, G. (1987). *American communication in a global society* (rev. ed.). Norwood, NJ: Ablex.

Fitzsimon, M. (1991). Public perception of war coverage: A survey analysis. In C. LeMay, M. Fitzsimon, and J. Sahadi (Eds.), *The media at war: The press and the Persian Gulf conflict* (pp. 86–95). New York: Gannett Foundation Media Center.

Ford, P. (1991, February 12). Pool system inadequate, western journalists say. *Christian Science Monitor, 83*, p. 3.

Fuller, J.F.C. (1920). *Tanks in the great war, 1914–1918*. London: Murray.

Funkhouser, R., and Shaw, E. (1990). How synthetic experience shapes social reality. *Journal of Communication, 40*, pp. 75–87.

Gallup, G. (1991, October). Confidence in major U.S. institutions at all-time low. *Gallup Poll Monthly, 313*, pp. 36–40.

Gantz, W. (1991, May). *Watching the war: Patterns of information seeking during a crisis*. Paper presented at the annual meeting of the International Communication Association, Chicago.

Gergen, D. (1991, March 11). Why America hates the press. *U.S. News & World Report*, p. 57.

Gigot, P. (1990, December 18). A great American screw-up: The U.S. and Iraq. *Wall Street Journal*.

Goldberg, R. (1991, February 8). TV: The antiseptic tube. *Wall Street Journal*, p. 18.

Golding, P., and Elliott, P. (1979). *Marketing the news*. London: Longman.

Goodman, W. (1991, September 27). David and Ben chat in shirtsleeves. *New York Times*, p. C30.

Goren, D. (1992). The Gulf war: The media dimension. (Unpublished manuscript.)

Gould, J. (1991, March). Is technology outstripping understanding? *RTNDA Communicator*.

Goulden, J. C. (1969). *Truth is the first casualty: The Gulf of Tonkin affair—Illusion and reality*. Chicago: James B. Adler, published in association with Rand-McNally.

Graber, D. A. (1990). Content and meaning: What is it all about? *American Behavioral Scientist, 33*, pp. 144–152.

Graubard, S. R. (1992). *Mr. Bush's war: Adventures in the politics of illusion*. New York: Hill and Wang.

Greenberg, M. R., Sachsman, D. B., Sandman, P. M., and Solomone, K. L. (1989, Summer). Risk, drama, and geography in coverage of environmental risk by network television. *Journalism Quarterly, 66* (2), pp. 267–276.

Greenberger, R. S. (1991, September 20). Iraqi documents show U.S. lawmakers in Baghdad visit didn't signal concerns. *Wall Street Journal*.

Group launches campaign to pull plug on CNN's Arnett. (1991, February 18). *Broadcasting*.

Gumpert, G., and Cathcart, R. (1985). Media grammars, generations, and media gaps. *Critical Studies in Mass Communication, 2*, pp. 23–35.

Gurevitch, M. (1989). Comparative research on television news: Problems and challenges. *American Behavioral Scientist, 33*, pp. 221–229.

Gurevitch M., Levy, M. R., and Roeh, I. (1991). The global newsroom: Convergences and diversities in the globalization of television news. In P. Dahlgren and C. Sparks (Eds.), *Communication and citizenship; Journalism and the public sphere in the new media age* (pp. 195–219). London: Routledge.

Guttman Institute for Applied Social Research. (1991). *Current survey for IBA during the Gulf war, January–March 1991*.

Hallin, D. C. (1986). Network news: We keep America on top of the world. In T. Gitlin (Ed.), *Watching television* (pp. 9–41). New York: Pantheon.

Hamblen, M. (1991, March). Satellite telephone the size of a suitcase. *Communicator*.

Hammond, W. 1988. *The military and the media, the U.S. Army in Vietnam*. Washington, DC: Center for Military History.

Harlow, G. D., and Maerz, G. C. (Eds.). (1991). *Measures short of war: The George F. Kennan lectures at the National War College, 1946–47*. Washington, DC: National Defense University Press.

al-Hayat. (1991, January 26). Beirut, Lebanon.

Head, S. W. (1985). *World broadcasting systems: A comparative analysis*. Belmont, CA: Wadsworth.

Henry, William A. (1991, January 14). Fencing in the messengers. *Time*, p. 17.

Heraldo De Aragon. (1991, February 1). Aragon, Spain.

Hertsgaard, M. (1991, January/February). Following Washington's lead. *Deadline: A Bulletin from the Center for War, Peace and the News Media*, p. 4.

Herz, M. F. (1958a). Ultimatums and propaganda to surrounded units. In W. E. Daugherty and M. Janowitz (Eds.), *A psychological warfare casebook* (pp. 397–402). Baltimore, MD: Johns Hopkins University Press.

Herz, M. F. (1958b). The combat leaflet: Weapon of persuasion. In W. E. Daugherty and M. Janowitz (Eds.), *A psychological warfare casebook* (pp. 562–566). Baltimore, MD: Johns Hopkins University Press.

Hess, S. (1984). *The government/press connection*. Washington, DC: Brookings Institution.

Hester, A. (1991). The collection and flow of world news. In J. C. Merrill (Ed.), *Global journalism: A Survey of international communication* (2nd ed., pp. 29–50). New York: Longman.

Hiebert, R. E. (1991, Summer). Public relations as a weapon of modern warfare. *Public Relations Review, 17*(2), pp. 107–116.

Hill, John W. (1975). Personal conversation with Marian K. Pinsdorf.

The history of the U.A.R. radio since its establishment in 1934 until now. (1970, August). *Arab Broadcasts*, p. 63.

Holsti, O. (1969). *Content analysis for the social sciences and humanities*. Reading, MA: Addison Wesley.

Horwitz, E. (1989). *The irony of regulatory reform: The deregulation of American telecommunications*. New York: Oxford University Press.

Howes, K.J.P. (1991, April). The globalization of communications. *Via Satellite, 48*, pp. 53.

Hudson, J.C., and Swindel, S. (1988). TV news in Saudi Arabia. *Journalism Quarterly, 65*, pp. 1003–1006.

Humphries, A. (1983). *Falklands war public affairs analysis*. United States Naval War College: Naval War College Center for Advanced Research.

In bad company: Censorship in the Gulf war. (1991, May 18). *New York Times*, p. 22.

Iraq to allow CNN satellite. (1991, January 26). *New York Times*, p. 5.

Issawi, C. (1963). *Egypt in revolution: An economic analysis*. London: Oxford University Press.

Jackson, S., and Jacobs, S. (1983). Generalizing about messages: Suggestions for design and analysis of experiments. *Human Communication Research, 9*, pp. 169–181.

Janowitz, M. (1958). Language idiom and accent in psychological warfare. In W. E. Daugherty and M. Janowitz (Eds.), *A psychological warfare casebook* (pp. 609–610). Baltimore, MD: Johns Hopkins University Press.

Johnson, H. (1991). *Sleepwalking through history: America in the Reagan years*. New York: W. W. Norton.

Jones, A. S. (1991, February 15). Process of news reporting on display. *New York Times*, p. A15.

Jowett, B. (Trans.). (1943). *The politics of Aristotle*. New York: Modern Library.

Kaiser, C. (1983, November 7). An off-the-record war. *Newsweek*, p. 83.

Katz, E. (1992, Summer). The end of journalism: Notes on watching the war. *Journal of Communication*, *42*(3), pp. 5–13.

Katz, E., and Dayan, D. (1985). Media events: On the experience of not being there. *Religion*, pp. 305–314.

Katz, P. P. (1982). Tactical psyop in support of combat operations. In R. D. McLaurin (Ed.), *Military propaganda: Psychological warfare and operations* (pp. 42–59). New York: Praeger.

Keen, P.G.W. (1991). *Shaping the future: Business design through information technology*. Cambridge, MA: Harvard Business School Press.

Kelly, T. W. (1991, September). Interview. *U.S. Naval Institute Proceedings*, p. 76.

Kleinwächter, W. (1991, October). National security versus the right to know. *Media Development*, pp. 5–6.

Knightley, P. (1975). *The first casualty*. New York: Harcourt Brace Jovanovich.

Koop, T. F. (1946). *Weapon of silence*. Chicago: University of Chicago Press.

Kroker, A. (1985). Television and the triumph of culture: Three theses. *Canadian Journal of Political and Social Theory*, *9*, pp. 37–47.

Kundera, Milan. (1991). *Immortality*. New York: Grove, Weidenfeld.

Landau, Saul. (1991, March). The real Nintendo game. *Progressive*, pp. 26–27.

Larson, J. F. (1986). Television and U.S. foreign policy: The case of the Iran hostage crisis. *Journal of Communication*, *36*, pp. 108–130.

Lee, J. A. (1989). Waging the real war in the media: Towards a content analysis of moral communication. *Canadian Journal of Communication*, *14*, pp. 37–56.

LeMay, C., Fitzsimon, M., and Sahadi, J. (1991, June). *The media at war: The press and the Persian Gulf conflict*. New York: Gannett Foundation Media Center, Spring.

Lemish, D., and Tidhar, C. E. (1993). Where have all the young girls gone? The disappearance of Israeli women broadcasters during the Gulf war. Paper presented at the ICA annual convention in Washington, DC.

Levinson, H. (1991). *Viewing of IETV broadcasts during the first three weeks of the Gulf war*. Guttman Institute for Applied Social Research. Publication No. HL/1142/H.

Lewis, A. (1991, May 6). 'To see ourselves' . . . The failings of the press in the Gulf war. *New York Times*, p. A15.

Lewis, J., Jhally, S., and Morgan, M. (1991, March). *The Gulf war: A study of the media, public opinion and public knowledge*. (Document No. P-8). Amherst, MA: Center for the Study of Communication.

Libre, Belgium. (1991, January 24). Liege, Belgium.

Liebes, T. (1992). Comparing the *Intifadeh* and the Gulf war in U.S. and Israeli television. *Critical Studies in Mass Communication*, *9*, pp. 44–55.

Linebarger, P.M.A. (1954). *Psychological warfare*. Washington, DC: Combat Force Press.

Lowy, J. (1991, March 22). Transcript of "War, the press and the first amendment." American Press Institute Issues Forum.

Lunt, J. (1984). *Grenada: A media assessment*. Maxwell Air Force Base, AL: Air War College.

MacArthur, J. R. (1992). *Second front, censorship and propaganda for the Gulf war*. New York: Hill and Wang.

Maitre, H. (1991, Summer). Journalistic incompetence. *Nieman Reports*, pp. 10–15.

al-Makaty, S., Boyd, D. A., and Van Tubergen, G. N. (1992, August). *Source credibility during the Gulf war: A Q-study of rural and urban Saudi Arabian citizens*. Paper presented at the Association for Education in Journalism and Mass Communication, Montreal, Canada.

Mander, M. S. (1987). Narrative dimensions of the news: Omniscience, prophecy, and morality. *Communication*, *10*, pp. 51–70.

Marlier, J. (1989). Fifteen minutes of glory: A Burkean analysis of press coverage of Oliver North's testimony. *Political Communication and Persuasion*, *6*, pp. 269–288.

Martin, F. P. (1987). *The military and the media*. Newport, RI: Naval War College.

Martin, L. J., and Chaudhary, A. G. (1983). Goals and roles of media systems. In L. J. Martin and A. G. Chaudhary (Eds.), *Comparative mass media systems* (pp. 1–31). New York: Longman.

Mathews, J. J. (1957). *Reporting the wars*. Minneapolis: University of Minnesota Press.

Mattelart, A. (1977). Cultural imperialism of the United States in Latin America in the era of the multinational corporation. *Langues Modernes*, *71*, pp. 129–143.

Matthews, L. J. (Ed.). (1991). *Newsmen and national defense*. Washington, DC: Brassey's.

McCain, T. A. (1992). Perspectives on policy, technology, and markets for Ohio's future telecommunications networks. In *Proceedings of the fall 1992 Symposium on Collaborative Strategies for Developing Telecommunications Networks in Ohio*. Columbus: Center for Advanced Study in Telecommunications (CAST), Ohio State University.

McCarthy, C. (1991, February 17). Not in front of the children. *Guardian Weekly*, p. 10.

McCormack, T. (1989). The 1988 Southam lecture: The texts of war and the discourse of peace. *Canadian Journal of Communication*, *14*, pp. 1–16.

McLeod, D. E., Perse, E., Signorielli, N., and Courtright, J. A. (1991, September). *Public perceptions and evaluations of the role of the media in the Persian Gulf war*. Paper presented at the Conference on Media and the Gulf War, Media Studies Project, Woodrow Wilson International Center for Scholars, Washington, DC.

McPhail, T. L. (1987). *Electronic colonialism: The future of international broadcasting and communication* (2nd ed., rev.). Newbury Park, CA: Sage.

McQuail, D. (1990). *Mass communication theory: An introduction* (2nd ed.). Beverly Hills: Sage.

The media in the 21st century. (1991, March 4). Seminar held at Fordham University Graduate School of Business Center for Communications.

Merrill, J. C., and Odell, S. J. (1983). *Philosophy and journalism*. New York: Longman.

Messagero Veneto. (1991, January 18). Venice, Italy.

Metcalf, J. (1991, August). The mother of the mother. *U.S. Naval Institute Proceedings*, pp. 56–58.

Metwally, E. A. (n.d.). *Historical survey of the Egyptian broadcast with background of pre-revolution period*. Cairo: Egyptian Radio-Television Federation.

Military obstacles detailed. (1991, July 13). *Editor and Publisher*, pp. 8–10.
Miller, J. (1991, January 22). Saudis try to cope with too few masks and too little information. *New York Times*, p. A7.
Mock, J. R. (1941). *Censorship, 1917*. Princeton: Princeton University Press.
Morgenbladet. (1991, January 25). Oslo, Norway.
Mossberg, W. S. (1991, February 28). U.S. used press as weapon. *Wall Street Journal*.
Mott, P. (1991, March). New king of the hill. *Quill*, pp. 14–16.
Mulvey, W. L. (1991, August). Inside media relations: Observations from Desert Storm. *U.S. Army Public Affairs Monthly Update*, pp. 1–5.
Al-Mussawar. (1991, February 1). Cairo, Egypt.
Nasser, M. K. (1983). News values versus ideology: A Third World perspective. In L. J. Martin and A. G. Chaudhary (Eds.), *Comparative mass media systems* (pp. 44–66). New York: Longman.
Nation Magazine v. U.S. Department of Defense, 762 F. Supp. 1558 (S.D.N.Y. 1991).
Nessen, R. (1991, January 12). The Pentagon's censors. *Washington Post*, p. A21.
Newsday. (1991a, September 12).
Newsday. (1991b, September 24).
Newsweek. (1991a, February 11).
Newsweek. (1991b, February 25).
Nimmo, D., and Combs, J. E. (1985). *Nightly horrors: Crisis coverage in television network news*. Knoxville: University of Tennessee Press.
No news: bad news. (1991, January 28). *Nation*, p. 75.
North, R. C., Holsti, O., Zaninovich, M. G., and Zinnes, D. A. (1963). *Content analysis: A handbook with applications for the study of international crisis*. Evanston, IL: Northwestern University Press.
Notes and comment. (1991, February 18). *New York Times*.
O'Brien, M. D. (1991). *A new threat to the nation's war fighting capability*. Newport, RI: Naval War College.
Officials discuss TV's impact on Gulf war. (1991, October 7). *Broadcasting*, p. 71.
Ogan, C. (1991). The Middle East and North Africa. In J. C. Merrill (Ed.), *Global journalism: A survey of international communication* (2nd ed., pp. 129–153). New York: Longman.
O'Heffernan, P. (1991). *Mass media and American foreign policy: Insider perspectives on global journalism and the foreign policy process*. Norwood, NJ: Ablex.
Paddock, A. H., Jr. (1990). U.S. military psychological operations: Past, present, and future. In J. Radvanyi (Ed.), *Psychological operations and political warfare in long-term strategic planning* (pp. 19–35). New York: Praeger.
Palestine department of posts and telegraphs annual report, 1935. (1936). Jerusalem.
Palestine department of posts and telegraphs annual report, 1936. (1937). Jerusalem.
Pavlik, J. V. (1990, December 28). Technological convergence in the newsroom. Gannett Foundation Media Center, Columbia University, New York City.
Pavlik, J., and Thalbimer, M. (1991, June). *The media at war: The press and the Persian Gulf conflict*. Gannett Foundation Media Center, Columbia University, New York City.
Peck, Chris. (1991, April 15). FOI report. *APME News*.
Peled, T., and Katz, E. (1974). Functions of the media in wartime: The Israeli home front in October 1973. In E. Katz and J. G. Blumler (Eds.), *The uses of mass*

communication: Current perspectives on gratifications research. Beverly Hills: Sage.

Pentagon rules on media access to the Persian Gulf war. Washington, DC: U.S. Government Printing Office.

Peters, N. J. (Ed.). (1992). *War after war*. San Francisco: City Lights Books.

Pilger, J. (1991, January 13). Myth-makers of the Gulf war. *Guardian Weekly*, p. 6.

Pinsdorf, M. K. (1989, Summer). Ordinary mortals: Journalists and management suffer some of the same deficiencies. *Business Journalism Review*, p. 56.

Pirsig, R. (1991). *Lila, an inquiry into morals*. New York: Bantam Books.

Press-bashing hero. (1991, March 4). *Newsweek*.

Price, B. (1942). Governmental censorship in war-time. *American Political Science Review, 3*, pp. 837–849.

Pyle, R. (1991). *Schwarzkopf in his own words: The man, the mission, the triumph*. New York: Signet Books.

The Quill. (1991, March).

The Quill. (1991, September).

Rabinowitz, D. (1991, February 11). Are reporters 'neutral'? *Wall Street Journal*, p. A10.

Radvanyi, J. (1990). Introduction to psyops. In J. Radvanyi (Ed.), *Psychological operations and political warfare in long-term strategic planning* (pp. 1–7). New York: Praeger.

Rana Blad. (1991, January 24). Oslo, Norway.

Ray, M. L., Sawyer, A. G., Rothschild, M. L., Heeler, R. M., Strong, E. C., and Reed, J. B. (1973). Marketing communication and the hierarchy of effects. In G. Kline and P. Clark (Eds.), *New models for communication research*. Beverly Hills: Sage.

Reed, F. (1991, February 5). Unasked questions. *Washington Times*, p. G3.

Reporters in the Gulf rally 'round the flag. (1991, April). *Die Zeit*. Hamburg, reprinted in *World Press Review*.

Robertson, H. E. (1991, May). *Military-media relations and Operation Desert Storm*. Speech at the Annual Awards Luncheon of the Chicago Publicity Club.

Robichaux, M., and Fuchsberg, G. (1991, February 1). Desert Storm demand buffets satellite-phone firm. *Wall Street Journal*, p. B2.

Roeh, I. (1989). Journalism in storytelling, coverage as narrative. *American Behavioral Scientist, 33*, pp. 162–168.

Rogers, E. (1986). *Communication technology: The new media in society*. New York: Free Press.

Rogers, D. H., Erickson, R., Winters, J. M. (1983). *The military and the media—A need for control*. Carlisle Barracks, PA: U.S. Army War College.

Rolo, C. J. (1941). *Radio goes to war*. New York: G. P. Putnam and Sons.

Rosenberg, E. (1991, March). TV and the Gulf war. *Quill*, pp. 17–19.

Safire, W. (1991, February 3). The balloon goes up on war words. *New York Times Magazine*, p. 8.

Salinger, P., and Laurent, E. Trans. from the French by H. Curtis. (1991). *Secret dossier, the hidden agenda behind the Gulf war*. New York: Penguin Books.

Schanberg, S. H. (1991a, March 22). Censoring for political security. *Washington Journalism Review*, pp. 23–26.

Schanberg, S. H. (1991b, March 22). Can this editor speak as a journalist? *Newsday*.

Schenck v. United States. (1919). 249 U.S. 47.

Schmeisser, P. (1991, March 18). How the press lost their Gulf war: shooting pool. *New Republic*, pp. 21–23.

Schudson, M. (1982). The politics of narrative form: The emergence of news conventions in print and television. *Daedalus, 111*, pp. 97–112.

Schwarzkopf, N. (1991, January-February). Televised press briefings during the Persian Gulf war.

Scolino, E., and Wines, M. (1992, June 27). Bush's greatest glory fades as questions on Iraq persist. *New York Times*, p. 8.

Scott, W. (1955). Reliability of content analysis: The case of nominal scale coding. *Public Opinion Quarterly, 19*, pp. 321–325.

Semetko, H. A., Blumler, J. G., Gurevitch, M., and Weaver, D. H., with Barkin, S., and Wilhoit, G. C. (1991). *The formation of campaign agendas: A comparative analysis of party and media roles in recent American and British elections*. Hillsdale, NJ: Erlbaum.

Sergeant, J. W. (1988). *Freedom of the press: A challenge to the operational commander*. Newport, RI: Naval War College.

Servaes, J. (1991). European press coverage of the Grenada crisis. *Journal of Communication, 42*(4), pp. 28–41.

Shaw, M., and Carr-Hill, R. (1991, November). Mass media and attitudes to the Gulf war in Britain. *Electronic Journal of Communication, 2*.

Shepard, G. (1991, March). The opening hours of the war. *Communicator*.

Shinar, D., and Stoicin, G. (1992). *Media representations of socio-political conflict: The Rumanian revolution and the Gulf war*. Paper presented at the IAMCR Conference, San Paulo, Brazil.

Siebert, F. S. (1952). *Freedom of the press in England, 1476–1776*. Urbana: University of Illinois Press.

Siebert, F., Peterson, T., and Schramm, W. (1956). *Four theories of the press*. Urbana: University of Illinois Press.

Simpson, Alan K. (1991, February 13). Reporters in Iraq spread Saddam's lies. *USA Today*.

Sims, R. B. (1983). *The Pentagon reporters*. Washington, DC: National Defense University Press.

Sloyan, P. J. (1991, January 13). The war you won't see. *Washington Post*, p. C2.

Small, W. J. (1992a). A report—The Gulf war and television news: past, future, and present. *Mass Communications Review, 19*(1–2), pp. 3–13.

Small, W. J. (1992b). *The Gulf war: Mass media coverage and restraints*. Miami: International Communications Association.

Smear from the whip. (1991, February 12). *New York Times*.

Smith, H. (Ed.). (1992). *The media and the Gulf war: The press and democracy in wartime*. Washington, DC: Seven Locks Press.

Smith, J. E. (1992). *George Bush's war*. New York: Henry Holt and Company.

Smith, L. D. (1989). Narrative analysis of the party platforms: The Democrats and Republicans of 1984. *Communication Quarterly, 37*, pp. 91–99.

Solomon, N. (1991, May 29). The media protest too much. *New York Times*, p. A31.

Sood, R., Stockdale, G., and Rogers, E. (1987). How the news media operate in natural disasters. *Journal of Communication, 37*(3), pp. 27–41.

Sowell, Thomas. (1991, February 5). Sound bite journalism. *Washington Times*, p. G3.

Sperry, S. L. (1981). Television news as narrative. In R. P. Adler (Ed.), *Understanding television: Essays on television as a social and cultural force* (pp. 295–312). New York: Praeger.

Spin control through censorship: The Pentagon manages the news. (1991, May). *Extra!*, pp. 14–15.

Stephens, L. F. (1991). The world's media systems: An overview. In J. C. Merrill (Ed.), *Global journalism: Survey of international communication* (2nd ed., pp. 51–71). New York: Longman.

Sterba, J. P. (1992, March 31). Japan inc. invades ink biz: New York Times drops period. *Wall Street Journal*, p. A14.

Stone, Emerson. (1991, March). News practices. *RTNDA Communicator*.

Straubhaar, J. D., Heeter, C., Greenberg, B. S., Ferreira, L., Wicks, R. H., and Lau, T. Y. (1992). What makes news: Western, Socialist, and Third World television newscasts compared in eight countries. In F. Korzenny and E. Schiff (Eds.), *International and intercultural communication annual* (Vol. 16, pp. 89–109). Newbury Park, CA: Sage.

Swanson, D. L., and Smith, L. D. (1993). War in the global village: A seven-country comparison of television news coverage of the beginning of the Gulf war. In R. E. Denton, Jr. (Ed.), *The media and the Persian Gulf war* (pp. 165–196). Westport, CT: Praeger.

Times Mirror Center for the People & the Press. (1991, January 31). *The people, the press, and the war in the Gulf*. News release, Washington, DC.

Toffler, A., and Toffler, H. (1991, May). War, wealth, and a new era in history. *World Monitor*, pp. 46–52.

Traber, M., and Davies, A. (1991, October). Ethics of war reporting. *Media Development*, pp. 7–10.

Tunstall, J. (1977). *The media are American: Anglo-American media in the world*. London: Constable.

Tyler, Patrick E. (1991, March 27). Schwarzkopf says truce enabled Iraqi to escape. *New York Times*.

Tyndall Report. (1991, February/March).

U.S. Advisory Commission of Public Diplomacy. (1991). *1991 report*. Washington, DC: U.S. Advisory Commission of Public Diplomacy.

U.S. Department of the Army. (1987). *Field manual (FM) 33-1: Psychological operations*. Washington, DC: Government Printing Office.

U.S. Department of the Army. (1992a). *Field manual (FM) 33-1: Psychological operations*. Washington, DC: Government Printing Office.

U.S. Department of the Army. (1992b). *4th psychological operations group: Leaflets of the Persian Gulf war*. Washington, DC: Government Printing Office.

U.S. Information Agency, Office of Research. (1973, August 30). Media habits of priority groups in Saudi Arabia—Part II Appendix. Research Report R-20-73A. Washington, DC.

U.S. Information Agency. (1975, December 12). *VOA audience estimate for Egypt, 1975*. Research report E-13-75. Washington DC: Office of Research.

U.S. Information Agency. (1984, December 18). *Radio Baghdad, BBC and Saudi radio leading foreign stations in Kuwait; VOA tenth*. Research memorandum. Washington, DC: Office of Research.

U.S. Information Agency. (1987, March). *VOA behind other international broadcasters in Bahrain and the United Arab Emirates*. Washington, DC: USIA.

U.S. Information Agency. (1991, February 14). *Foreign radio listening rates high in four Arab Gulf nations; VOA increases audience during crisis*. Washington, DC: USIA.

Vatcher, W. H. (1958). Appeal to General Ushijima. In W. E. Daugherty and M. Janowitz (Eds.), *A psychological warfare casebook* (pp. 403-404). Baltimore, MD: Johns Hopkins University Press.

Venanzi, G. S. (1982). *Democracy and protracted war: The impact of television*. Maxwell Air Force Base, AL: Air War College.

Waldman, P. (1992, March 5). Western-style mass entertainment is dished out to Arab viewers via MBC. *Wall Street Journal*, p. A10.

Waldman, P. (1992, March 24). Arab states revel in the squabbling of U.S. and Israel. *Wall Street Journal*, p. A12.

Walker, D. C., Wicks, R. H., and Pyle, R. (1991, August 8). *Differences in live coverage between CNN and the broadcast networks in the Persian Gulf war*. Presented at meeting of the Association for Education in Journalism and Mass Communication, Boston.

Wallis, R., and Baran, S. J. (1990). *The known world of broadcast news: International news and the electronic media*. London: Routledge.

Wall Street Journal. (1991, January 21). P. C12.

War boosts CNN ratings. (1991, January 28). *Broadcasting*, p. 23.

War takes its toll on networks. (1991, March 4). *Broadcasting*, pp. 27-30.

Washington Journalism Review. (1991, April).

Washington Post. (1991, May 14).

Watson, L. (1989). *Should members of the military be concerned about television news coverage of military operations?* Fort Leavenworth, KS: U.S. Army Command and General Staff College.

Weaver, R. (1990). The politics of storytelling: The effects of dramatistic structuring in daily current affairs television. *Media Information Australia*, *57*, pp. 12-18.

Weissert, R. F. (1991, Spring). Hero of Desert Storm information systems. *Army Communicator: Voice of the Signal Corp*, *16* (2).

Who won the media war? (1991, March 18). *New York*, pp. 20, 29.

Wicker, T. (1991, March 20). An unknown casualty. *New York Times*, p. A29.

Wiehe, V. (1986). Scientific technology and the human condition. *Journal of Sociology and Social Welfare*, *13*, pp. 88-97.

Williams, P. (1990, December 14). Memo to Washington bureau chiefs of the Pentagon press corps.

Williams, P. (1991a, February 20). Statement before Committee on Government Affairs, U.S. Senate, p. 3.

Williams, P. (1991b, March 14). *A Gulf war media review*. Remarks to the National Press Club, Washington, DC.

Williams, P. (1991c, Autumn). The press and the Persian Gulf war. *Parameters*, pp. 2-9.

Winograd, T., and Flores, T. (1988). *Understanding computers and cognition: A new foundation for design*. Norwood, NJ: Ablex.

Witness to war: Images from the Persian Gulf war from the staff of the Los Angeles Times. (1991). Los Angeles: Los Angeles Times.

Wober, J. M. (1990, October). *Viewers' opinions of continuing television coverage of the conflict with Iraq*. Independent Broadcasting Authority Research Report. London: IBA.

Wood, J. (1991, July/August). Desert sounds: International broadcasting in the Arab world. *IEE Review*, pp. 275–280.

Woodward, R. (1991). *The Commanders*. New York: Simon & Schuster.

Woollacott, M. (1991, September 2). Saddam on TV—Another view. *Guardian Weekly*, p. 8.

Zelizer, B. (1992). CNN, the Gulf war, and journalistic practice. *Journal of Communication*, *42*(1), pp. 66–81.

Zettl, H. (1989). The graphication and personification of television news. In G. Burns and R. J. Thompson (Eds.), *Television studies: Textual analysis* (pp. 137–164). New York: Praeger.

Zoglin, R. (1991a, February 25). Just whose side are they on? *Time*, pp. 52–55.

Zoglin, R. (1991b, March 11). It was a public relations rout, too. *Time*, p. 56.

Zorn, J. (1991). Demonizing in the Gulf war: Reading the archetypes. *English Journal*, *80*, pp. 44–46.

Index

About the Contributors

M. DAVID ARANT is an Assistant Professor in the Department of Journalism at Memphis State University. A former journalist, he is a doctoral candidate at the University of North Carolina at Chapel Hill, where his dissertation addresses the constitutionality of the military restrictions on the press in the Persian Gulf War.

DOUGLAS A. BOYD is Professor, College of Communications, University of Kentucky-Lexington. He has been a Fulbright Professor of Mass Communication, Cairo University and the American University in Cairo, Egypt. He is the author of *Broadcasting in the Arab World*, and coauthor of *Video Cassette Recorders in the Third World*. Boyd's research appears in numerous international scholarly and professional journals.

LINDA JO CALLOWAY is an Assistant Professor in the Information and Communication Systems program at the Fordham University Graduate School of Business Administration. She has been a visiting scholar at the Computer Science Department in Fudan University, Shanghai, and has taught at Fordham University's Dublin campus in Ireland. Her research interests concern the application of new information technologies to mass media settings. Her research has appeared in information systems and public relations journals.

REBECCA A. CARRIER is a doctoral student in speech communication at the University of Illinois at Urbana-Champaign. Her work concerns the social and political aspects of mass communication. Before beginning graduate study, she worked as a producer and writer for National Public Radio and United Press International.

MIKE CHANSLOR is a doctoral student in the Department of Communication at the University of Oklahoma who has written on the topics of media coverage and political advertising effects. His current work addresses the role of image in political advertising.

ROBERT M. FISCHBACH is Associate Professor of communication at Central Connecticut State University. He has conducted research in television and culture, counselor training as interpersonal persuasion and AIDS Education and Awareness. In addition to continuing his research on the Gulf War, he is currently working on the development of a counselor training model.

JEROLD L. HALE is an Associate Professor of speech communication at the University of Georgia. His research interests include communication and social influence and analysis. He has published studies on persuasive message effects. He has served as guest instructor in the PSYOP Officers Training Course, John F. Kennedy Special Warfare Center and School, at Fort Bragg, North Carolina.

MARK HOVIND is a doctoral student in the Department of Communication at the University of Oklahoma who has written on the topics of media coverage and political advertising effects. His current work addresses political campaign strategies.

LYNDA LEE KAID is Professor of communication at the University of Oklahoma, where she also serves as director of the Political Communication Center and supervises the Political Commercial Archive. Her research specialties include political advertising and news coverage of political events. A Fulbright Scholar, she has also done work on political television in several Western European countries. She is the author and editor of several books and journal articles, on various aspects of political communication.

DAFNA LEMISH, is the director of the Center for Education and Communication and senior lecturer at the New School of Media Studies at the College of Management, Tel Aviv. Her areas of specialty include media literacy, children and television, and media gender portrayals.

THOMAS A. MCCAIN is Professor of communication and journalism at The Ohio State University where he also serves as the codirector of the Center for Advanced Study in Telecommunications. He is a past editor of the *Journal of Broadcasting and Electronic Media*, serves on the editorial boards of numerous national and international communication journals, and has written widely on topics concerning media and society relationships. His current work addresses the interdependent nature of communication technologies, economics, and public policy.

ROGER MYRICK is a visiting instructor of business communications in the College of Business Administration at the University of Oklahoma, where he is also currently a Ph.D. candidate in the Department of Communication. His dissertation work focuses on AIDS messages directed at gays and lesbians.

JAY M. PARKER is a major and career U.S. Army officer. He is currently assigned to the 9th PSYOP Battalion (Airborne) (Tactical) at Fort Bragg, North Carolina. He previously served as commander of the PSYOP Training and Doctrine Development Company at Fort Bragg and as an assistant professor of politics at the United States Military Academy at West Point. His academic specialization is in U.S. foreign policy in East Asia.

MARION K. PINSDORF is Associate Professor at the Center for Communications and Media Management in the Graduate School of Business at Fordham University. She has held executive positions in corporate communication with Hill and Knowlton, Inc., Smithkline Beckman, INA, and Textron. She is the author of *German-speaking Entrepreneurs: Builders of Business in Brazil South* and *Communicating When Your Company Is Under Siege, Surviving Public Crises*.

CYNTHIA ROPER is a doctoral student in the Department of Communication at the University of Oklahoma. She has written on the topics of political debates, media coverage, and political advertising. Her current work deals with crosscultural comparisons of political communication.

LEONARD SHYLES is Associate Professor of communication at Villanova University. He has published his research on political communication and media in numerous political science and communication journals and books. In addition to continuing his research on the Gulf War, Shyles is working on an analysis of the 1992 presidential campaign.

WILLIAM J. SMALL is Dean of the Graduate School of Business at Fordham University in New York. He is also the Felix Larkin Professor of Communications and director of Fordham's Center for Communications. He has served as news director at WLS, Chicago, and WHAS-AM & TV in Louisville. He went to CBS News as Washington Bureau Chief and later became senior vice-president in charge of hard news. He left CBS to become president of NBC News and later, UPI. He is a past president of Radio Television News Director's Association (RTNDA) and Society of Professional Journalists (SPJ) and came to Fordham in 1986.

DAVID L. SWANSON is Professor, Associate Head, and Director of Graduate Study in the Department of Speech Communication, University of Illinois at Urbana-Champaign. A past chair of the Political Communication Division of the International Communication Association and the Rhetorical and Communication Theory Division of the Speech Communication Association, he is coeditor of *New Directions in Political Communication* and coauthor of *The Nature of Human Communication*. His research on the social and political aspects of mass communication has appeared in numerous volumes and journals. His chapter in this volume is part of a larger comparative study of television coverage of the Gulf War in some 30 countries around the world.

CHAVA E. TIDHAR, is the director of research at the Israel Educational Television, Ramat Aviv, and a senior lecturer at the graduate school of education at Bar Ilan University, Ramat Gan. Her areas of specialty include television literacy, television and the family, television gender portrayals, program evaluation, and thinking and learning processes.

NIKOS TRIVOULIDIS is a doctoral student in the Department of Communication at the University of Oklahoma. His research interests include the analysis of international films and televised political communication campaigns.

MICHAEL L. WARDEN, a lieutenant colonel in the U.S. Air Force, is currently assigned to the Office of Public Affairs, U.S. Air Force, the Pentagon. He is a doctoral candidate at the University of North Carolina at Chapel Hill, where his research concerns the military's decision-making process that shaped the press coverage in Grenada in 1983.